# A Beautiful Game

# A Beautiful Game
## International Perspectives on Women's Football

**Jean Williams**

*Oxford • New York*

First published in 2007 by
**Berg**
Editorial offices:
1st Floor, Angel Court, 81 St Clements Street, Oxford, OX4 1AW, UK
175 Fifth Avenue, New York, NY 10010, USA

Berg is the imprint of Oxford International Publishers Ltd.

**Library of Congress Cataloging-in-Publication Data**

Williams, Jean, 1964–
A beautiful game : international perspectives on
women's football / Jean Williams.
p. cm.
Includes bibliographical references and index.
ISBN-13: 978-1-84520-674-1 (cloth)
ISBN-10: 1-84520-674-6 (cloth)
ISBN-13: 978-1-84520-675-8 (pbk.)
ISBN-10: 1-84520-675-4 (pbk.)
1. Soccer for women—Cross-cultural studies.
2. Soccer—Social aspects—Cross-cultural studies. I. Title.
GV944.5.W54 2007
796.334082—dc22
2007037049

**British Library Cataloguing-in-Publication Data**

A catalogue record for this book is available from the British Library.

ISBN 978 1 84520 674 1 (Cloth)
ISBN 978 1 84520 675 8 (Paper)

Typeset by Apex Publishing, LLC, Madison, WI
Printed in the United Kingdom by Biddles Ltd, King's Lynn

**www.bergpublishers.com**

# Contents

# Illustrations

# Acknowledgements

As Julie Burchill never said, just because you visit a BSSH conference, it doesn't make you a historicist. Knowing a few great sports historians helps though, and is all the more privilege. My indebtedness to past and present colleagues at the International Centre for Sports History and Culture is evident in both the time to complete the research and in providing much-needed context. In particular, Matt Taylor's comments on a first draft of the manuscript were characteristically generous, perceptive and thoughtful. Especial thanks to Dil Porter. Quite apart from benefitting from his professional expertise on a daily basis, you have to respect someone who signs off conversations with senior people by shouting 'Up the Os' down the phone without malice intended or offence, presumably, taken. I am grateful for the patience of commissioning editor, Kathleen May, at Berg; her successor, Hannah Shakespeare; and to Emily Medcalfe, who kindly worked on the design and marketing.

The research was funded by a two-year João Havelange Scholarship awarded by CIES, the International Centre for Sports Studies, University of Neuchatel, and funded by Federation Internationale de Football Association, FIFA, the international governing body of football. Professor Jean Louis Juvet and Jérôme Champagne, Deputy General Secretary FIFA, have been most supportive. Given that the findings are broadly critical of the federation, it is perhaps a sign of the maturity of their confidence that they would fund research of this kind and allow me access to the archive. In particular, Tatjana Haenni, Mary Harvey, Arno Flach and his colleagues at the documentation centre made useful suggestions. Clearly, in their generous hospitality, they helped the process of research without necessarily agreeing with the conclusions drawn from it, and for that I am acutely grateful.

My largest obligation, nevertheless, remains to the women, men, girls and boys who participated, principally to celebrate their love of football. Collectors of women's memorabilia to whom I am grateful include, in no particular order, Sue Lopez, Gail Newsham, Dr Colin Aldis, Sheila Rollinson, Laurence Prudhomme-Poncet, Peter Bridgett, Angela Moore (aka 'the chief'), Dennis O'Brien, Julien Garises, Elsie Cook, Jess Macbeth, Winnifred Bourke, Bente Skogvang, Becky Wang, Nancy Thompson, Ali Melling, Debbie Hindley, Barbara Jacobs, Shawn Ladda, plus Jacob Hickey and Rachel Bowering at the BBC, to name but a few.

The topic has a long and personal history for me because, at age eleven, going on twelve, I just couldn't understand why my good friend Annette Astley was no longer allowed to represent the school when she was, in that very matter of fact way that children calculate others' ability, the best player. 'Nessie' didn't seem to be offended then and took up other sports. I still mind. Not least because Barwell FC under eleven's striker is called Sophie. Fortunately, I am continually inspired by my own set of sporting heroes—Kelly, James, Natalie, Tom, Kirsty and Lee. My biggest thanks, as always, is to Simon.

# Abbreviations and Acronyms

| | |
|---|---|
| AAA | Amateur Athletic Association |
| AFA | Australian Football Association |
| AFC | Asian Football Confederation |
| AIAW | Association for Intercollegiate Athletics for Women |
| ALFC | Asian Ladies' Football Confederation |
| AWSA | Australian Women's Soccer Association |
| CAAWS | Canadian Association for the Advancement of Women in Sport |
| CAF | Confédération Africaine de Football |
| CFA | Chinese Football Association |
| China '91 | FIFA Women's World Championship 1991 |
| CONCACAF | Confederation of North, Central American and Caribbean Association Football |
| CONMEBOL | Confederación Sudamericana de Fútbol |
| FACA | Football Association Coaching Association |
| FA | Football Association (English) |
| FAI | Football Association of Ireland |
| FAW | Football Association of Wales |
| FAWPL | Football Association Women's Premier League |
| FFA | Football Federation Australia Ltd |
| FIFA | Federation International Football Association |
| FIFA U-17 WC | FIFA Under Seventeen World Championship for Men |
| FIFA U 19 WC | FIFA Under Nineteen World Cup for Women |
| FIFA U 20 WC | FIFA Under Twenty World Cup for Women |
| FSFI | Federation Sportive Feminine Internationale |
| HOF | Australian Soccer Association Hall of Fame |
| HK$ | Hong Kong Dollar |
| IAPESGW | International Association for Physical Education and Sport for Girls and Women |
| IOC | International Olympic Committee |
| ISF | International Sports Federations |
| LFAI | Ladies' Football Association of Ireland |
| Korea DPR | Democratic People's Republic of Korea (North Korea) |
| Korea Republic | Republic of Korea (South Korea) |

| | |
|---|---|
| LTA | Lawn Tennis Association |
| MLS | Major League Soccer |
| NAIA | National Association of Intercollegiate Athletics |
| NCAA | National Collegiate Athletic Association |
| NOC | National Olympic Committees |
| NSL | Australian National Soccer League |
| NSWWF | New South Wales Women's Federation |
| OFC | Oceania Football Confederation |
| PFA | Professional Football Association |
| RMB | China Yuan Renminbi |
| ROC | Republic of China (Taipei) |
| ROCFA | Republic of China Football Association (Taipei) |
| SFA | Scottish Football Association |
| SGAS | State General Administration of Sports in PR China |
| SWFA | Scottish Women's Football Association |
| UEFA | Union des Associations Européennes de Football |
| USSF | United States Soccer Federation |
| US$ | United States Dollar |
| WCA | Women's Cricket Association |
| WFA | Women's Football Association |
| WFAI | Women's Football Association of Ireland |
| WNBA | Women's National Basketball Association |
| WNSL | Women's National Soccer League |
| WRFU | Women's Rugby Football Union |
| WUSA | Women's United Soccer Association |
| WWC '99 | Women's World Cup 1999 |
| WWC '07 | Women's World Cup 2007 |

# Introduction

## From *A Game for Rough Girls* to *A Beautiful Game*
### Dusting the Mirror of Women's Football

When the 2007 World Cup was allocated to PR China, the country which had staged the first official competition for female players in 1991, the president of the international governing body of football, Federation Internationale de Football Association (FIFA), Joseph 'Sepp' Blatter, remarked that women's football was 'returning to its roots'.[1] The Asian philosophy of revisiting, of continually 'dusting the mirror', informed this investigation into the international status of women's football. While the transnational themes are mainly new, it has also been an opportunity to review some ideas previously discussed in *A Game for Rough Girls*, particularly with regard to the female game's sometimes controversial image. Reappraising the topic with a broader focus, the study develops the thesis of women's involvement as fundamental to the history of association football at the same time as acknowledging localized and globalized tensions in its progress. If China is officially recognized by FIFA as the 'cradle' of football, then it seems appropriate perhaps that it should stage the fifth competition, when the Women's World Cup, as one commentator put it, 'comes home'.[2] This periodization is to be resisted. When women players of the late nineteenth century and the early decades of the twentieth took to the football fields in each of the four case study countries covered here (the United States, PR China, England, Australia), they were self-consciously challenging the paradigm of the association code as a 'manly' game. Roughly between the 1890s and the mid-1920s, the strategy was to lobby and seek space in the social milieu; then, until the late 1950s, it became to protest exclusion of various kinds, after which time women's associations formed and the sports authorities challenged before a process of merger and integration in the 1990s. The complex and changing context of football around the world across these phases also textures the history which narrow assumptions of the modern nature of women's interest obscure. Not least, the fragmented nature of the source material on which the story depends indicates that women's football has had, in national and international terms, a pretty rootless existence. Given the longer view, supposedly world-wide tournaments organized by sporting associations of the 1990s can be seen each as more a departure than a homecoming.

The diffusion of association football as part of a British mercantile colonial legacy is disputably a process whereby the simplicity of the game enabled the format to remain largely the same, while different cultural and social meanings were given to it.

Football has arguably been a global sport since the first (men's) World Cup competition was contested, in 1930, and if this view is accepted, the internationalization of female play appears at least sixty years behind the mark.[3] As the finalists of the 2007 tournament indicate, it is debatable whether association football is a global sport for women, though the arguments around globalization, modernization, imperialism, dependency theory and world system theory as they relate to football are not the focus here.[4] Rather, the scope and character of female representation at the event raise questions around issues of national identity, citizenship, freedom of labour, social inclusion and the sports media, as well as football as a leisure and business pursuit. Clearly, it has also diversified into a variety of other codified forms on both a local and an international basis. The decision to launch the new brand architecture for the international federation at the 2007 Women's World Cup tournament (WWC) reflects a concern to unify the potentially confusing emblems and logos of FIFA's multiplying competitions and projects. The need to market international football, in particular the women's game, as part of a diverse but coherent brand strategy, as the trademark term World Cup becomes used more extensively, presents an evident challenge.[5]

The 1999 Women's World Cup (WWC '99) tournament in the United States was the most high-profile women's sporting event staged and had a symbolic significance beyond sport itself in reaching a world-wide audience. As with many women-only tournaments and female events in international sports contests, there was a degree of cynicism expressed in the popular and sporting media regarding the audience viability and profitability of the proposed schedule prior to its launch. Two old sporting myths were bandied about: Didn't we already know that the TV and live audience would not be there because women will never be as popular as male athletes because of their physical limitations in less competitive contests? Who would want to watch women's soccer in the country where American football dominates print and televised media? Yet it became an event which illustrated that, given opportunity, a big enough stage and the right kind of story, women's sport can draw. The fan base ranged from a bashful Clinton to rather more innocent young enthusiasts clutching soccer Barbies. The final in particular was a family affair; both for the public unity of Bill, Hillary and Chelsea (albeit behind the protective glass of the press box) and for the soccer moms and dads who made up a large proportion of the 92,000-strong live audience. However, in spite of the world-wide television viewers, front-page headlines, full major stadia and degree of public recognition, the myths endure in the minds of those cynics who now seek to dismiss 1999 as an aberration, especially following the different atmosphere of the 2003 tournament, which was relocated from PR China to Los Angeles at short notice due to the SARS outbreak. So to what degree might the macho myths have been challenged and confirmed by WWC '99? What are the implications of this for WWC 2007 and beyond?

First, not all aspects of the return to China, it is hoped, will be nostalgic. There is a sufficiently sustained history of women's football across national boundaries without the need to invent a tradition of newness. The four case studies, of the PR China, United States, England and Australia, outlined here make both country-specific and comparative points. With the Women's World Cup 2007 emblem, FIFA enters a new era in the branding of the international association. The FIFA two-globes symbol now becomes an in-house identifying mark, while the new logos comprise both competitions and projects reflective of the proliferation of activities of the governing body. This is a concern. Beach Soccer, Futsal and Interactive World Cups vie with development projects and with men's and women's World Cups for attention and interest in one code, let alone the crowded sports market. Meanwhile, in the Vision Asia programme, specifically designed to extend the market share of all aspects of football on the continent while simultaneously promoting the place of Asian football on the world stage, women's football is one of eleven 'players' identified as priority for development.[6] In the quickly changing place of football in the creative industries and in the rather more staid atmosphere of the sports governing bodies that are managing that transformation, the place of women's football has possibly been conceded as a priority since the 'Future is Feminine' pronouncement of 1995 by Blatter.

Second, though the United States, PR China and Australian case studies may provide models for future developments, such as their respective pioneering World Cup and Olympic events, there are a number of barriers to the acceptance of women's sport more generally (and leisure-based physical activity) that prevent the realization of potential opportunities. Attempts by various agencies to create sports opportunities for women have had rather a slow-burn effect in the late twentieth century because of these enduring attitudes and century-old systems. As a European exemplar, the England case discusses a missed opportunity to host a World Cup in the 1970s, against a wider backdrop of continental networking and support for women's teams going back at least to the 1920s. Some of the ambiguities of the European situation were reflected in the social and cultural attitudes which produced the least successful of the Women's World Cups, in Sweden in 1995 (the only one for which the English team had qualified before 2007). The organization was marred by divided spectator support and match statistics due to FIFA tampering with the introduction of a time-out system at a major championship where none had been used by the teams before. With the highest use of nine time-outs in six matches, the United States came third; the eventual winners, Norway, used three in six and the team they beat in the final, Germany, used none. The principle of sharing the scheduling with another multisport tournament and the time-out trial perhaps unsurprisingly became notorious among players, more so for the English team as they missed out on going to the 1996 Atlanta Olympic Games, though they had qualified as quarter finalists, Roseli's goal for Brazil earning them the eighth place by default.

> Success hankers after affirmation. Because the dazzling debut in China had been such a triumph in 1991, expectations for the 2nd Women's World Cup were running high. We can say from the start that a comparison of the two events gave rise to positive results,

not least among the referees where women were in the majority. Some of the terms and conditions had been changed this time: 90 minutes of play instead of 80 in China, a full group of 20 players instead of 18, three points for a win, and the experiment with time out. Making a direct statistical comparison is therefore a little more difficult, but in spite of these slight changes an upward trend was, on the whole detectable.[7]

While the total number of spectators in China '91 was 510,000, with an average of 19,615 per match, Sweden managed 112,213 and 4,316, respectively, with a pretty dismal 17,158 at the Stockholm final. Little wonder, maybe, that it was the most bad tempered of the women's events so far, with eleven sent off.

As the chapter on Australia shows, it is easy to overlook the very recent nature of some increase in female participation and the precariousness of what might be called progress. The presentation of women's football as part of an international sports festival in the Sydney Olympics 2000 as part of the 'best ever' Olympic Games much longed for by enthusiasts, administrators and supportive journalists. This took place in context of an ongoing debate about the place of cricket, rugby codes and Australian Rules football as national and manly sports while soccer players are generally regarded as 'soft'. This may not necessarily prevent an increase in participation. For instance, in 1986, there were approximately 50,000 female soccer players in the US compared with about 8 million today. It is hard to believe too that it was only when the first FIFA World Championship for Women's Football was announced, in 1991, that the United States Soccer Association was able to get government financial support to form a squad or that during the preparation for that tournament the side played as many international games as they had totalled in the previous decade.[8] Yet, unlike football in the UK, the rise in female soccer in the US is part of a pattern of an increase in school and college sport for girls and young women which has been dramatic: in thirty years, from one in twenty-seven to almost one in two. The reasons for this are many, but, most crucially, engendered budgets have been tied to civil rights legislation. This has obliged educational institutions and sports governing bodies to provide opportunities as a right rather than as a service, something that has yet to be enacted in the UK but that European courts could help to reinforce via gender mainstreaming policies in the future. The alliance of astute individuals and government reform is an example of how radical change can bring about increased outcomes. The more liberal view, prevalent in the UK, that improved participation will eventually lead to a more fundamental change in the status and position of women's sport, including football, has produced slower effect. For example, in 2006, a cross-party Parliamentary committee concluded that, despite being enjoyed by millions, women's football still suffers from both cultural and practical barriers and targeted a ruling preventing mixed football after age eleven as in need of amendment. Its remit could extend, however, only to a suggestion to the Football Association that it revise its views.[9]

The most obvious point to make here is that the countries referred to as case studies are diverse and by no means intended to represent, or misrepresent, continents or the whole women's football community. Nor are they a single entity because of a range of geographical, climatic, linguistic, social and cultural circumstances, resource allocation, infrastructure differences and so forth. However, as we examine each and ask broad questions about a single sport played by women, some specific answers emerge. Part of the subject is the need for further, more localized research in order to set the work attempted here in context of varied experiences in each country. This may seem to be such an obvious thing to say that a generalist could have hazarded the same view. However, it is part of a growing reconsideration in academia that women's football has a history of at least 100 years' duration, even if a largely un-acknowledged, marginalized and overlooked one. Especially significant in the era of spin has been the way that groups of women and men who initiated competition (in forming 'unofficial' national and international associations and arguing for a world cup tournament, for example) have largely been written out of authorized histories.

The 'image problem' of women's football, in large part created in the twentieth century by those sports organizations that codified, regulated and promoted the as-sociation game in the nineteenth, has obliged those same concerns to employ public-relations professionals in the twenty-first to undo some of the spoil. Admirable for its directness, if not for a sense of delicacy or accuracy, the single most frequent question from undergraduates researching the topic is why women's football has a reputation as a 'gay' sport. It is easier to ask than to answer. Reinvention of old myths about female physical inferiority in new slogans appears to imply that the project on which the publicists are employed has more to do with damage limitation than reparation. Confounding the eternal sceptics, meanwhile, remains an endeavour for the female player today, though with good fortune not to the same degree as it was for her great grandmother. The cynicism may be enduring but the expression of disdain is not changeless. Those who defended a manly image in 1921 with a ban on women's teams playing on Football League and Football Association-affiliated grounds were as much of their age as those who see media hype as a means of sports development in an era of the 'celeb diet', size zero and the 'instant' make-over in the West. Questions about women's participation on an international scale may not be so superficial, image-based or straightforward to address. Mohammad Ehsani, for example, in his work on women's football in Iran, details their participation in alley and street games, which led to a national team hosting international competition in Amdjadieh stadium in 1971 and a surge of popularity until the 1979 Islamic revolu-tion, followed by a return to some futsal in 1993.[10] If female football players continue to negotiate the circumstances of their culture, place and time, progress within and across national boundaries can sometimes be too easily assumed.

Part of the re-appraisal has involved going over events and chronologies again to see that, sometimes, in *A Game for Rough Girls,* facts, and consequently the inter-pretation, were just plain wrong. The case of a World Cup for Women is the most significant example of this, and, consequently, it receives considerable treatment here as a section of the introduction in its own right, as well as in all four case studies.

In the United States, England, Australia and PR China, Hong Kong and Chinese Taipei individuals active in unofficial female football associations lobbied for a tournament well before FIFA felt able to sponsor such an undertaking. The support of the FIFA president Dr João Havelange was then overstated, and the matter questions the place of social equality in the single model of sports federation regulation rather more than:

> FIFA embodies in its constitutional form the most direct democracy within the International Sports Federations. It can accomplish its mission and reach its goals however only if each one of you personally contributes to the cause by not only working for the development of football but also (and foremost) by strictly respecting the FIFA Statutes and Regulations. The decisions of the International Football Association Board (the authority governing the entire football family) regarding the Laws of the Game [sic]. Only such respect will allow us to progress together and keep the interest in our sport going thereby enabling football to play its conciliatory part and also to unite the youth all over the world.[11]

In addition to judgments about a simple, wrong story about women's participation in football in the past, there were also omissions of brevity, an instance of which is the role of the Olympic Games in terms of national and international development, particularly significant in Australia, the US and PR China. It could also be noteworthy in England. There is much talk of having a British women's team at the 2012 Olympics in order to benefit from a 'home nation' allocation in the competition (with England qualifying for the Women's World Cup in 2007, a berth by merit is a possibility for the first time since their appearance at the 1995 final competition in Sweden). It is widely rumoured that Scotland have already declined to be involved.

Without access to the FIFA-held archival material, the more complicated picture of agitation, negotiation and resolution was not previously available, and their help in providing this critique has been invaluable. Methodologically, this collection also gave the starting point for following up leads with individuals who were active in both national associations and women's football. There has been a price to pay for what might be seen as privileging documentation over people, though.[12] Oral history is less in evidence here. Responding to a colleague who observed that 'women academics tend to rely more on oral history', my reply was that it is often because we are obliged to (while also resenting the implication that this is the scholarly equivalent of cosy fireside chats compared with which visiting an archive is working at the coalface of credibility). The interest isn't primarily a pragmatic one, though. Writing *A Game for Rough Girls* using mainly the archival and newspaper sources would have produced a possibly very short, no doubt altogether different, book. Using some of the 'official' collections in repositories is an extension of the wish to reflect the community by using at least some of their own words, though here it is more in dealing with patrician international bureaucracy gradually made uncomfortable by its remoteness than in dealing with the joy of actually playing. The themes which were treated in some depth there, namely competition, community, memory and oral history, are less in evidence than the global and professional issues around international elite female competition. Nevertheless, they inform the country-specific examples. Even so, referring to a previous work in the introduction to another could be seen as overly reflexive. Leaving this judgement to the reader, my hope nevertheless is for the two works to interrogate use of source and of depiction. When João Havelange wrote the following extract in announcing one of several 'first' FIFA world tournaments for women, the subtext is perhaps more telling than the message:

> As President of FIFA, I welcome all participants to this World Women's Invitational Football Tournament 1984 to be staged in Taipei and congratulate the Chinese Taipei Football Association on their initiative, this particularly in the moment when FIFA has decided to organize in the near future a World Tournament for the National Teams in Ladies' Football. We wish you every success and trust that this Tournament will be held in a true sporting spirit.[13]

Whether having stalled since a previous tournament had been held in 1978 in Chinese Taipei or on a number of subsequent occasions could be seen as sporting, it did at least mark a moment.

In trying to 'consult the archive in an avowedly political manner consistent with refiguring, that is as a site of power, remembering and forgetting,' it is also necessary to see how and why these collections have such authority,[14] to polish the mirror so that the image of the women's football community is more revealed. This means deconstructing the context in which the archive is given primacy as well as presenting contradictory and corroborative evidence, itself part of the construction of their credibility and privilege. Accepting that this is a large part of the story doesn't also mean consenting to see it as the most remarkable element. Nor does it also entail accepting that there is not much to tell about the time before the sports' authorities saw fit to collect some of the material available. The assortments themselves are flawed, as there have been thousands of participants over a 100-year history of which postcards, photographs, films, programmes, scrapbooks, letters and so on give a glimpse but hold back as much, if not more, than they reveal. Though a substantial body of writing exists in archives recorded by some of the prestigious participants, the minute books are often equally elusive, if less poignant than the privately-held material.

Going to the holdings of the various sports bodies involved dealing not just with custodians of primary material but also with self-appointed defenders of a public image of the sport. Their various treatments of some documentation as systematically collected and processed (and most related to women's football not so valued) entails physically storing and preserving the evidence in a way that presents it as of the past. This spatial, temporal and hence symbolic defence of some documents, records and artefacts as valuable and others as of little consequence is a skewed and self-conscious construction of history.

Harry H. Cavan, OBE, senior Vice President and Chairman of the FIFA Committee in 1984, protests rather too much support and activity, for example, in his greetings to the President of the Chinese Taipei Football Association:

> The Policy of FIFA is to encourage the development and progress of Women's Football throughout the World. The National Associations affiliated to FIFA, have been directed to ensure that Women's football organisations come within their jurisdiction and also, that they are given all possible assistance. Already the Confederations of FIFA have organised International competitions for women players, with outstanding success.[15]

Defence of the 'official' documentation is tied to the survival of evidence, which in turn helps to bolster the credibility of the institutions' sporting tradition. It was possible to look at FA Minute books at Soho Square, for example, or FIFA Women's Committee meeting minutes. Apart from valuable material held in private hands, the English Women's Football Association collection from 1969 to 1992 lies with an individual, unthematized, unrecorded, relatively unimportant as information. Much of the same can be said about women's regional, national and international tournaments in the other case-study nations. The lack of significance, the irrelevance, makes its own point about proclaiming a golden future compared to the past in constructing a public-relations-driven present for women's football. Some things have not changed, therefore. With access to more official documentation than was available in the first study, the role of historical forces in defining contemporary circumstance became strengthened as a theme. The processes of the establishment of national and international sports governing bodies meant that women's sports have been required to adapt their traditions in return for a degree of legitimacy in integrating with them, and examining this has been instructive, if not exactly enlightening. This is treated as a subsection in this introduction in terms of developing a theoretical model which explores the partial assimilation of women as one of negative integration. Those who don't like their history to be informed on this theoretical score have been given advance warning that they may wish to look away, not exactly now, but at least to make a cup of tea at the halfway stage of the Introduction.

The launch of a logo for a Women's World Cup in 2007 without the image of a woman (particularly without 'the ubiquitous ponytail') is a significant departure. On the one hand it is to be welcomed because it implies a move away from a Westernized, white bias and the heteronormative symbolism of long hair as indicative of youthful femininity. It is at least a reminder that public performance by women, in any of the cultural industries, not just sport, is a contentious issue, related to the physical presentation of women's bodies in society. Specifically with regard to football, the social meaning of the game as a national sport, a site of resistance, as evidence of Western progressive values or as colonial import have all affected women's access to it. What the abstracted logo doesn't undo is the title of the Women's World Cup, and this raises the question of how this symbolic 'difference' might be understood. In spite of outright hostility, neglect and scepticism, evidence suggested that there was a growth in the women's football community in the early twentieth century and a more considerable revival in the later decades, albeit not in a uniform manner. It goes without saying that there is considerable variation in countries as well as huge contrast across continents. Local, national, regional and global factors apply, so the material covered here is necessarily selective, and successive studies will elaborate or accentuate other people, places and themes. For the sake of consistency, major achievements and challenges in each case enable discussions of continuity and change for women in the sport.

The United States is the longest case study on four counts: first because of the number of female participants, second because of the achievement of the national team, third because of the link with the Olympic Games and fourth because of the staging of WWC '99 and the establishment of a media-owned professional league Women's United Soccer Association (WUSA). The effect of the 1972 Title IX Equal Education Amendments Act legislation has been to make college campuses the primary force in women's elite soccer in the US. Though it has always been under threat, a danger which remains to this day, in conjunction with other equity legislation, the principle of Title IX was to tie finance to opportunity and to give recourse to the legal system should this be denied. Nevertheless, as has been shown with the English Sex Discrimination Act, legislation in itself is not necessarily useful until its application serves reform. Education-based participation and elite development are not the only defining features of female soccer in the PR China and the US, as the live audience support at Women's World Cup 1991 and 1999 showed. In America, England, PR China and Australia, community and recreational leagues which operate parallel with but distinct from those in educational facilities, provide a reservoir of talent, enthusiasm and interest made up of those who participate and those who facilitate their involvement. Most of this participation is also crucially financially self-supporting in drawing on subscriptions to individual teams and leagues. Even sceptics would concede that this is a sizable demographic.

However, it is possible to overstate the unique features of the US cohort, and the remaining three chapters illustrate continuities. While sympathetic to the use of hegemony as a way of understanding women's access to aspects of football and marginalization from others, the evidence seems not to support the view that women's soccer is the counterpart of, let alone outperforming, the men's game in spite of the success of WWC 99, the collegiate system, the US women's National Team or a mass of participation. The case of PR China is one of the shorter chapters; while attempting to set a wider context for the women's sporting alliances in Asia, it also looks at the potential size of the population for participation as the country looks forward to the Women's World Cup in 2007 and the 'sporting mega-event' of the Beijing Olympiad, in 2008. Women's football has come under the Chinese FA since the mid-1980s, when there were approximately 300 women players. By 1996 there were around 800 women players, mostly students. Considerable elite success with this limited number of participants is a quite different form to describe. Also, one of the more unfortunately brief appraisals is the Australian case. The women who played in the green and gold in Sweden in 1995 came from clubs in Japan (Panasonic Bambina), Italy (AFC Agliana), Denmark (Fortuna Njorring) and England (Liverpool), as well as Marconi, Queensland Academy, Goonella Bah, Eastern Suburbs and Sydney Olympic. The lack of strength in depth of the sport, indeed whether it can be called a national sport, is reflected in the number of women players who go abroad to develop their game. However, there are emerging sources and a degree of interest to make this a much larger enquiry. Exploring the issue of time, people and place in cultures less close to my own is wonderfully difficult. While the limitation of linguistic skills is evident in the case of PR China, a lack of immersion in US and Australian culture is also clear. Some clear links between timelines, the novelty of women's play, the selectivity of participants and the problems of delivering elite competition emerged as themes to unite the very different examples. When John Economos, the 'best (journalist) friend women's soccer in Australia has had,' according to one of the correspondents in the pages of *Australia Soccer Weekly*, wrote to FIFA asking about a Women's World Cup in 1986, he got much the same reply that was given to the English professional Sue Lopez and to the journalist Ted Hart in 1971; to Mrs Jeffra Becknell of New Jersey, USA, in 1981, and a much less polite one than the Asian Ladies Football Confederation (ALFC) received the same year. The gist of this was that football activities are 'only possible through the National Associations and the Confederations'. The fact that they had been busy not organizing these events seems to have escaped notice. Meanwhile, examples like the ALFC and the Federation of Independent European Female Football (FIEFF), formed in 1969, meant that control of national teams and international competitions was to remain contentious for some time. Upon creating an 'official' England team after the Football Association ban on women's football was lifted, in December 1970, the Women's Football Association in England immediately threatened to 'ban' both players who jeopardized their amateur status by playing professionally and those who had played for the now illicit representative national eleven.

The broader context of the position of the women's game in relation to the men's is significant in all four cases.[16] Those who link female participation with a perceived feminization of the game which, in turn, limits its appeal to elements of the male population overlook statements such as the following priorities of the US national association: 'The national team is governed by the USSF. All national teams are treated alike and given the same consideration within the US structure (exception US male national team).'[17] The argument takes the case in isolation and particularly neglects issues of professionalism, especially as a matter of international gendered labour markets. What we do not have in terms of the 'cultural capital' of women's football, in the cases referred to here or anywhere else, is a women's professional league with the same prestige, sponsorship or support as any of the male domestic leagues around the world, and the country-specific reasons for this link women's history, sports and particularly the popularity of association football. In the same way, though FIFA tournaments for women are now rather belatedly titled World Cups, the flagship international competitions for women's football are less prestigious, glamorous and economically valuable than equivalent male events. Unable to attend the launch for the 2007 event, Sepp Blatter sent FIFA's director of development, Mary Harvey, and Sun Wen, a star of WWC'99 and FIFA ambassador for women's football, to deputize. Impressive as these women are in their own right, it is perhaps unimaginable that the normally forthright FIFA president would find himself indisposed at the launch of a World Cup (for men). The loss of the feminine in the sloganeering about the future of football is no great one, provided that it does not also involve devaluing of women's participation (currently only 10 per cent of FUTURO development funding is to be spent on developing female involvement, for example) in an increasingly diversified portfolio.[18]

M Ann Hall's borrowing of the term 'leaky hegemony' to characterize the history of women in sport as cultural resistance is partially useful across all four case studies.[19] However exactly what constitutes that hegemony in each differs. This is not just because some are 'football countries' (England), while others are passionate about the so-called indigenous forms (Australian rules, American football) and yet more have a militaristic individualized sporting ethos (PR China), as some generalizations would have us believe. How, when and where groups of women football players participate in and across societies can be understood as issues of access to education, leisure, resources and transport, which in turn impact on culture. To give an example of this, the high profile of Mia Hamm in the US and a handful of veteran National Team players from 1999 to 2003 should not draw attention from the lack of professional opportunities for women, which have meant their only option was to try to launch their own league in an already crowded sports market, as was the case with WUSA.[20] In each case, both the resistance of the dominant culture to change (of which sport is an economic, social, symbolic, political and social project, among others) and, usually, smaller adjustments to the prevailing mores are implied by women's participation in football. Consequently, though there has been some shift in attitudes that women ought not to participate in contact sport which seem to have begun to change as late as the 1970s in terms of what we might call significant numbers of participating women, residues of these ideas remain at the same time as new forms of specialization have taken place.[21] This has led international federations that took over women's football during that decade to argue that there are specific female-appropriate forms of play requiring exclusive and explicit conditions for women to be able to compete 'equitably'. There are significant pockets of mixed competitive play; most notably adult co-ed leagues in the United States, elements of youth sport in Oceania, Europe and Asia, where mixed play is up to age 18, and various gradations of mixed football as a game only for children (where the age limit is interpreted according to the context). This variety of regular participation exists unacknowledged by the direction of FIFA, as it were, compared to relatively high-profile cases of individual women reportedly signed to professional men's clubs.[22]

US women National Team players may well be better known to the public than their male counterparts, but those men may trade relative domestic anonymity for markets where their skills will make them millionaires and household names. The next generation of Mias (let alone Suns, Kellys and Cheryls) faces trying to launch a franchise as vehicle for their talent, in addition to earning a living.[23] The gendered career of football players has the effect of placing (at least) a double burden on elite women who have been obliged to be involved in constructing the framework of competition in addition to providing sporting spectacle. In examining the contemporary situation then, the perceived 'newness factor' of women's football requires critical evaluation because football (implying men's and male 'youth') and women's football (also involving girls) is a semantic reflection of the problem of how to accommodate female play.

FIFA and the Olympic Movement, like the national football associations, possess mechanisms that provide channels of mobility for members of in-groups and close them to others. This is not new.[24] Alice Milliat, who played football for the French Femina side during World War One, became secretary of the Federation Sportive Feminine Internationale (FSFI) in 1921.[25] At the 1923 all-male International Olympic Committee (IOC) congress, members voted to assume control of athletics and to offer five track and field events in the 1928 games. The International Amateur Athletic Federation (IAAF) Administrative Committee for European Athletics also decided to manage women's events in 1924 but voted against the inclusion of women's events before reversing the decision. By 1928, the longest women's event, the 800 metres, had been banned because of its supposedly exhausting nature and did not reappear until 1960. This wrangling over whether to acknowledge, let alone encourage, women's athletics ended in 1934 with assimilation of women's groups into international bodies and a loss of influence for female administrators. Milliat nonetheless stayed friendly with the English Dick, Kerr players for some years and took part in several contests between England and France.

The methods of excluding 'lady' athletes such as the 1921 ban on female football in England and a failure to incorporate women players into football associations combined with an absence of self-governing bodies. The latter are notable by their absence in each case-study nation prior to the 1960s, particularly surprising at international level. In other sports codes and in physical education generally, women formed such organizations. A limiting factor in both the construction of tradition and the development of the sport has been the lack of these coordinating groups run either by or for women from which an international network could develop. The Olympic examples show that the antipathy was not specific to football as a sport or bureaucratic attitude, but women's football has been particularly affected. Procedures of incorporation and assimilation were mirrored fifty years later in the century as FIFA assumed reluctant and gradual control of women's football from the 1970s. It was to take until 1996 for football to become an Olympic women's sport.[26]

Female teams were calling themselves world champions seventy years before there was a FIFA Women's World Cup, and so there's a need not to focus too narrowly on just four examples. What emerges from the attempts to develop an international women's tournament in England, the US, Hong Kong, Mexico, and Italy in the 1970s, before an official World Cup was deemed viable by FIFA, is that its attitude with regard to women and football developed out of a strategy conflict in its position as international federation. After the first phase of women's interest in each case-study nation, which seems to have peaked in the early to mid-1920s for country-specific reasons, there appears to have been steady but uncoordinated interest before the mid-1950s and an accelerated growth from the early 1970s on. Laurence Prudhomme-Poncet has discussed the shape of this history of women's football in France from 'the very beginning 1917 to 1937 and the second age since 1965'.[27] This view of neglect for almost thirty years is somewhat at odds with the emerging evidence. While thoroughly prepared for someone to show a much wider uptake, we are aware, for example, of the Dick, Kerr tours to Belgium, France, and the US from 1920; Stoke versus Femina in Barcelona in 1923; women's games in schools in China in the 1920s; matches between England and France (for example in Blackpool in 1937) and, in addition, matches in South Africa in the 1930s, which drew quite large crowds: 'Down in South Africa, the girls have taken up football and loud cries of "Soccer" ring the welkin.'[28] There seems to have been a resumption of international interest and competition after World War Two, though there was also domestic women's football during it, for instance between electrical engineers (team name the "Bright Sparks") and munitions workers (the "Great Guns") in England and college games in the US which had continued since the 1920s. International games took place, including one between the Canadian and the Norwegian Air Force teams in 1944; Bolton beat Edinburgh 7–1 in 1946, and there were several England versus France fixtures, for example in 1949. There had been evidence of women's games in Australia in the 1920s and 1940s, but whether these were domestic or international games is unclear, and some of the earlier matches followed Aussie rather than association rules.[29] Manchester Corinthians formed in 1949 and were first associated with Bert Trautmann in 1951 when he presented them with the Festival of Britain trophy. In 1957 the team toured Germany with Trautmann as interpreter.[30] This was followed by tours of Portugal in 1957–1958, Madeira in 1958, South America and Ireland in 1960, Italy in 1961, and Morocco and North Africa in 1966. Many of these exhibition and charity matches were organized by the International Red Cross and were played on major grounds in front of large crowds.[31] Women's games in US and Canadian colleges began to develop networks in the 1950s, and isolated events such as the domestic women's match at Kisumu Kenya in 1964 to mark Prime Minister Kenyatta's discussions of independence made the press with, appropriately, the Minister for Justice, Tom Mboya, as referee.[32] Slavia Praha and CKD Slany played in a Czech tournament that looks to have been a regular event of the 1960s, including a 'Gingerbread Heart Final' in 1969. By this time, the growth increasingly concerned international sporting federations. For example, on 17 May 1968 sixteen Italian women's football teams had announced the formation of the first women's football federation, in Viareggio.[33] There were also individual causes for concern, as twenty-seven-year-old Claudine Vidal, who by 1971 had enjoyed considerable success as a goal scorer in Uruguay, was at the centre of a fortnight-long controversy because the (men's) Sud American club of Paysandu, 200 miles northwest of Montevideo, had planned to play her as a centre-forward. In addition, there were widely reported news stories of the inappropriateness of football for women such as that reported by Dr Natalya Grayevskaya, chief of the Soviet Sports Federation:

> 'It could give them varicose veins and, worse, damage the functioning of the sexual organs ... A woman's pelvis is not just a firm support for the spine and lower limbs. A hard ball kicked there could damage organs protected by the pelvic ring.' She recommends any one of 48 allowable sports ... published by the Ministry of Health, answering the complaint of an irate male sports fan who said he was disgusted by the sight of two women's teams playing last summer.[34]

By the 1970s it simply wasn't a viable option for FIFA to ignore women playing the game and to hope that they would go away. The still-young commercial revolution that began to happen in football in the decade couldn't obscure this recreative and competitive community, which had grown in spite of lack of access, opportunity or enthusiasm from established sports federations, as this broader survey indicates.

What does seem to be clear in terms of setting an agenda for the following chapters is that women's football has had to reconcile itself to the single-structure model of sport whereby one international federation (in this case, FIFA, founded in 1904) controls the activities of constituent members (national football associations), which are grouped by region into affiliated confederations (the six are the Asian Football Confederation (AFC); Confédération Africaine de Football (CAF); Confederation of North, Central American and Caribbean Association Football (CONCACAF); Confederación Sudamericana de Fútbol (CONMEBOL); Oceania Football Confederation (OFC); and Union des Associations Européennes de Football (UEFA)).[35] The supposedly democratic basis of one country one vote coexists with a wealthy, powerful, centralized executive with a dual responsibility for regulation and development. The federation expects and reinforces that affiliates will participate only in competitions sanctioned by them at the national, regional and international levels. If women's associations began to form in the late 1960s, the emergence of this new leadership, like the growth in female participants, created a community cohesion requiring acknowledgement. It seems therefore to have prompted something of a contradictory progress as the women's game became gradually institutionalized but without effectively being commercialized.

This single-structure model has been particularly strengthened by Olympic recognition of FIFA's control of football. This has had a symbolic and, importantly, economic impact in all four countries discussed in the succeeding chapters. Briefly, this has meant that women's football associations seeking to arrange international competitions have been encouraged (if one takes a polite view) to align with FIFA as the only body recognized by the International Olympic Committee. The processes involved in this arbitration are case-specific, but the effect of interventions has been to require those active in women's football to make the adjustment. This is not to say that concessions have not been made on both sides, but, as a wealthy and prestigious international nongovernmental organization with strong associational links with other international sports bureaucracies, FIFA has centralized power over world football that other bureaucracies in sport support. On an international level, it reinforces a point made by Matthias Marschick in reference to the systematic processes in Austrian football: 'The massive exclusion however, is masked by a front of tolerance.'[36] The veneer of progressivism remains at the core of the procedural anxieties of football's national and international governing bodies, almost without exception.[37] It also raises some ongoing issues about amateurism, professionalism and related commercialism of the women's game. The issue of commercial viability is routinely treated in women's sport more widely by the sporting press as a case of 'I'm not a chauvinist, but I know a chap who might be.' For example, Pat Cash's discussion of the All England Club's eventual award of equal prize money: 'Whatever they say in public, male players will resent pay equality at Wimbledon' and, less candidly, a remark by Hugh McIlvanney, citing a comment by the late Mark McCormack, founder of IMG whom he considers the most significant pioneer of sports marketing: 'Women tennis players should get down in thanks and pray each day to whomever they believe in that they play the Grand Slams at the same time as the men. To sell women's tennis on its own terms has nowhere near the same attraction.'[38] The possibility of double-header games for men's and women's teams has been trialled in a number of cases, but, as will be discussed, the divide between 'football' and 'women's football' is carefully guarded.

The trade-off for the women's football community in being belatedly accepted by the structures designed to oversee men's football has been an increase in support for 'official' World Cup, Olympic, confederation and national competition in return for accepting a degree of regulation. The developments have been so considerable that it could seem curmudgeonly to point out that, on occasion, this has meant the loss of long-standing tournaments which have formed part of the history and culture of the international women's football community, while in other cases these existing arrangements have been revised to form current competition. It is not, however, ungracious to point out that the majority of women's and girls' involvement has relied on, and continues to depend upon, the efforts of an extraordinary number of volunteers and enthusiasts even where elite forms of the sport have benefitted a great deal from co-option. Outlining this in a brief historical overview in each chapter gives some sense of both country-specific and international networks.

This is both blessing and curse because at the everyday sporting level, the degree of autonomy available to those volunteering and to paid facilitators of female play is considerable. Part of the creativity celebrated by women players interviewed for this study is reciprocated and amplified by those who help to create club identity, competitive events, recreational tournaments and the many other initiatives. The cascade of information, rules and regulations sent down by the decision-making authorities is then adapted, interpreted, overlooked or ignored (the widespread problem of getting qualified referees to oversee competitive matches is one example). However, at the commercial and, by extension, the competitive pinnacle, we could be more careful in asking those who make decisions on behalf of this hardworking community about justifiable and indefensible sporting and profit-making policies.

The most obvious of these and one which affects football as both leisure and competitive sport and as a multibillion-pound business is the question of the partial assimilation of women players, coaches and administrators, though in what might be called the ancillary occupations related to sports science there has been some growth of opportunity for women. In characterizing the process as one of negative integration, I suggest that there are four main reasons for this situation. The first is that the national associations and international federations delayed the incorporation of women as long as was feasible. Circular letter 142 of 1970 asked FIFA member nations to comment on the status of women's football, including whether it was recognized at all in each member country. When it became clear that there were international female competitions with a degree of media interest, the risk of losing control of part of the sport forced the rather unwilling bureaucrats to review their position. A conciliatory approach to resolving legitimacy crises, such as the Asian Ladies Football Association episode discussed later, meant that co-option of the women's game was a pragmatic response handled in a diplomatic manner.[39] Since then, the structures of men's football have become the frameworks onto which women's participation has been partially grafted, including the adoption of women's competitions which may have existed before merger.

The second reason concerns how partial the integration will remain if it is based on the equal-but-different model, which in the context of the last decade of the twentieth century saw increasingly specialized functions around the elite male game including, but not limited to, sports law, sports medicine, commercialization and mediatization. Given the moderate ambitions of these bureaucracies for the women's game, it is highly unlikely that it can aspire to the same market share, media coverage and so on. The third point is that the use of the terminology 'football', generally taken to mean top-flight professional aspects of the game, and 'women's football' reflects a wish to maintain binary opposition between the two. If, for example, we see reference to youth football, futsal, and so on, to demonstrate a variety of initiatives to increase participation, many of these are, by implication, male youth development, men's futsal, male beach soccer and so forth. Women's and girls' concerns are maintained as a niche. The fourth reason for using the term is to indicate that the processes used are far from transparent and open, particularly to women administrators who perhaps facilitated play before the interest of various national and international associations. 'Negative integration' is meant therefore to characterize structures, attitudes and processes from the 1960s to the present.

This links the subject with discussions of diffuse status characteristics and expectations over and above sport and unrelated to the athletic body. The postulate that higher-status individuals will be judged more competent regardless of performance attracts attention to the narratives around justifying that distinction and the processes of reinforcing it. If your interest in football is rather more about the beautiful game than feminist-informed theory, what is the advantage in describing male/female interaction in terms of status rather than as an expression of physical characteristics? The different but equal logic currently popular in the United Nations and EU directives calling for equitable access to sport and recreation as a human right, discusses availability of gender-specific opportunity. The dysfunctions of power and prestige implied by ordering status along lines of sex are beyond questions of regular sport and recreational activities for which 'equality' sometimes acts as shorthand. Treating this as a question of normalizing prerogative and influence is intended to make these processes conspicuous. As *The Times* reporting *La Republica* put it, reactions of 'astonishment to mild hysteria' followed when the former international centre-forward Carolina Morace, 'who is blessed with blonde curls and long legs', was appointed to coach third-division Italian side Viterbese in 1999. A law graduate from Venice, Morace had one of the highest international strike rates in women's football before her retirement. *The Times* correspondent was able to effectively distance himself from the fuss in Viterbo: Italians had accepted women pilots, soldiers, and cabinet ministers, but the idea of a female football coach 'could be a step too far ... this punctures the last male taboo in Italy.'[40] Whenever a woman player or coach is signed to a male team, these modest avatars of the unthinkable and the unmentionable provoke this question of status. What kind of equality is desirable and is it possible to have too much?

When looking at the case of a World Cup, while equivocal, then, it can't be denied that the overall gains for women's football have been considerable. Even at a practical level, events like the Women's World Cup 1999 require the support of an array of international partners with considerable expertise in presenting first-class tournaments. Women's current position in football has developed out of historical frictions between the authoritarian, expansionist and mercantile functions of national and international associations. In other words, a distinct phase is identifiable whereby the 'problem' no longer lies in women's partaking per se but in how expectations of that participation are managed. The year 2006 saw the launch of fifteen FIFA Ambassadors for Women's Football. The terminology indicates the sense of a dilemma as they aren't ambassadresses but represent and promote a gender-specific game. Why not ambassadors of football (who happen to be women)?

> I am writing to thank FIFA for conducting the recent seminar on women's football ... I was relieved to hear you say that you had not informed the New Zealand Football Association that they were to take over the running of New Zealand women's football, and that you were happy after being assured that we are affiliated to the NZFA and go through them for all international matters and dealings with FIFA. It appeared to me that this situation was most acceptable to yourself. I would be most grateful if you could please put this in writing to the New Zealand Women's Association.[41]

The autonomy once enjoyed by those who organized the sport for women has been the trade-off for those who see themselves as acting 'for the good of the game', and this has meant intervention at the national and international levels. Perhaps unsurprisingly given the gains, most women administrators who have a part in that infrastructure remain a good deal more optimistic than I about this and strongly supported the single-structure model but with more women chosen on merit. Certainly, there is sufficient support for this view to make breakaway or independent women's organizations seem a thing of the past in view of the wealth, prestige and international recognition linked with football. Rather than fight old battles, women administrators and players disaffected by the current situation have tended to withdraw from sport altogether with the question of a meritocracy by whose definition left in the air. However, as we have seen with the format of WWC '99 and the creation of WUSA, there is an impetus for women's elite competition that lies outside sport, and these other protagonists have sometimes had a more ambitious agenda than the achievement of mere respectability. The mutual adjustment of women's football and the sports organizations that took control of it (where they have taken control) continues.

Since it appears that women's football has accelerated participation rates in the 1990s, most of the young women and girls interviewed for this book thought that this would be a continuing trend, bringing with it increased visibility and recognition. FIFA has opted for a policy of encouragement rather than compliance over the issue of whether there is any women's football overseen by the various national associations. In a not isolated case, one colleague from Tanzania was still having difficulty in gaining recognition for women's football at all and in particular her status as administrator in 2005, so it is good to see that nation join the FIFA rankings for women's football even if it is an overdue inclusion.

It remains a moot point whether women can and may play football under what circumstance. Like many aspects of women's lives, this surveillance over what they can, should and ought to do with their bodies (and by implication not) is the subject of much regulation and control. Yet, when speaking to women and girls who play football, this tension is not usually central to their view, which instead combines personal fulfilment, pleasure and absorption with camaraderie. In theoretical terms, it seems a little patronizing to say that they are creating meaning in football through their involvement at the same time that they are reinforcing female-appropriate behaviour because so many were willing to celebrate a variety of relationships formed through the sport. The sensitivity to stereotypes from those operating outside the sport can mask the multiple experiences of players and also the active support of those outside the game or on its periphery for the women in it. Women in football seem to enjoy the challenge of their overlapping and multiple experience of the body as players. So while an essentialist masculinity and femininity is upheld in the official and elite forms of the sport, this distinction is by no means universally accepted, lived or upheld through play.

It also appeared that a vital part of the solidarity was an acceptance of the multiple experiences of gender configurations of both other women and men players.[42] The altruism of players was informative to me as an academic trying to reflect their experience (though I'm not such a fan as to want to pretend that all are equally pleasant, kind, tolerant or interested in football). That is, my concern here is not women's football solely at the level of the individual or at the level of the social systems which intersect with it. It would seem artificial to separate these two elements. More absorbing is the plasticity of the social locations and of the constitution of gender in a variety of contexts. Neither gender nor sport is fixed; what are the multiple practices and meanings of women and football? Of course, limiting this study to 'wimmin's sport' is embedding it within a normalizing classification of identity production, and we should go beyond this to look at what men and women's multiple practices of football are. This would be a large undertaking, requiring a considerable budget and a great deal of stamina. A starting point might be to look at the male contribution to the women's game because the history of women's football indicates that it has not been a very sexually-segregated one in most countries. Some of the material here is drawn from that cohort, but this isn't that study. The focus is the ideological terrain that is under contestation, the manner of the struggle and sources of tension because women want to play.[43]

There also seems to be an assumption of late that the regulatory and commercial functions of the sport can be divided, and, though 2007 will see another new departure in that all participating women's teams will be financially rewarded for providing World Cup entertainment, important future questions about the viability of the women's game remain. The football 'family' was rather more of a gentleman's club until the 1990s. Now, for example, both Sepp Blatter and Lenhart Johansson have less courteously called for women to move into new markets for sponsorship.[44] Are women being asked to earn their keep by breaking the sport into new markets, or is there still a concern about their financial viability? Will it be of the right kind? This new emphasis on the commercialized aspects of the game is in contrast with the early phase of integration which held back the women's game in a variety of ways across the globe. There appears to have been a contradictory attitude in FIFA that women's football needed protection from pursuing the 'wrong' kind of marketable future and a feeling that the 'correct' type of for-profit activity was financially unviable. A tone of romantic paternalism is evident throughout. Following FIFA circular letter 142 of 1970, the first UEFA committee to look at the international status of women's football was set up in 1971 on the occasion of the extraordinary UEFA Congress of Monte Carlo, with the first conference on women's football staged in March 1973 with the participation of just nine member associations.[45] The discussions centred upon information received from twenty-three member associations following a survey carried out by UEFA. The summaries reveal a reported 111,000 players in the Federal Republic of Germany, 26,000 in Denmark, 11,000 in the Netherlands, 9,400 in Sweden, 6,000 in France, 4,000 in England, 3,000 in Finland, 2,500 in Belgium and Hungary and undisclosed numbers in Czechoslovakia, Switzerland, Austria, Iceland, the German Democratic Republic, Romania and Wales. The first eight had national championships and the remainder regional competitions.

Given Norway's prominence today, the lack of evidence of women's play there is a notable exception, as is the 'illegal' semiprofessional Italian league unrecognized by the national association where 'the payment of considerable transfer fees for good players was indeed a common fact.'[46] Of the twenty-three member associations who had replied, five were in favour of international competition for representative teams and five for club teams; five felt it was too early, and eight were not in support. Consequently, no arrangements for international competition were made. Another meeting in Rotterdam followed in 1974, and there was no further action until November 1977, when UEFA felt obligated to raise the questions again because, ironically, international tournaments in Europe, Asia and North America had proven so popular with women's teams from a range of nations. National associations were repeatedly asked to restrict participation to FIFA- and UEFA-approved tournaments, which in turn had to be recognized and approved by the relevant national association. UEFA then resurrected the women's committee in 1980 after compiling the responses to the earlier questionnaire. By then, the policy of not approving existing intercontinental competitions but failing to create officially-sanctioned events was obviously ineffective, so, coincidentally, a UEFA conference was scheduled on the same day as a conference in the valley of Aosta, Italy, which looked set to organize yet another unofficial women's invitational cup. There had been sufficient interest in 1979 for twelve national teams to participate in the Italian tournament, for example, a fact that was registered in the minutes of the 1980 UEFA conference as a cause for concern.[47]

So-called friendly or invitational tournaments had grown since the Coppa Europa per Nazioni in 1969 and 1979 (Italy), the Coppa del Mondo in 1970 (Italy), the Mundualito in 1971 (Mexico), the Women's Asian Championship from 1975 onwards (various), and an unofficial Women's World Cup contested annually with the exception of 1972 and 1973, plus numerous international tournaments in North America during the 1970s. So, does the evidence indicate a conspiracy of inaction, unwillingness or incomprehension? Was this primarily a wish to prevent commercial exploitation, a fear of financial difficulty, qualms over the loss of control of part of the sport, or a preservation of the more professionalized aspects of football as essentially masculine? It seems that all of these elements were present, but the written records, which indicate several unminuted meetings which punctuate the formal gatherings, tend to support the view that restrictions imposed for the good of the game or women's place in it (and out of it) were used to prevent well-financed tournaments for which approval was sought. For example, a 1973 letter sent by the WFA secretary Pat Gregory proposed a pilot Women's European Competition of four countries supported to the tune of £5,000 by the cutlery manufacturers Viners.[48] The correspondence over this proposal went back and forth between the WFA, the Football Association, UEFA and FIFA from August 1973 to July 1974. After agreeing that the tournament would be open only to representative teams and those women's teams recognized by their respective national associations (which effectively prevented Italy, arguably one of the most competitive teams, from participating), a deal was reached. FIFA recorded no objection to the sponsorship or the tournament provided that it was played according to the laws of the game and the existing regulations, though the phrasing of the correspondence changed as the 'project' became a 'problem' by January 1974.[49] The sticking point was that Viners were to make no profit. The words 'international' and 'world cup' also seem to have caused some consternation. The Women's Nordic Championships, for example, ran as an official tournament and was left well alone from 1974 to 1982 as an important precursor to European-wide female competition.

The Second Conference on Women's Football, in 1980, began by rehearsing well-worn themes.

> The last article on the Provisions of women's football concerns international competitions played outside Europe. The participation in such competitions is only possible with the consent of UEFA and the approval of FIFA. The restrictions in question had to be included on account of the fact that 'so-called' World Championships for women's teams have been staged on two occasions by inofficial organizations without the approval of FIFA and UEFA ... As spokesman for the Austrian FA Dr Gerö addressed the Conference by stating that Women's Football is known in his country since 1935, but that the Austrian FA has only intervened in 1973 out of fear that profit-seeking organizations or private individuals not affiliated to the Association would start to organize matches for women's teams. The Austrian FA felt responsible to protect football from any unwelcome influence, which could be a challenge to the ethics of sport.[50]

At the conference, four of the twenty-nine delegates were women; unsurprisingly, Pat Gregory, Hannelore Ratzeburg, of Germany and Ellen Wille, of Norway were there. The acceleration of interest across Europe since 1973 is notable. The Federal Republic of Germany had 380,000 women and girls playing in 2,252 teams; Sweden had 50,000 females registered in 3,000 teams; Denmark claimed 27,000 players in 1,034 teams; France reported 16,000 registered players in 727 clubs; Norway had

10,000 women in 650 teams; England had 6,000 players in 261 clubs, and Italy reported a decline of interest with 2,000 players and 57 teams in Switzerland. While the figures for Finland (2,500 participants in 51 clubs) and Belgium (2,000 players) dipped slightly, there was also evidence of interest in Austria, Portugal, Scotland and Wales. It perhaps indicates the distance of UEFA from women's participation that each association present was asked to describe the timing of the women's season, which in all cases ran concurrent with the traditional sporting calendar of winter leagues and summer tournaments. The conference closed with a unanimous motion to support women's football to the extent that 'UEFA, in accordance with its fundamental policy of fostering football in general, would not refuse its financial support to a competition for women's teams. This did not mean, however, that UEFA would now be prepared to act as host and to take charge of all the costs, but it would support energetically the National Associations or relevant organizations in their efforts.'[51] It would appear however that the Women's Football Association of Italy would not be classified as 'relevant' because 'As everybody knows this Association is extremely active on an international level. Certain machinations such as the strong commercialization of sports, the attempts to attract foreign female players etc. had led to great problems in the past ... The President is therefore confident that the inconsistencies still existing could be eliminated within a short time.'[52] This language of intrigues was not enough, however, to convince the international federation to adopt the same policy with regard to a world championship event.

What is most telling about this response to the idea for an official tournament is that the international association was under pressure from several invitational competitions, which claimed to be a world cup of sorts, and these are explored in the following chapters. So there was a tension within the federation between those who wished to facilitate a degree of international competition for women, as the UEFA attitude indicates, and those who seemed to wish it would all go away. This may have been a vestige of the old amateur/professional divide where there was a genuine belief that another football tournament would flood an already challenged market, or it could have reflected prejudice. As ever, the ambitions of the women's football community at more local levels were focussed to sharper effect. For example, Women's International Soccer (WINS) organized tournaments in Los Angeles and combined these with conferences to discuss 'the development of competition nationally and internationally, the need to establish a national and international communications network, women as coaches and referees, how to organize better tournaments, and the current movement to get soccer into the 1984 Olympics'.[53] The response to this from FIFA is a view of American 'exceptionalism' with quite a different interpretation, as it explained:

> There are some countries where the national associations took no action, mostly because they were of the opinion that women's football does not exist in their country ... It is true that in the United States especially, quite an astonishing number of private enterprises take advantage of the development of the game in this area to set up conferences,

organisations, competitions and to make money out of soccer. You are certainly aware of the fact that, as a whole, the approach to the game in the United States is different from other parts of the world. Not the sporting competition as such is important, it seems that much more the possibility of earning money is the reason for their interest in soccer ... if, in a determined country, the national association does nothing to control women's football then it is obvious that private enterprises try to take it over.[54]

It also becomes apparent from the response to Pat Gregory, who had supported the request for Olympic recognition in 1980, that for strategic and competition reasons FIFA would not support WINS's aims for that tournament. That is, negotiations had already taken place in which it was agreed that in exchange for maintaining the number of teams in the men's Olympic Final competition, the introduction of a women's event would be postponed. Conveniently, the standard of female play was also not considered good enough.

May we recall only a couple of years ago, the IOC discussed the problem of team sports with the competent international federations. On that occasion, the number of teams as a whole (by this we mean for all team sports) was reduced. FIFA was granted the previous number of 16 teams for the final Competition provided that, at least for the time being, women's football was not introduced as an Olympic team sport. In the internal exchange of views with all committees concerned, FIFA came to the conclusion that at least for the time being the standard of women's football was not such that this branch of our game should be presented at Olympic Games. May we also recall that it was FIFA's interest and FIFA's decision that in the sixties women's football was officially recognized. National Associations in membership were encouraged to take women's football under their umbrella and prevent business men and promoters from introducing women's football not mainly as a sporting event but much more to make money.[55]

It is peculiar that where national associations took no action 'because they were of the opinion that women's football does not exist in their country', there was also a worry regarding the lure of the female game for private enterprise.

Two elements prevent an indulgent attitude toward this 'If we don't recognize it, it doesn't exist' syndrome. The first is that there was an absurdity in regarding organizations such as WINS as requiring oversight by the relevant national association, which had the effect of smothering such developments as could have taken place. Those who did recognize women's associations encouraged them not to attend WINS conferences because it was unclear whether they were affiliated. Nevertheless, as the 1985 UEFA survey indicates, there was very little football for school-age girls at this time, and so without the networks developed by women's teams (affiliated or not), the international growth of the sport would have been very much slowed, let alone the rate of growth in individual nations.

The second element is that it does not support a view in which national or international federations led the way in supporting or developing the game as a sport or as a commercial enterprise, and each case study goes only some way toward outlining this. There wasn't a rush of female participation in the 1990s which the sports bodies facilitated, encouraged and assisted. A more extensive network and time frame contextualizes the willingness to quantify female participation as part of the success story of the international federation in fostering competition. The current narratives about the difficulty of presenting female play to live and mediated audiences therefore become part of an ongoing story, a large part of which has been a sizable degree of unofficial endeavour because of official inactivity. On looking through the correspondence spanning forty years, the 'can do' attitude of the various members of the international women's football community is met with a 'we'd really rather not thanks' from those bureaucrats time and again. Refreshingly, the can-doers' determination was sufficiently organized that the federation's response became 'we're already doing that' by 1983, though it took a further eight years to organize. The gradual acceptance of a Women's World Cup doesn't really support the view of Havelange as a visionary of women's future in the game. Instead, it is largely because of that lobbying and activism that we have the current range of international competitions for women. Before going on to give examples of how that community is constituted in the chapters, the tone is set by referring to arguably the most significant of these in terms of strategy, lobbying and sheer persistence.

Based in Hong Kong, the Asian Ladies Football Confederation had caused some anxiety not least because, as the name indicated, they wished to be affiliated with FIFA as an entity in their own right. The Executive Council of this body included representatives from Indonesia, India, Japan, Malaysia, the Philippines, the Republic of China and Thailand. The standing committees comprised some of these executive members but also other officials, and the organization appeared to involve twenty to thirty individuals with a turnover of around 50,000 Hong Kong dollars (HK$) in the 1980s.[56] After protracted negotiations which were widely covered by the press from 1968 on, by the end of September 1984 the ALFC had become a federation and, as such, the women's committee of the AFC.[57] The success of this affiliation led FIFA to once again insist that 'control is really carried out by the National Association, especially with regard to the international activities of women's football, be this at club or national association level.'[58] Cumulatively, these events put pressure on FIFA to control the large women's tournaments at a time when it was little interested in developing its own. It is not the ALFC alone that forced this change but more likely the proliferation of international tournaments, suggesting a general degree of commercial viability regardless of the financial success of each.[59]

So, as early as 1983 and more frequently by 1984, Havelange was speaking in the media about a FIFA-hosted Women's World Cup, which he indicated would be staged in 1985 (then 1986, then 1987; eventually it became the 1988 Guangzhou event) and biennially thereafter. There was a meeting in September 1983, for example, at which FIFA officials outlined the costing and organization of a two-week Women's World Cup to be contested in either 1984 or 1985 by eight teams and costing 1,750,000 Swiss francs.[60] There was a proposal at the 1986 Congress, but this appeared to formalize a situation that had already been agreed to as a precedent. It seems that the level of interest in this subject was sufficient to overcome the more conservative elements within FIFA that had made the 1981 report, which is referred to in detail in the chapter on England, though it was to take a decade to host a full World Cup event. The ALFC may not have had considerable size or scope, but it did spur the AFC to host an invitational tournament for women and for the idea of a Women's World Championship to become a commonly referred-to topic thereafter. The motion sent by Norway at the 1986 Congress to initiate an official Women's World Cup also included the proposal to gain acceptance as an Olympic sport and was supported by Denmark and Iceland.[61] The minutes of the Congress in Mexico indicates that Ellen Wille 'suggested that the official report of the General Secretary pay in future more attention to Women's football [sic]. She requested that FIFA do more for Women's Football, particularly as far as refereeing was concerned but also in the form of international women's tournaments. President Havelange thanked Mrs Wille for these suggestions but drew attention to the fact that FIFA was already dealing with this topic.'[62] In 1987 at a meeting with Peter Verlappen, General Secretary of the AFC, participants arrived at the conclusion that there was a need for a test tournament for 'ladies' that year, followed by the first world tournament the following year. The test tournament was to be played by eight teams with four from Asia, the sixteen-team tournament to include six AFC, six UEFA, two Oceania and two CONCACAF teams.[63] It is evident from the subsequent correspondence that the second of these events was to be a rehearsal for the first official FIFA Women's World Cup.

Minutes of the 46th Ordinary Congress indicate that the 1986–1988 Activity Report was opened by a representative from the Canadian Soccer Association, Fred Stambrook, who congratulated FIFA on staging 'the first international women's football tournament. At the same time he expressed his consternation at the negative implications in some remarks made on women's football in FIFA News, such as, for instance, that it was asking too much of women to use ball no. 5 and that it was intended to reduce their playing time.'[64] Both suggestions had repeatedly been debated and questions raised about whether women could cope with playing for a full ninety minutes with a size five ball, and these remained issues at the first FIFA symposium on women's football, in 1992, after the championships had been held.

In what sense is there justification for seeing the return to China this year as a departure rather than a return? For the first time in the history of the FIFA Women's World Cup, in 2007 bonuses (totalling $6 million US) will be paid to the teams, with the champions earning $1 million US and those in from ninth to sixteenth place earning $200,000.[65] As the argument moves on to examine the case-study situation across diverse political, social, cultural, geographic and economic examples, ambiguity and equivocation remain strong influences. At the same time, in the past fifteen years, since the establishment of a Women's World Cup, comparison of key themes and new contexts dusts the mirror a little more in revealing the previously hidden picture of individuals and groups who might constitute an international women's football community. At the core of the argument are two principles of which the example of the World Cup negotiations is meant to provide illustration. The first is that it is possible to focus too tightly on contemporary developments at the expense of understanding how historical forces continue to shape those events. How have women players and their (practical and moral) supporters reconfigured their ideas and representations to take account of expanding or contracting markets, changing economic conditions and new demands for labour and leisure? What are the specific challenges to historians of women's football posed by nationalism and ethnicity? The second principle is that women's football as a leisure pursuit, sport and business should not be isolated from a study of the wider trends affecting these issues. What is the relation between what we can know about women players in any local situation and what we can know about women broadly and comparatively? What are the current economic and political relations of world football that affect women players? The interconnectedness of these two ideas reflects intricate patterns both in and between countries and sets of countries.

## Notes

1. Sepp Blatter, *FIFA News*, 19 March 2006.
2. Nan Yong, 'Full Speed Ahead', *FIFA News*, 1 September 2006, available at http://www.fifa.com/.
3. However, in terms of the history of international football, the 1934 tournament in Italy and the 1938 World Cup (for men) hosted in France have been argued to be localized rather than international events. See, for example, Matthew Taylor, 'Global Players? Football Migration and Globalization 1930–2000', *Historical Social Research,* 31, no. 1 (2006): 7–30.
4. See, for example, John Bale and Joseph Maguire (eds), *The Global Sports Arena: Athletic Talent Migration in an Interdependent World* (London: Frank Cass, 1994); Pierre Lanfranchi and Matthew Taylor, *Moving with the Ball: The Migration of Professional Footballers* (Oxford: Berg, 2001); Taylor, 'Global Players?'.
5. These competitions include FIFA Beach Soccer World Cup; FIFA Interactive World Cup; Blue Stars/FIFA Youth Cup; FIFA Club World Cup; FIFA Futsal World Cup; FIFA U-20 Women's World Cup; FIFA U-17 World Cup and the FIFA U-20 World Cup.
6. Vision Asia is the Asian Football Confederation's grand plan for a continent-wide programme to raise the standards of Asian football at all levels—on the field of play, in administration or in sports science. It was launched in September 2002 by AFC President Mohamed Bin Hammam. See, for example, http://www.the-afc.com/english/, accessed 12 January 2005.

7. FIFA, *Statistics: 2nd FIFA Women's World Cup Sweden 1995 5–18 June* (Geneva: Zollikofer, 1995), p. 5. Continuing the confectionary theme, the Second FIFA Women's World Championship for Women's Football '95 Sweden was 'presented by Snickers'.

8. See for example an analysis in USA Team Statement *China '91: 1st FIFA World Championship for Women's Football for the M&Ms Cup* (Zurich: FIFA, 1991), p. 51.

9. House of Commons Select Committee Second Special Report: Women's Football 25 July 2006. The Committee published its Fourth Report of Session 2005–2006, on Women's Football. The Committee has now received responses from the Department for Culture, Media and Sport, the Football Association and the Football Foundation; see http://www.publications.parliament.uk/pa/cm200506/cmselect, accessed 19 October 2006. For the FA Consultation see TheFA.com, a national online consultation, consisting of ten different questionnaires targeting adult players, coaches, referees, parents and teachers, as well as those whose involvement until now has been more recreational.

10. Mohammad Ehsani, 'The History of Women's Football in Iran', *Women, Football and Europe,* University of Central Lancashire, 14 June 2005.

11. João Havelange, 'Address by the President', *45th Ordinary Congress of FIFA,* Mexico City, p. 5. So animated did the Swiss Football Association President, Heinrich Röthlisberger, become that after fourteen years of 'guiding the fate of world football ... in his inimitable style: magnanimously, perspicaciously, diplomatically but unflinchingly ... in recognition of João Havelange's services towards a better understanding between the peoples of the world, for his efforts to create a fairer sport and his dedication to the Third World, I wish to ask this FIFA congress to propose him as a candidate for the Nobel Peace Prize.' Minutes of the *46th Ordinary Congress of FIFA*, 1 July 1988, Zurich, p. 19.

12. Douglas Booth, *The Field: Truth and Fiction in Sport History* (London: Routledge, 2005).

13. João Havelange, *World Women's Invitational Football Tournament Chinese Taipei Football Association,* 11 September 1984, FIFA Correspondence File, Zurich.

14. Douglas Booth, 'Sites of Truth or Metaphors of Power? Refiguring the Archive', *Sport in History,* 26, no. 1 (April 2006): 104.

15. Harry H. Cavan, *World Women's Invitational Football Tournament Chinese Taipei Football Association,* 11 September 1984, FIFA Correspondence File, Zurich. He continues: 'The Chinese Taipei Football Association has the full approval of FIFA to organize this World Women's Invitational Football Tournament to be played in Taiwan and it is my privilege and honour to convey the congratulations of FIFA to the Association for this excellent initiative. I offer sincere best wishes to the Organising Committee and all the women players, for a happy and successful Tournament and which will contribute much to the

progress of women's football in the World.' Havelange oversaw the reintegration of the People's Republic of China into the FIFA family 'without the stautory rights of the Football Association located in Taipei being infringed upon ... The solution passed by the Congress of 1978 was accepted by acclamation in 1980. Consequently, it was also adopted by a series of International Sports Federations, notably the International Olympic Committee.' Havelange, 'Address by the President', p. 4.

16. For a more in-depth discussion of this issue see A. Markovits and S. Hellerman, *Women's Soccer in the United States: Yet Another American Exceptionalism,* in F. Hong and J. A. Mangan, *Soccer, Women and Sexual Liberation: Kicking Off a New Era* (London: Frank Cass, 2003), pp. 14–30.

17. This is one example given in USA Team Statement, *China '91: 1st FIFA World Championship for Women's Football for the M&Ms Cup* (Zurich: FIFA, 1991), p. 53. However, there is a history of differential treatment for men and women national team players since this time; see http://www.womensoccer.com/refs/comment99.html, accessed 12 March 2006.

18. For examples of FIFA development programmes and FUTURO in particular, see http://www.fifa.com/en/development, accessed 12 January 2005.

19. Hall acknowledges borrowing this term from Susan Birrell and Nancy Theberg, 'Feminist Resistance and Transformation in Sport', in D. Costa and S. Guthrie (eds), *Women and Sport: Interdisciplinary Perspectives* (Champaign, IL: Human Kinetics, 1994), p. 263. See, for example, her discussion of cycling as both a means of increasing the mobility of women and a factor in changing dress codes; she also addresses how these relate to enduring myths about essential female qualities.

20. See for example the latest children's book by Mia Hamm, with the illustrator Carol Thompson, entitled *Winners Never Quit!* (New York: Byron Press Visual Publications, 2004).

21. When Russia hosted the 2006 female youth tournament, it was known as the FIFA U 20 Women's World Championship. The next proposal is the creation of a FIFA U 17 Women's World Championship, which, according to the Executive Committee, will have its inaugural edition in 2008.

22. In December 2004 Maribel Dominguez reportedly signed to play for the Mexican men's side Celaya. In 2003 Italian team Perugia announced it had made an offer to the German World Cup winner Birgit Prinz; the club had previously tried to sign Sweden's Hannah Ljungberg, which would have made her the first female player in Series A.

23. It also strikes me as incongruous to differentiate between recreation and competition, as Markovits and Hellerman do in statements like 'participatory recreation almost always superseded the drive for competition over a long period, at least until the 1970s,' when in terms of access to sport generally and football particularly, the principle of female access to competitive and/or

recreational opportunities was bitterly contested. The evolution of women's soccer accelerated after the 1970s, but the sports market in which it developed altered radically too.

24. The Australian Olympic Committee stated that the word 'Olympic' could not appear anywhere on the Australian Women's Soccer Association Calendar for 2000. Their objection arose because players were either semi- or unclothed, and the AWSA agreed to remove any association with the Olympic Games. See for example http://www.womensoccer.com/refs/austrcalendar, accessed December 2003.

25. For more detail on the role of Madame Milliat see M. Leigh and T. Bonin, 'The Pioneering Role of Madame Alice Milliat and the FSFI in Establishing International Trade for Women', *Journal of Sport History,* 4, no. 1 (Spring 1977): 72–83; and L. Duval, 'The Development of Women's Track and Field in England: The Role of the Athletic Club, 1920s–1950s', *The Sports Historian,* 1, no. 21 (2000): 1–34. In the 1928 Olympic Games, the five women's events were the 100 metres, high jump, 800 metres, discus and 4 x 100 metres relay. The 800 metres was banned after this until 1960. The FSFI's world championships, held from 1922 to 1934, offered a fuller programme to female athletes.

26. Though intriguingly the ITN website has REF: BP020759158729, ' "Football's a Girl's Game". Italy 12 July 1959', the intertitle reads 'Various shots Italian women's football squad doing exercises on pitch. Various shots girls practising shooting at goalkeeper—they're very good! The team will take part in the national women's football tournament during the next Olympics'; see http://www.itnsource.com, accessed 12 August 2006. This could have been a Rome v Naples match held also in 1959.

27. Laurence Prudhomme-Poncet, *Histoire du football feminine au XXème siècle: Espaces et temps du sport* (Paris: L'Harmattann, 2003).

28. BP13113092624, 'Eve's Film Review', no. 493, available at www.itnsource. com, accessed 11 July 2007.

29. BP13113092624, 'Eve's Doing', Pathé, 13 November 1930, available at http://www.itnsource.com.

30. REF: BP010157149729, 'Women's Football in Stuttgart 1', January 1957; REF: BP050857149724, 'Germany and United Kingdom Ends with Draw 1–1', 5 August 1957; REF: BP010158154511, 'Millions Take a Breather', 1 January 1958; available at http://www.itnsource.com.

31. See Sue Lopez, *Women on the Ball: A Guide to Women's Football* (London: Scarlet Press, 1997), pp. 21–22, for oral history accounts from some of the players involved in these tours. See also Pathé newsreel of Bert Trautmann at what may have been the final match of the tour won by Corinthians 4–0.

32. REF: BGY505160012, 'Kenya: Prime Minister Kenyatta Tells of Independence Ruse', 4 August 1964; http://www.itnsource.com, accessed January 2006.

33. 'Sports in Brief', *The Times,* 18 May 1968, p. 8.

34. 'Woman's Place Not on the Football Field', *The Times,* 30 September 1972, p. 4.
35. This single-structure model is by no means common to all sport, for example.
36. M. Marschik, 'Offside: The Development of Women's Football in Austria', *Football Studies* 2, no. 1 (1998): 69–88.
37. The most notable exception could be argued to be Norway.
38. Pat Cash, 'Easy Money', *The Sunday Times,* 25 February 2007, Section 2, p. 20; Hugh McIlvanney, 'Women Not Equal to the Task', *The Sunday Times,* 25 February 2007, Section 2, p. 27 Both are textbook examples. I especially like the phrase 'just £30,000 less' in describing Amelie Mauresmo's winnings compared with Roger Federer's in 2006, not meaning 'a great deal practically.' McIlvanney clearly operates in a rarefied climate. Forget tennis, maybe it's time to take up journalism.
39. Christiane Eisenberg, Pierre Lanfranchi, Tony Mason, and Alfred Wahl, *100 Years of Football: The FIFA Centennial Book* (London: Weidenfeld and Nicholson, 2004), ch. 9, for a discussion of this issue.
40. 'Macho World of Italian Football', *The Times,* 23 June 1999. After two league games, Morace resigned, claiming too much interference from the team owner Luciano Gaucci before being appointed coach to the Women's National Team 2000–2005.
41. Jenny Bray, 'Women's Soccer Association of New Zealand (Inc)', *Letter to JS Blatter,* 9 November 1992, FIFA Correspondence File, Zurich.
42. Jaques M. Henry and Howard P. Comeaux, 'Gender Egalitarianism in Coed Sport', *International Review for the Sociology of Sport,* 34, no. 3 (1999): 277–290.
43. Henry and Comeaux, in ibid., suggest women's football to be the primary beneficiary of Title IX (p. 278); Jessica Gavora, *Tilting the Playing Field: Schools, Sport, Sex and Title IX* (San Francisco: Encounter Books, 2002), p. 5, says that Title IX has gone too far in benefitting female athletes generally and soccer players specifically.
44. 'Backlash over Johansson's remarks'; available at http://news.bbc.co.uk/sport1, accessed 17 June 2005.
45. Minutes of the First UEFA Women's Football Conference, 22 March 1973, Zurich, p. 2.
46. Ibid.
47. Minutes of the Second UEFA Women's Football Conference, 19 February 1980, Zurich, p. 8.
48. There was to be an unofficial women's European Championship in 1979 and official Championships from 1984.
49. Correspondence Files, FIFA, UEFA and the Football Association; letter from Dr H Käser to Mr T Croker, 17 January 1974, FIFA archive, Zurich.
50. Minutes of the Second UEFA Women's Football Conference, 19 February 1980, Zurich, pp. 5–6; grammar and spelling as per the original document.

51. Minutes of the Second UEFA Women's Football Conference, 19 February 1980, Zurich, p. 21.

52. Minutes of the Second UEFA Women's Football Conference, 19 February 1980, Zurich, p. 22.

53. Women's International Soccer, 3 June 1980, WFA Correspondence Files. At the UEFA conference on women's football the same year, member associations were asked not to support this initiative as it was not recognized by the United States Soccer Federation.

54. H Käser, Secretary, FIFA, to Glen Kirton, Football Association, 30 May 1980, FIFA Correspondence File, Zurich.

55. H Käser, Secretary, FIFA, to Pat Gregory, 17 June 1980, FIFA Correspondence File, Zurich, to the Women's Football Association; WFA Correspondence Files.

56. By 1985 the national associations affiliated with the Asian Ladies Football Federation included Hong Kong, India, Indonesia, Japan, Korea, Malaysia, Philippines, Singapore and Sri Lanka.

57. The events briefly referred to here are covered in more depth in the chapter on China in this text.

58. Sepp Blatter, General Secretary, FIFA, Circular 338 to all associations, 22 June 1984, FIFA Correspondence File, Zurich.

59. The 1979 Italian tournament is often cited as being financially disastrous, but it was not so for the participating teams. Rather, the hosts bore the costs, but the financial problems affected the organization of the competition.

60. Walter Gagg 'FIFA Proposition pour l'organisation d'un tournoi mondial de feminin pour equipes representatives', pp. 8–9, FIFA Correspondence File, Zurich. The allocation of places was slightly different from that in the other proposals, being AFC 2 berths, CAF 1, UEFA 3, CONCACAF 1, CONMEBOL 1.

61. FIFA, 'Willy Simonsen Norges Fotballforbund', Item 4, Oslo, 30 December 1985, FIFA Correspondence File, Zurich.

62. FIFA, *Minutes of the 45th Ordinary Congress Mexico City*, 29 May 1986, FIFA Correspondence File, Zurich, p. 8.

63. FIFA, *Minutes of Meeting with Peter Verlappen, General Secretary AFC*, 17 April 1986, FIFA Correspondence File, Zurich, p. 1.

64. FIFA, *Minutes of the 46th Ordinary Congress*, 23 September 1983, Zurich, p. 10.

65. FIFA, 'FIFA on Target for Women's World Cup 2007', 16 October 2006, available at http://www.fifa.com/.

# The Girls of Summer, the Daughters of Title IX
## Women's Football in the United States[1]

When a girl learns to make a sacrifice at home in the same manner as she makes a sacrifice hit on the ball team, the play programme has certainly made a definite contribution. This transfer may be hard to secure but not impossible. A girl who plays on any team soon learns to respect the rights of others, the opinion of others, and the rules of the game. A girl must learn that it is more important to win respect from an opponent than to win a game, and that sportsmanship does not end with the playing of the game but carries over into all of life's situations.[2]

Said the Sporting Goods Journal last year: 'Sporting goods dealers have suddenly become awakened to the fact that there is more profit in playing for the trade of the ladies than in catering exclusively for men.' The growing participation of women in sport during recent years is as striking as the change from bloomers of 1900 to the shorts of 1935. It may or may not be an exaggeration to say that women play many games today to be seen in costume; but the point is that they play.[3]

The Olympic closing ceremony in Athens in September 2004 could be interpreted as marking the end of a chapter for women's association football in the United States. The US team flag-bearer was the triple Olympic medallist Mia Hamm, star player of the women's national soccer team and the professional women's league (Women's United Soccer Association), twice World Cup champion, five times national player of the year and Nike-sponsored icon. The Women's National Team had won gold; a victory that made up in small part for the semifinal exit in the 2003 World Cup (defeated by the winners, Germany, 3–0) in Los Angeles. The following ten-game 'Fan Celebration Tour' served as a last opportunity to see Hamm, Julie Foudy and Joy Fawcett in a women's national team that had transcended sport and had made front-page news. Kristine Lilly and Brandi (it's not about the bra) Chastain also toured, though Michelle Akers did not.[4] The six had been part an exclusive club known as the '91ers; the team which won the inaugural FIFA Women's World Cup, in 1991, in China. Though Akers retired from international football after the US repeated the victory in the 1999 World Cup Final at the Rose Bowl, in Los Angeles, she preceded Hamm as the figurehead in a team which at that point had never placed below third in any of the seven senior women's events and had won two World Cup titles and two Olympic gold medals. The 1999 World Cup final was a record-breaking event, with 93,000 spectators and world-wide TV coverage. The twenty women of the US squad were sufficiently well known to found the WUSA professional league in what has been called the most competitive sports market in the world shortly after. Perhaps uniquely, Mia, Julie, Joy, Kristine, Brandi, and Michelle (along with Briana, Tiffany and Carla) rose to levels of fame with the US public which make surnames unnecessary. Had the golden age of women's football in the US lasted a short thirteen years? Perhaps a more important question, what was to be the legacy of the 91ers? Would they be consigned to history as the daughters of Title IX, 'not merely great athletes and fierce competitors, but also the embodiment of the beneficiaries of a federal law'?[5]

Most commentators would be surprised to find that women's association football has been part of the social and cultural history of the United States of America for almost a century. However, ethnographic and historic approaches to the study of women's soccer increasingly indicate this to be the case. The consensus that soccer became established in the 1950s as an intramural sport is changing as new evidence emerges.[6] What is more widely known is that there has been a dramatic increase in the number of women players since the 1970s. It is difficult to believe that thirty years ago there were approximately 50,000 American female soccer players, whereas the current figure is estimated around 9 million.[7]

In 1972, Congress provisionally passed the Equal Rights Amendment, though its ratification has been an ongoing complicated obstruction. In the same year, it passed Title IX of the Education Amendments to the Civil Rights Act of 1964, a relatively straightforward commitment to gender equity for federal-funded education programmes: 'No person in the United States shall, on the basis of sex, be excluded from participation in, be denied the benefits of, or be subjected to discrimination under any education program or activity receiving Federal financial assistance.'[8] The broad application of this led, first, to the 1975 implementing regulations and later, to the 1979 Title IX Athletics Policy Interpretation. This introduced the three-part test of proportionality, a demonstrable commitment to expanding opportunities and a satisfaction of the interests and abilities of the historically underrepresented sex.[9] The correlation between the introduction of Title IX, the broader social and cultural change related to it and an increase in both female sport and participation in education is compelling: in 1970, one in twenty-five North American school-age girls were involved in school sport, whereas by 2006 one in three participated. 'The ten most frequently found college varsity sports for women are in rank order: basketball, volleyball, cross country, soccer, softball, tennis, track/field, golf, swimming and lacrosse. Soccer exhibits the greatest growth of any sport in the last 27 years. It is now offered for women on 88.6% of the campuses while in 1977 it was only found on 2.8% of the campuses. Soccer has increased 40 fold since.'[10] The wider factors that have contributed to the success of women athletes have clearly impacted on the development of association football (also called soccer interchangeably here). However, this is not as straightforward as the figures suggest. The subject also includes political lobbying, legal changes, the enforcement of equal-rights legislation in education and negotiations with sports governing bodies. It is also worth reminding ourselves that for some commentators the paradigm has shifted so far in favour of women that they can now be viewed as 'creatures of entitlement—the welfare queens of the sports world. The fact that portraying these remarkable athletes as [such] ... diminishes their achievement never seems to occur to those feminists who use them for a political agenda.'[11] However, just why soccer has caught the imagination of female players in the United States and how that enthusiasm has been historically produced is particular to football as a sport, a leisure activity and a profession. That there *is* now an entitlement under Title IX is clear, but there was little evidence of women soccer players queening it during field visits in 1999, 2001 and 2003, be they the stars of the US National Team and Women's United Soccer Association or Little League players. Establishing the sport for women in the US has not been a history of the handout. Very little has been given that has not been carefully asked for, shrewdly lobbied in favour of and defended on behalf of the women's football community. Questions are therefore raised instead regarding whether there has been a commitment to, let alone fulfilment of, egalitarian principles.

The word most used by academics to discuss the history of female participation in association football in the US is 'success'; perhaps a stereotypical American aspiration. This seems peculiar because, on an international scale, as a sport and administrative entity, it remains a largely male preserve, both in performance and in concept. Mark Zeigler, a journalist who has covered the sport favourably over a number of years, summed up the range of forces against its success in 2003: 'WUSA folds. Hurricane Isabel. Injuries. Competition from NFL, college football, baseball. Aging stars. SARS forces Cup form China. Distractions. The rest of the world is catching up.'[12] This raises the distinct but related enquiry: can our understanding of women's soccer in the United States be best grasped by focusing on recreational play, elite-level international competition or the collegiate system? The obvious response is all these and more, not least the extent of co-ed participation, which seems to operate under some kind of FIFA radar which picks up high-profile cases of women signing to professional men's teams.[13] The following chapter describes some of the formal and informal arrangements, as well as the conceptualization of the game by players, administrators and the media during the history of women's football in the United States of America. Casting a net this wide perhaps inevitably leads to more holes than connections. Nevertheless, it is difficult to share the certainty of Markovits and Hellerman regarding the thesis of 'American exceptionalism', with regard to either women's participation or the broader case for association football:

> Indeed, it has only been in recent years that the national teams of Brazil and Germany have joined the United States, China and Norway at the pinnacle of women's soccer. And the reason is obvious: women succeeded precisely in countries where soccer was not completely occupied by men, and thus did not fully constitute what we have termed

(in our previously published studies on sport) 'hegemonic sports culture'. Put another way, the men's game did not dominate in the United States, Norway and China at anywhere near the level it has in the countries where the men's game constitutes the absolute core of hegemonic sports culture.[14]

While agreeing that several aspects of the sport are peculiar to the US case, this analysis seems epigrammatic rather than encompassing. I take the point that the history of men's participation in association football has to be part of the story (one which has been treated more extensively here than in my previous work) and the usefulness of ideas of hegemony, questions of periodization and specificity remain. Is the recent rise of female participation such a distinct time in the history of association football in the United States? In what ways has women's soccer 'succeeded'? Rather than an insulated constant, hegemonic sports culture may have a core, but it is rarely absolute. There appears instead to be a series of practices which can accommodate (even a considerable) female presence while defending sport as primarily a masculine preserve. The perception of soccer as less macho than American football and ice hockey, less authentically naturalized than basketball and baseball, still deals with competing masculinities. The dialectic, the processes themselves, may be particularly difficult to try to capture against which, seeing the growth of women's soccer as somehow socially certain or natural is a too-neat conclusion. As Stephen Hardy has indicated, with regard to team sports, 'the particular forms of any sport, in any historical period, are hardly inevitable derivatives of some *zeitgeist*. They are the products of conscious decision making that cries out for more historical investigation. If rulemakers create a special product—the game form—that may exist as a commodity, it is also true that their product seldom exists in isolation.'[15]

The early historical period, especially collegiate women's soccer in the 1920s on, raises uncertainty about exceptionality as it is argued that 'participatory recreation almost always superseded the drive for competition over a long period, at least until the 1970s.'[16] The binary nature of these two forms of play seems overstated. While agreeing that there was not the same degree of formal organization and 'rationalization' of women's football, it seems useful to examine the forms that women's participation did take. Even though women physical educators may have intended the games as recreation, it doesn't follow that an element of competition was excluded or that the primary motivation for participants could be predetermined. We know that women's football attracted some measure of spectatorship and enthusiastic participation in the 1920s, yet remained relatively uncommodified until the 1970s. The notion that some kind of male 'soccer vacuum' inevitably drew in female participation and enabled women to achieve in the sport appears to overlook the sense of agency most apparent from the evidence. The finality of the past tense in the definition of exceptionalism characterizes the women's game as uniform, stable and established. Female participation at around 40 per cent in the US is astonishing, exceptional and worth celebrating, yet even as an enthusiast it seems optimistic to suggest that it has more cultural capital than male aspects of the game and this question of 'overall weight' for debate in the chapter.

Markovits and Hellerman are not alone in emphasizing a lack of male professional soccer leagues as relating to female participation. Browsing the web sites of serious soccer fans and academics, for example, there is more than a little indignation about soccer's less highly masculine and scientific appeal than the perceived indigenous legitimacy of American football, for example in response to 'sweepers performing domestic chores'.[17] Most notably in this line of argument, Sugden and Tomlinson contend that 'It has been convincingly argued that not only is soccer in the USA the sport of minority ethnic communities, of the middle-class educational institutions—but it is the sport, at its most spectacularly successful level, of women. This has caused great problems for the game in gaining acceptance in the still so-macho and nativist sports culture.'[18] The success referred to appears to be the establishment of FIFA-sponsored World Cup and Olympic competitions; particularly the US Women's National Team's achievements in these competitions. Before this, Germany, Italy, France and Asian women's organizations oversaw tournaments (which eventually led to the creation of a World Cup tournament for women under the FIFA umbrella) in which the achievements of women from some traditional football countries are much more evident. So how are we to judge success? What elements of public sports space have women soccer players historically occupied?

Arguing for a longer periodization and more intricate investigation leads me to question the neatness of dependency theories especially, which suggest that a kind of soccer void leads to female achievement. Accepting the concept of a core of hegemonic sports culture and that football constitutes that core in some countries is one thing. Extrapolating from a lack of domination of male professional soccer leagues in the US sportsscape to female prosperity, without regard to the wider context of national and international sports culture, is another big leap altogether. In spite of these two fundamental critiques (one over how to measure and demarcate continuity and change, the second about whether to focus primarily on micro or macro elements of the gendered construction of sport), the argument does offer useful consideration of why soccer was a less popular sport for some groups and the processes of absorption into US culture. Critics of my 'more questions than answers' approach will no doubt be frustrated by the evidence here which shows both the increasingly visible ties between women's participation and historically remote events often located in the private rather than the public domain. Women's participation in association football is not always best viewed as primarily relating to the status of male versions of the sport. Soccer has not been 'completely occupied by men' since its codification as a sport in the nineteenth century and arguably before. By extension, there are also questions of consistency across nations. There may be some continuity with the China case study, for example, as was suggested earlier, but there is also considerable difference.

Successive male professional association football leagues have been launched in the United States since the nineteenth century. The first established league began in 1894 and operated less than a month, perhaps leading to a view that the sport struggles to assert itself. The American League of Professional Football (ALPF) could hardly be called national and was owned by a group of baseball entrepreneurs.[19] This ongoing narrative of success-failure in view of the 'big three and a half' of American football, baseball, basketball and ice hockey sets a wider framework for the relative underdevelopment of the sport for women in the same decades. The United States American Soccer League (ASL) was formed in 1921, and professionals from Scottish, English and Irish leagues made up the majority of the players, with the best-known declinee, Dixie Dean, refusing to leave Everton for the New York Giants in 1928.[20] For some historians of association football, the 'golden years' of US soccer were the decade of operation of the ASL (1921–1931).[21] This was followed by several unsuccessful attempts to establish professional leagues until the creation, in 1968, of the North American Soccer League (NASL), which operated for almost twenty years. A dependence on 'imports' also arguably affected the image of North American Soccer League. The historic migration of talent has led to the perception that later franchises like Major League Soccer (MLS) are populated as retirement circuits for foreign stars.[22] This is obviously a larger and more complex issue related to migration than can be covered here, and because the focus is on women's sport, three elements pertain. The first is the link between traditional football countries and postcolonialism, particularly the attempt to set association rules as a 'manly' sport but less violent than rugby and some perceived indigenous codes (American rules, Australian rules). The second are the informal networks which formed in the absence of more rationalized structures, and the third is the relatively late intervention of the state into matters of women's health and education. For all the theories about an American exceptionalism and a wider rejection of the association code, the examples later in this chapter show that individuals and groups made particular choices, often for very specific reasons. The chapter argues a need for a more rigorous connection of overarching theory and the study of those individual experiences.

Are we perhaps being led by the rather obviously monumental intention of much sport myth-making in wishing to focus on the few at the expense of the many? If, as historians of the 'people's game', we are faced with possibly the largest mass of participation at competitive and recreational level, in which youth play is facilitated by an army of volunteering soccer moms, dads and community coaches, in which an increasing number of women are able to achieve an education as well as athletic excellence and in which a variety of marginalized groups can compete in a celebratory manner, might we call the current status of association football in the United States some kind of an arrival? Though not wholly democratic in its appeal, as for example, the number of black and Asian women players (or nonplayers) indicates, the weight of opinion favouring the thesis of exceptionalism perhaps requires more critical consideration.[23] Accepting the achievements mentioned doesn't also mean assuming either that there is only so much to go around or that women are somehow privileged in the US case study, let alone that this somehow damages the image of the sport as a whole.

The longer historical view suggests that the antipathy of societal and cultural attitudes to female competition in contact team sports, not least among the national and international sports administrations, is a continuity which soccer in the US shares with other nations world-wide. Markovits and Hellerman's disquiet over both resistance and accommodation of marginalized elements leads them to ask a question very pertinent to this study: 'Why should a world that was created by very particular social forces and their interaction between 1870 and 1930 define hegemonic sports culture?'[24] It may well be that some women national-team players are better known to the US general public than some male equivalents, even after the success of the men's squad at recent World Cups. It may also be that these very intelligent, media-savvy women commentated on national television during the 2002 men's World Cup. However, it does not follow that 'nowhere else is women's soccer the cultural equivalent of—or even superior to—the men's game, as it is in the United States.'[25] There are factors within the international administration of football, in the attitude and management of US Soccer, in the mediatization of sport in America, in the entertainment marketplace of which sport is an element and in social and cultural history that preclude such straightforward explanations. If we *were* to take professional sport as the primary indicator of success, US male soccer players are able to compete in a very lucrative international marketplace for financially well-paid and prestigious careers in professional leagues and World Cup competitions. Elite women players, iconized as Nike-sponsored heroines or not, face a quite different set of career options.

A history of women's soccer in the United States would have to include the more obvious recreational aspects as well as the competitive elements. The range runs from pick-up games to youth leagues, school and college soccer teams, the Olympic competitions, the national team and the professional league. That would be a larger study—a very welcome book. This case study has space to focus on only two of the consequential trends for women's soccer in the United States: the constantly growing base of collegiate female players and elite achievement in international competition. The two issues are interconnected in that the current elite women are in the main, young, well-educated college students or graduates. Julie Foudy, for example, is a veteran of three Women's World Cups and gave up a graduate career in medicine at Stanford to concentrate on soccer. There is admittedly much that this doesn't include. Youngsters can get into soccer through community-based programmes catering to all levels of ability using both public school facilities and community fields. In this way, organized participation develops outside school settings at the same time that female recreational and competitive educational programmes are increasingly coordinated within. The institutional development of American football players through school and college programmes may, on the one hand, marginalize soccer players to the community field and recreational park, but the combination of the participative ethos and the appropriation of the 'pick-up' tradition means that it is not unusual to see a game where green spaces exist in US towns and cities. As with other case-study nations, players I spoke to did not always differentiate between playing for fun and playing in a challenging competition but enjoyed both.

The Olympic name perhaps means more to some sections of the American population than the football World Cup tournament. Elsewhere, as FIFA has grown in power during the century and the World Cup has become increasingly mediatized, the importance of the Olympics to male international football competition has decreased compared to, say, club and Confederation-sponsored cups. Over the past twenty years, the importance of women's sport in the Olympic movement has increased, and the women's Olympic programme has been enlarged in cooperation with the respective International Sports Federations and the Organizing Committee. Women made their Olympic debut as athletes in 1900, in Paris, but it took until 1996 for a women's football competition to be included.[26] The global status of the 'world's most popular team sport' logically depended upon the inclusion of a female competition, as FIFA President Havelange, a long-serving member of the IOC, was aware. Though now all sports seeking inclusion to the Games must include women's events, FIFA's characteristic caution in developing women's competition meant that football lagged behind less globally popular sports and disciplines in achieving full medal status (joined by softball, mountain biking and beach volleyball) in 1996. The USA won the gold medal in 1996 and 2004 but was beaten in the final by Norway in 2000.

The relationship between the Women's World Cup and the Olympic Games has been further cemented as the former tournament serves as a qualification system for the latter. So, for example, the seven quarter-finalists of the 1999 WWC tournament and the host Olympic country in 2000, Australia, were guaranteed a place; a similar scenario to the expanded ten-team event in Athens in 2004 and the twelve-team competition in 2008 in PR China.[27] In this way, the Olympics provide the second most important international competition between the quadrennial World Cup tournaments for women in terms of creating a television and live spectacle. Until such time as confederation and club championships for women are more fully developed, Olympic competition looks set to remain significant in the international calendar of women's football. This is particularly pertinent to this case study as the success of Women's World Cup 1999 followed the 1996 Olympic final, which had created the largest live audience for a women-only event.[28] Considered in this light, the men's World Cup of 1994, the Atlanta Games in 1996 and the Women's World Cup in 1999 are key moments in the continuing attempt by FIFA to sell the world's most popular sport to one of the major underexploited markets. In short, Women's World Cup 2003 re-presented soccer as a spectator sport to the United States in the fourth significant tournament in nine years.[29]

Consequently, Women's World Cup 1999 brought together stakeholders interested in making this a momentous event for women's sport in areas of marketing and publicity. The role of US Soccer was, for example, critical as the US Soccer Foundation, set up to administer the profits from the 1994 World Cup tournament, granted a $2.5 million loan to the Women's World Cup Organizing Committee in 1997.[30] Five of the eight members of the Women's World Cup board of directors had positions with US Soccer, and one with the International Olympic Committee. The implications for the international culture of women's football were potentially considerable, but the 2003 tournament was relatively less successful and, if the US *is* the largest commercial market for women's soccer, then the demise of the WUSA professional league just before kickoff all the more depressing. The 1999 organizing committee sought to capture large live audiences in mainstream auditoria with an ambitiously planned single-sex, single-sport event that would also sell well to the media. It built on the Olympic tradition in the United States by making the live and televised event sensational, and it adroitly disseminated the opportunity to spectate as a family-friendly activity. This grass-roots marketing effectively included many who had been excluded from the men's World Cup in 1994, most notably by the pricing policy. The timing was significant for women's sports generally and for association football for women in particular. The implications of Women's World Cup 1999 for the international profile of women's football therefore went beyond women as consumers and producers of soccer in the United States. In this sense, it went way beyond the notion of entitlement to puncture some myths about the popularity of women's sport and the popularity of soccer with the American public. This had advantages for women who wished to play and caused problems in the subsequent marketing of the sport, as some of the negative media coverage of WUSA and the 2003 tournament indicated.

Perhaps mindful of the 'so-macho' and nativist elements, Women's World Cup 1999 promotional material used the metaphor of family throughout. This is evident in marketing strategies used to promote women's football in the United States and beyond. In conversation with Lauren Gregg (a national team player, the first woman full-time national coach to the Under 20s team and the assistant coach of the Women's National Team from 1989 to 2000), we debated whether there was culture-changing potential in the cumulative effects of 1996, 1999, and WUSA or whether the shift had taken place. Gregg was an assistant coach for the USA at the 1991 FIFA Women's World Cup in China, at the 1995 FIFA Women's World Cup in Sweden, and she assisted the squad that won the gold medal at the 1996 Olympic Games. At the time of our interview, she was head of player personnel for WUSA, responsible for balancing the composition of American and foreign players in each of the eight franchise teams.[31]

JW   How did WWC 99 impact on WUSA?

LG   The wheels were in motion long before the WWC 99. Many felt that it was central to us being successful. While, in many ways, that is true, I do believe that we have been on ascension for many years with several key platforms that ultimately made this possible. If we hadn't won the World Cup in 1991, perhaps, we would not have had women's soccer in the Olympics five years later. Winning the first gold there caught America's eye ... and yes, WWC 1999, what an amazing event. The momentum from that was so important to a successful launch in 2001. It helped to catapult our stars and the international stars into the public eye. The media ran with it and that served the sport in some vital ways. But, as I said, the WWC did not stand by itself. The climb was underway and it assured we were where we needed to be.

JW   The WUSA draft system has been beneficial to the play of European players (evident in the UEFA Championships). Are there plans to extend the numbers of foreign drafts after the 2001 season?

LG   We want to establish the best women's professional league in the world. In order to do that, we need to attract and secure the best players in the world. Without question, this past year, we had an incredible core of international stars. We intend to continue to strive for this standard of excellence through the addition of international players.

JW   Dan Cox called WUSA a league with 'culture changing potential'. What aspects of US sporting culture has it begun to change?

LG   Certainly, it is proving that women's sports can draw and women can be professional athletes. We are in part a product of Title IX, and, in turn, we will have a ripple effect as well in the future for women's sports not only in the US but, we hope, around the world. Our goal is to grow the game worldwide and show the incredible appeal of the Women's World Cup in 1999 was not just a phenomenon but also a cultural shift. The shift has already begun. It is now not only acceptable to be a female athlete but it is admired and revered. That is new. But boys and girls will grow up in a world not knowing another way. Boys and girls both have role models in female athletes, and the WUSA is providing an arena for women's soccer players to thrive in.

JW   What is the greatest barrier remaining for WUSA as a league?

LG   Again, I feel one of the greatest challenges of any professional soccer league in our country is to sustain it over time.

JW   From your other professional experience—what singles out women's soccer as a viable market?

LG   It started with the accessibility of our national team. We really reached out to the fans, the young people and the country. We told our stories and became vulnerable. We brought people along our journey. Whether it is a male athlete, a female athlete, a family, a young aspiring athlete or any young person for that matter, people can relate to us because we are so available and willing to share our story. Our passion is palpable and contagious. It tells young people you can do and be anything. Look at us, we love what we do, we work hard and we excel because of it.

JW  Will there be a competing league in the next four years?

LG  I cannot foresee a league within the US competing directly. Germany, Norway, Sweden and China all have very competitive leagues that are developing players. Certainly the wonderful difference for us is the financial backing we have. That makes an enormous difference and we are fortunate to have the investors we do and their belief in what we can accomplish together. Although we want our other leagues to push us to be the best we can and vice versa. Competition only makes you better. And for sure, we believe there will be competition cropping up around the world. And that is exactly what we want. We have never grown the game by ourselves.[32]

As Gregg had been placed in a position to see the elite developments around 1991 and subsequently, at the professional level, until 2003, the conscious accessibility of the national team is a significant theme which could be developed in terms of the image and status of the women's game.

The organizers of Women's World Cup 1999 had a particular view of the cohort of the American public that would be attracted to the event. For example, a grass-roots Development Director was appointed to tap into a potentially underexploited demographic pool to translate the fan base to stadium and television consumers. Investors and sponsors were offered a wider spectrum of potential consumer by such strategies, and this opened up new relationships, particularly with those companies not traditionally interested in sports sponsorship. The phrasing in the excerpt about vulnerability and accessibility indicates that, seeking a specifically domestic, family-oriented market, Women's World Cup 1999 used the success of the US women's team to attract audiences perhaps excluded by other premier events. Of course, the traditional sport fan may not have been interested in a women's competition even if the World Cup title was meaningful to them. Nevertheless, the athletes of the American team acted as eloquent ambassadors and media spokespersons for the tournament. White House support for the US team was featured in daily newspapers, and the Clintons, honourary co-chairs of the competition, appeared in person to support the championship, including at the final.

This twin strategy of appealing to a core fan base of the grassroots participative community and differentiating the product from professional male competition appeared to work for the tournament itself and for the launch of WUSA. Building upon the of the success women's football final in the 1996 Olympic Games, the express aim was 'to make the 1999 Women's World Cup a breakthrough event before the turn of the century to inspire the next generation'.[33] The participative element and elite endorsement were combined through out the marketing campaign. For instance, 'soccer families' were offered discounted packages of tickets twenty months before the tournament began. It is worth remembering that the financial success of 1999 was in large part due to ticket sales, with estimates of half the total 650,000 tickets sold before the spring of that year. In the spirit of familial cooperation, the women's professional basketball league WNBA helped promote the event by publicizing it and also by scheduling important matches to achieve minimum overlap.

An example of how one Women's National Team player passed into United States popular culture confounds common-sense logic about the limited appeal of sports women in the media, and as commercial properties. By the late 1990s, Mia Hamm, the US National Team's number 9 player, shared the limelight with Michael Jordan in the so-called consciousness industries of commercial sporting products and their media spinoffs as the second most important Nike-sponsored athlete.[34] However, as with leading female figures in others of these industries, the image of equal but different is construed as female athletes, including soccer players, are absorbed into these trades. Nike Air Jordan shoes have created a story: The advertising campaigns are in tune with an MTV generation to whom these promotions sell the expensive shoe as a symbol of Michael Jordan. Hamm's image is subtly different because, though she too is an aggressive winner at the pinnacle of her career on the field, the target market for sales of related gear is more likely to be young girls, their soccer moms and dads. So the focus is altogether a more wholesome, less urban, and more straightforward personal endorsement. If wearing transcendental-quality Air Jordans on the streets is a sign that you would like to be as bad as Michael, wearing Nike M9 boots on the pitch signifies that you'd like to be as good as Mia.[35] As with Lauren Gregg's summary, the image is of hard work, celebrating effort and excelling because of that investment. If Jordan is a larger-than-life brand, then Hamm is a very human heroine.

What had changed by 2003? Had the next generation merely grown up and out of the game? Given the successful launch of the Women's United Soccer Association franchise, in 2001, an altered public perception of the female athlete appeared to be in evidence, as Gregg's optimism reflects. Yet this professional league shows how women's sports are now intrinsically linked with culture, commerce and the media, not least commercial network television's ownership of the league. Even so, the size and composition of television audiences assumed critical importance for the continuation of the franchise itself. The reason for this is that, in an unprecedented step for women's sport, sales of advertising space became the principal source of revenue, followed by sponsorship income and syndication fees. There were a number of commercial, cultural and sporting successes in WUSA's operating years. Culturally, it built upon the historical appeal of the Atlanta Olympic Games and the Women's

World Cup 1999 in Los Angeles in presenting young, female, elite soccer players to the American public as worthy of interest in their own right as media stars. The draft of United States team members across the franchises supported by foreign stars made good sporting sense in terms of the competitiveness of individual games and the community focus of the league as whole. The problem of convergence with a wider public as an innovative commercial product was to prove a difficult one to solve, as the responses from Barbara Allen, the first-year chief executive officer, to my questions as she prepared to leave the role, indicate.

JW  What do you feel has been the single most significant achievement of WUSA?

BA  I feel the most significant achievement was the fan attendance and satisfaction ratings. The attendance throughout the season was above the plan projections. The satisfaction ratings from fans in exit interviews was extremely positive and reinforced that the fan experience was excellent—the quality of soccer as well as the overall entertainment/family fun.

JW  Could you identify an area which has surpassed your own expectations for the league and one which you thought fell short?

BA  The area that surpassed my expectations was the significant effort made by the players to connect with our fans—I knew the players were willing to work hard to reach out, but their willingness to sign autographs and do community events was outstanding, beyond what other sports leagues get from their player base. We fell short in convincing fans to tune in to the television broadcasts—lower ratings that we would have hoped for on a national basis and in the team cities with a few exceptions.

JW  How would you describe the developing public profile of the league?

BA  World-class soccer played by athletes who are committed to the sport, to the fans and to helping young women realize their dreams. I think the women in the WUSA have continued what they started as a part of the World Cup and the Olympics—they are providing strong role models for women's sports as viable, legitimate sport. The quality of soccer represented in the WUSA—we really have the world's best players as a part of the league playing the world's favourite sport (if not America's!!).

JW  Dan Cox called WUSA a league with 'culture changing potential'. What aspects of US sporting culture has it begun to change?

BA  The belief that women are marketable athletes and the belief that soccer can be entertaining to a US audience. I would love to help young women believe that there are significant opportunities for women in the field of sports—as athletes, as sports marketing managers, as event or operations staff, as referees, as coaches—the possibilities are boundless! I think the WUSA will help to bring soccer to life, to make it a more popular sport within the US and that the WUSA can help promote women's soccer around the world.

JW  What is the greatest barrier remaining for WUSA as a league?

BA  Turning a dream into a viable business. Getting the economics to work for a sustainable business is very challenging. Startup businesses often have long paths to profitability as do sports leagues. The responsibility will be completely transitioned to the new smaller organization.[36]

As a media product the games drew good live attendances and as a televised sporting spectacle they were relatively inexpensive and easy to produce with elements of skill and chance with a predominantly female cast (though team coaches were predominantly male). By the end of the first season the commercial viability was challenging, with the league seriously underestimating set-up costs and failing to tie in advertisers for extended periods or to obtain repeat contracts with existing marketing partners. In sporting terms, the draft was extended to leading scorers and other 'stars' not necessarily Women's National Team players. Beyond the mercantile aspects, the cultural significance of the league has had a paradoxical legacy so far. The League was a great innovation, but the suspension of operations just as Women's World Cup 2003 kicked off meant that a shadow was cast over the tournament. Many of the mainstream sponsors for World Cup events had established agreements with FIFA, so were consequently under no obligation to promote the women's game but had the right to representation as public relations hospitality. In a situation where few sponsors are willing to invest to the same extent as for male sport, this inability to cultivate discrete and committed partners for women's soccer events remains a trial for the future of international and professional competition.

Even though relocation of the tournament from PR China at late notice was the overriding factor in the relative lack of success of the 2003 competition compared to that of the 1999 Women's World Cup, it produced a resounding media chorus of 'I told you so' which appeared to be relished all the more after the exit of the US team in the semifinals.[37] Women's World Cup 1999 had an ambitious aim and was a success. However many front-page articles and programme minutes were eventually given over to the tournament, the cynicism of sports writers and pundits remained bitterly enduring. Before the 1999 tournament, we were told it would never happen, and now that it had, we were told it was a one-off. The line went that supporters would not continue their interest in events outside the US and then post-Sydney because the US National Team were no longer the Olympic gold-medal holders. The suspension of WUSA trading shortly before the kickoff of the Women's World Cup in 2003 seemed to encourage the sceptics, and the momentum of 1999 appeared to have stalled.[38] Certainly the scale and success of Women's World Cup 1999 contributed to the impetus for a professional women's league, drawing on some of the marketing techniques that proved so successful in Los Angeles. However, the difference between a tournament and a league meant that sponsors and supporters that participated in 1999 faced a rather more conservative market in the altered economic atmosphere after 9/11 in which WUSA was attempting to operate. This said, the influence of the 1999 competition on the international configuration of women's football, and for that matter women's sport, remains likely to be far reaching.

What, though, of the broader history of women's participation in association football? The tension between North America as the largest developed sports market in the world and the perceived failure of association football, most notably in the establishment of a permanent professional league, continues to intrigue commentators. Nathan D Abrams's response to this is to argue it is marginalized but not excluded because it is the sport of 'immigrants, aliens, "outsiders" and youngsters'.[39] Whether women are implied as aliens or outsiders, the apparent popularity of football in certain school and universities in the late nineteenth century meant that association rules took a long time to become the mass-participation game which marks its reputation today.[40] It would be too simplistic to say that where football first flourished, for example in New York, Philadelphia, Chicago, St Louis, Milwaukee, and districts of California, as well as in Canadian cities such as Toronto, Montreal and Winnipeg, women's teams developed, too, though these areas were to be significant.[41] In 1880 the Canadian Western Football Association was founded in Toronto, Canada, by clubs including the 1904 Olympic Champions, FC Galt, and this became the Dominion of Canada FA in 1912.[42] In 1884, the American Football Association was organized in Newark, New Jersey, and some years later, originally founded in 1913 as the United States Football Association, the U.S. Soccer Federation was formed. Due to internal tensions and external rivalries, the organization has been known by three different names: U.S. Football Association (1913–1944); U.S. Soccer Football Association (1945–1973) and, since 1974, U.S. Soccer Federation. As the evidence indicates, enthusiastic individuals and groups of like-minded educators meant that local association code competitions took place either as one-offs or over a number of years. From the mid-nineteenth century, as football was moving toward codification, large population changes occurred which affected the spread of football as a sport. If the US received more than 30 million immigrants from Europe between 1820 and 1924, many from Ireland, Italy and other parts of southern and eastern Europe, the steamships no doubt helped with the professional competition established in the 1920s for men's teams as well as the 1922 Dick, Kerr Ladies tour. What isn't clear about this tour is whether it was a catalyst for women's football in the US or whether it punctuated an already growing interest. If there were teams in Canada in 1922, Frost and Cubberly's *Field Hockey and Soccer for Women* was published in 1923, and there is evidence of women's college participation from 1924, why is there little evidence of female college football before the Dick, Kerr tour?

This period of expansion also correlated with a change in women's access to education plus with political and reform movements. As in Britain, the US factory system had a strong cotton-textile industry. Women moved into the paid labour force in unprecedented numbers. Between 1867 and 1929 the population of the United States grew, the number of marriages increased and the divorce rate rose, so the most significant changes to women's status combined the economic underpinnings of companionate marriage and gave women power to retain their own property and children if they chose to leave.[43] In the final decades of the nineteenth century, American 'New Women' were agitating for improved economic, social and political conditions in an era of rapid change, especially regarding popular entertainment.[44] This made arguments about what kinds of behaviour were appropriate for the female sex in sport one of several controversies quite beyond decorum and in a wider debate about the definitions of American woman and manhood. A better race for the nation meant that doctors became most interested in those aspects of women's lives which threatened reproductive health, and this influenced ideas of procreative fitness and vitality as constituting the primary aspect of female adulthood. Birth control, education and professionalization, it was thought, could harm women's fertility and fitness, which, because they were the mothers of the race, became an issue of some importance for the whole of society. The Athletic Girl was the focus of much public debate on both sides of the Atlantic, and it is in this environment that soccer became established but failed to grow to the same extent as field hockey, basketball, golf, tennis or other sports for women.[45] Celebratory portraits included a sun-tanned or rosy-cheeked modern young women whose figure and outlook on life were enhanced by regular exercise, particularly outdoors.[46] Progressive-era activists argued that immigrant and working-class youth could learn about self-disciplined teamwork in church leagues, welfare programmes, school curricula and settlement tournaments. Consequently, soccer was just one of many new 'healthful' forms of recreation and certainly not the most important. If the superior athletic clubs for women allowed exclusive sociability, working-class girls had to arrange for recreational time in relation to their employment and to the availability of space in city and public-school playgrounds.

As the number of women in college grew from 11,000 in 1870 to 85,000 in 1900, women physical educators became established in newly created PE departments.[47] Links between higher education and women's athletic programmes began in the late 1880s when the Morrill Land Grants Act of 1862 established more than seventy 'land grant' colleges, as they came to be known. These included those which would become known as the Seven Sisters (Mount Holyoke Female Seminary in 1837; Vassar in 1861; Wellesley in 1870; Smith 1871; Bryn Mawr in 1885; Barnard in 1889 and Radcliffe in 1893), so-called because they were founded with the express purpose of providing higher education for women.[48] The Seven Sisters colleges supported physical education as part of an 'all-around' ethos but sought to protect themselves and their pupils from undue controversy by emphasizing participation to the extent of allowing class-based, club and intramural activities only.[49] Well-equipped gymnasiums and playing fields were built on campuses, and in 1895 Vassar staged the first all-girl track event.[50] In the early 1900s Mount Holyoke, Radcliffe, Smith, Vassar, and Wellesley, among others, emphasized physical education in their curricula to counter claims about the physical incapability of women students. Clearly there were various interpretations of the respectability of physical culture involving regimented drills or exercises and 'rough' activities, including competitive games, as in Europe.

The credibility of 'refined' as opposed to 'rough' games became a wider social issue and affected college education because of the association of certain pursuits with class identity. Mixed-sex games undertaken in the latest fashionable outfit for fun, fresh air and socializing were considered to be sophisticated, especially if accomplished at an exclusive venue.[51] These were rarely contact or large-team sports and included skills like riding, archery, swimming, tennis, golf and croquet. Late-nineteenth-century opponents of higher education for women had begun to use pseudoscientific arguments to suggest that intellectual effort would damage women's reproductive functions. Moderate exercise was especially designed to prevent exploitation of vulnerable sexuality. Like many other aspects of female emancipation, participation in vigorous games was considered by some to be incompatible with true 'womanliness'. Students may not have agreed with the policies, particularly the ban on intercollegiate sport, but intramural activities intended to limit competitive strain also provided opportunities for physical programs well away from public spectatorship, which may have caused even more criticism. Opportunities may have been circumscribed, but a college education allowed time and space for sport, which were luxuries many working-class girls did not have. By the late 1920s, women physical educators and their allies continued to call for moderate and female-appropriate forms of physical culture. However, the number of African American athletes, working-class participants and, increasingly, young competitive female players challenged the idea of the 'nice girl' in sport.

During the period of the modernization of sport, roughly from the 1870s to the late 1930s, we know very little about the cultural 'sports space' of female children and youths in football, especially street football, as one of many recreational games and pastimes. Before this time, Native American women played a form of folk football, but more remains to be researched about the purpose and function of this activity and the 'married'-versus-'single' games in small communities which appear to have continued during this time. However, the early college intramural programs could be interpreted as the first games to be recognized as sport or organized recreation as the ethos of a healthy body in a healthy mind was borrowed. One of the earliest references to women playing football found so far is a small excerpt in *The Radcliffe Magazine* for October 1918:

> Radcliffe Athletic Association (RAA)
> Madeline Ellis 1915, President
> Elizabeth Chandler 1916, Vice President

Charlotte Bruner 1917, Secretary
Martha Noll 1915, Treasurer

On October 24 the RAA gave a welcome to 1918 in the form of a field day, with tennis, football and hockey as the main attractions Edith Parkman, '17 won the tennis championship. On October 29 the hockey team played against Sargent. Radcliffe 3; Sargent 6. C.B.[52]

There is also reference to a student piece called *The Beginning of a Football Game*, seemingly based at Harvard with a description of what reads like a rugby scrum, so whether the reference in the excerpt above is to the association code is unclear.[53]

By the early 1920s women were playing soccer as part of intramural programmes and became sufficiently established to produce books like Frost and Cubberley's *Field Hockey and Soccer for Women* and the *Smith Book of Soccer*. Hockey was more popular, though both were introduced to the US from Europe at about the same time. Like hockey, football was perceived by some woman educators to lead to possible injury. On the one hand, a case for fairly energetic exercise was made, but, on the other, competitive sports which involved some degree of contact were perceived as potentially damaging. Ethel Perrin's foreword to Frost and Cubberly's book opines, 'There could be no better training for a vigorous and healthy girl than three years of soccer, followed by three years of field hockey in the high school. Then she will be ready for any form of outdoor sport when she enters college.'[54] Ladda has suggested that the histories of field hockey and soccer are closely intertwined in connection with college competition but is unsure why a Field Hockey Association was founded at Bryn Mawr in 1922 and yet no such organization was created for football. Quite why wielding a hockey stick should have been more feminine than playing football is still also to be explained while hybrid examples indicate there appears not to have been a broad consensus on this. As Perrin notes, in some cases soccer is seen as a preparation to the more violent field hockey. Writing in 1929, Marian Knighton, a physical educator at New York University, was so much in favour as to suggest that football should be 'compulsory in all of our physical education schools for women'.[55] Lee has suggested that in the 1930s nearly 60 per cent of colleges that took women students had soccer in their physical education programmes.[56] What is also significant is the effect of the formation of a Field Hockey Association on the sport's increasing popularity, which in turn drew more members to the organization. In any case, it appears that intensely competitive play was hampered more by the view of intercollegiate competition as undesirable than by the image of the sport of football as somehow unfeminine. The administrative structure, rules, regulations and policy imperatives surrounding female physical education, however, reflected quite particular social and cultural values in the late nineteenth century. One way that women's football acquired a dubious status in both Europe and the US was a link between sport and the Rights question. Whether early women players on either side of the Atlantic were politically motivated or fashionable enthusiasts the very early games, be they 'pick up' arrangements on campus or set fixtures, are difficult to document from sources in the public domain.

There are two elements to the collection of documentation in the various college archives that require consideration, though. The first is that the extensive nature of the collections entails frustrating search for small reward. The club and intramural nature of the games on the one hand means that an oblique reference will be made in a letter or student diary to a game which is referred to as football or soccer. This makes it difficult to assert categorically that it was played according to association rules. This might seem to be an overly sophisticated treatment of source material that was specifically created to be disposable or private. Nevertheless, incidental material from college collections has been kept by archivists, and the range of material is considerable. The second aspect is consequently a need not to overemphasize college participation just because the material is there for the grateful researcher. The participation of women outside college in the US in the 1800s and early 1900s is harder to describe because many of the games and matches were short lived and transient, perhaps played by those without a privileged enough background to have their artefacts collected. This is an even more obscure search for less return but a necessary one, if only to avoid the assumption that college soccer was the main or only form for women in this early period.

A key event as these games were developing was the establishment of a National Convention of the American Physical Education Association, in Springfield, Massachusetts, in 1923 which sought to squash competition, especially of the intercollegiate kind, as undignified.[57] The collegiate system affected subsequent forms of play for more than fifty years. For instance, though women's athletic programmes promoted the formation of relatively stable teams playing regular competitive matches, these were usually 'interhouse, interclass and intramural' components of physical-education provision. The majority of women's athletics departments (which often combined with or stood in place of physical education departments) had little interest in intercollegiate team sport which, some held, focussed on the best players rather than physical fitness fostered through egalitarian participation. Some colleges went so far as to ban this aspect of competition, so the role of college soccer for women was both to incorporate the game into the daily life of the institution and to prevent systematic forms of rivalry based on geographic and organizational representation (until the early 1970s). It appears unlikely that it was wholly American attitudes toward competitive sport which produced an antipathy to women's football.

This format proved to be significant for the tour of Dick, Kerr Ladies to the US and Canada in 1922, as the English team expected that they would play other women. It is unlikely that interest from the United States was the only spur for the Dick, Kerr tour to the United States as, by 1921, the English FA had declared that the game was 'unsuitable' for women and banned them from playing on the pitches of FA and League affiliates. The ban spread across Britain quickly and prevented the evolution of organized competitive participation in schools and beyond. One Scottish newspaper reporting the effects of the ban suggested the female player in the United States as a more amenable type than her British counterpart, and this perhaps referred to college-based women's football.

> The action of the Football Association in passing a resolution considering the game unsuitable for females, would appear to have a good deal of support. Even among women generally, the playing of football by the sex is far from being popular ... In America girls are not allowed to play unless they have been medically tested and the gymnastic instructor is always a qualified medical man. The trouble is that the type of woman who wants to play football here won't be medically examined.[58]

However, at the annual general meeting of the Dominion of Canada Football Association, held in Winnipeg, in early September 1922, the coming arrival of Dick, Kerr Ladies was debated and a motion was passed to the effect that 'We do not approve of the proposal of Ladies Football'.[59] The minutes of the meeting reflect the same bias against the women's game as shown in England, and the existing Canadian women's soccer clubs were banned from competing. Consequently Dick, Kerr's crossed the border into the United States fully expecting to play against female teams but eventually played against men's professional teams.

Wider migration patterns appear to have influenced working-class women's football just as they provided the male players for the launch of the American Soccer League in 1921. Of course, women moved to the area for industrial work rather than football. Some teams that made up the American Soccer League were backed by companies such as the Scottish-owned J & P Coats, in Pawtucket, Rhode Island, which provided work for Lancashire women with mill experience and their families.[60] Consequently, when Dick, Kerr visited in autumn, they expected matches in Canada and the United States in front of audiences partly made up of migrant workers from Lancashire cotton towns.[61] The *Pawtucket Times* had reported a game played by Dick, Kerr against Leeds watched by a crowd of 15,000 a year, before so there is evidence of interest in women's teams before the tour, but more remains to be found.[62] Matches were arranged in Baltimore, Boston and other New England locales, Chicago, Detroit, New England, New York, Philadelphia, St Louis and Washington, DC. In addition to playing against men's teams from the leading professional league of the time in the US, Dick, Kerr also visited, and were aware of, college women playing association rules, for example, at two Baltimore colleges particularly. It's unlikely therefore that Smith's record of women playing from 1924 reflects the first instance, but it does suggest a growth of interest in several institutions of college women's football at around this time. For example, 'Sports in Women's Colleges', published in 1932, mentions Mount Holyoke's introduction of soccer to complete the fall outdoor program, and 'Athletic Activities at MHC' notes that soccer was initiated on campus in 1924/1925.[63] A note in the same collection states that the Fiske-Harrington award, established in 1983/1984, was named after two members of the class of 1926 who were active in soccer.[64]

What neither the Smith nor Mount Holyoke examples show is why Dick, Kerr didn't play against existing US women's teams. Given the Dick, Kerr form of competition before the 1921 FA ban on Football League grounds and clubs affiliated to the Association, perhaps the organizers hoped to use football in the United States to present the team to a new audience in a professional or semi-professional context. That is, having been used to playing in front of large crowds on the grounds of professional teams until December 1921, the team was undertaking an experiment in replicating that format in the US even if it meant playing against men's professional teams. This is speculation, as it isn't recorded either in the press or in the private collections what the intention was. However, it was allowed and apparently jointly promoted by Mr Zelickman, a representative of the United States Football Association, which was in turn perhaps keen to distance themselves from the Dominian attitude. It is indicated that the USFA were hospitable to the point of replacing Zelickman with Mr Barnall for the remainder of the tour when the accommodation was less than pleasant.[65] It may have been that the popularity of association rules was new enough for college girls to be learning the sport but not yet up to Dick, Kerr standards, but it also shows the fame of the team and a point on sporting nationalisms.

The invitation to the Preston team does not appear intended to show the limits of American women's soccer or to expose college women to extremely competitive matches against working-class women. Instead, a kind of gentlemanly exhibition format involving guest elite women players and professional teams ensued. Again it suggests the need to resist projecting current attitudes onto historic events. The matches appear to have been well supported at between 10,000 and 45,000 spectators, with considerable numbers of women taking advantage of cheap entrance fees to attend. Were this to take place today, the media coverage can only be imagined; as we are in a post-'battle-of-the-sexes' age it would perhaps tend toward the unedifying. In contrast, an elegant balance of competition, spectacle, (male and female) gentlemanly sporting conduct and lively spectator support appears to have been arrived at.

One of the points raised by the tour is the wider presentation of the team to the live and mediated sporting audience. The crowd and hospitality in New Bedford, Fall River, and Pawtucket, Rhode Island, were especially noteworthy, as was the number of women attending as spectators at all the games. For example, 45,000 spectators at the Philadelphia Baseball Ground saw Florie Haslam, Jennie Harris, Molly Walker and Lily Parr win against an American Olympic Women's Relay team before kickoff, and media interest in Lily Parr was considerable.[66] The tour lasted nine weeks, and Dick, Kerr played against some professional players and otherwise reasonably good league teams, so the experiment was held to be a success though some of the wins have been described as victories for gallantry. They opened with a 6–3 loss to the Paterson Silk Sox F.C. but drew with the J & P Coats and the Fall River Marksmen and defeated the New Bedford Whalers.[67] The press reports are delicately phrased, and the change in tone across the three following excerpts is notable as the tour progressed:

> Jauntily togged out in light athletic suits familiar to the followers of soccer football, the women, bobbed hair held in restraint by outing caps, trotting out on the field shortly before 4 o'clock to the tooting of horns and wild acclaim of the crowd. Winning the toss, the women kicked off and displayed expertness in the free, open style of play which distinguishes the English from the more aggressive and somewhat rougher yankee tactics. Sweeney of Paterson made the first try for goal and Fullback Lee failed in a display of backheeling. Mlle Carmen Pomies of Paris, champion javelin thrower for 1920 and the only 'foreigner' in the team was goalkeeper and saved the situation. The Jersey forwards for a time adopted the policy of constantly feeding out to the ends and this kept the women on the run, winding several. Jennie Harris, at inside right, and the smallest of all the players, soon showed herself to be the speediest. Her passing was splendid and the way she followed up would put many a veteran male to shame. The other outstanding figure among the English girls was Lillie [*sic*] Parr at outside left. Her driving from the wing and the accuracy of her shots left little to be desired.[68]

> A record crowd of soccer fans will undoubtedly witness the exhibition game between the Dick, Kerr International Ladies Football Team of England and the J & P Coats team of the American Soccer League at Coats' field on Saturday afternoon. Nearly 5000 tickets have been sold to date, and it is believed that the attendance will go over 10,000. The visiting aggregation is much different than others that have played in exhibition games here ... the game played by the women was remarkable from the fact that the team had been off the ship only five hours when it took to the field ... The game at Paterson last Sunday was a revelation to soccer fans in that vicinity and expert soccer writers for New York papers were loud in their praise.[69]

> Dick Kerr's team of English women soccer stars played a 4–4 tie with the J & P Coats team at Coats' Field Saturday afternoon before a crowd that was lined 10-row deep around the confines of the field. Balmy weather and the unique attraction of seeing in action the first women's soccer eleven to invade this country were contributory factors to one of the largest attendances ever witnessed within the enclosure. At least 9,000 witnessed the contest. The bonny girls, clad in regulation uniforms, were no real match for the Coats eleven and yet they succeeded in outwitting the team to the extent of pulling out a tie. It was clearly evident from the start of the contests that the home men, with commendable chivalrous intent, were out to annex no more goals than was absolutely necessary. Easy scores were forfeited through the employment of devious tricks such as booting the ball over the net of offside [*sic*]. Yet Coats intended to win, perhaps by one or two scores. In the last few minutes of time, however, the girls played brilliantly and on Miss Parr's lift led by a 3–2 count. Just before the end of things Gallagher netted the ball for the last home tally. Whether or not the Coats could have run up a big score is immaterial, as the vast crowd seemed perfectly satisfied with the termination of the game

and gave the girls a great ovation. The contest was one of the biggest attractions ever staged on Coats Field. When the girls' team ran out ... a battery of cameras were trained on the black and white figures [*sic*]. Every fan stretched his neck to get his first glimpse of the team that has conquered the best in Europe and is over here to garner further laurels. The girls were real business-like and did no more posing than was required by the persistent photographers. After the shooting of two group pictures, the members fell to booting the ball around by way of getting in trim. Many of the girls discarded their caps at this stage and disclosed tresses bobbed in the prevailing fashion.[70]

The degree of coverage of which the three excerpts are a small range indicates that the events caused considerable media and spectator interest. What remains unclear is the process of casual games for children and youths, recreation and competitive matches and the blend of participation and camaraderie that is evident in the scrapbooks of the British and French players of this time. The matches took place in a ceremonial atmosphere, with local dignitaries in attendance. Teams were accompanied out on to the pitch, half-time entertainment was provided and the games were followed by civic receptions. Distance may have lent a more accepting attitude toward women players. Nevertheless, the free choice of supporters in opting to attend games rather than participate in another leisure activity was part of the construction of a reciprocal relationship which linked players, albeit foreign female guests, with the host community.

Alice Mills left England for the United States immediately after the 1922 Dick, Kerr's tour, and her extended family settled mainly in Konch, Massachusetts, and Pawtucket, Rhode Island. With the passing of the 1921 Immigration Act, for the first time numerical restrictions were placed on immigrants of each nationality, and the link between the life in the US glimpsed by the players and the life back at home looked perhaps more difficult. Many of the women at Dick, Kerr (known by then as English Electric Ltd) lost their jobs at the factory after returning from the tour in 1923, though a celebratory dinner was hosted by the firm at which the prized possession of a football signed by President Harding was photographed along with some of the players. It's difficult to know whether the tour harmed women's football more than it helped it because, while spreading the word abroad, Dick, Kerr were notable by their absence at home. Following their return, women's football became less spectacular, though players still moved to join the team.

Some left, as in the case of Alice Mills, since, having begun work at twelve in the textile mills of Preston, it was relatively easy to find work as a weaver in the mills of Pawtucket. Her extended family continues to live in the Massachusetts/ Pawtucket area, and though she retired from football when she married in 1925, her daughters, twenty-two grandchildren, and twenty-six great grandchildren have continued the soccer tradition in the family. As a mother of six, who was joined by mother, brother and sisters (she was the eldest of five), Alice found the opportunity to visit the States in 1921 to be life-changing on several levels. It is perhaps unsurprising therefore that, into the 1940s and 1950s in the Pawtucket region, we find college teams playing local women (the Pawtucket Rockets), some of whom were in their thirties and forties. Is it too much to hope that a retired 'World Champion' was among them?

However, though the tour was significant in these ways, it did not lead to a level of rationalization or spectator support of women's football for some considerable time. While some of the great rivalries of male college sport were well established as annual fixtures, the women's colleges preferred a sisterly athletic isolation.[71] Instead, during the first six decades of the twentieth century, women's collegiate soccer was primarily gym class, informal pickup games and college intramural competition.[72] Nevertheless, the emerging sources support a view that it was enthusiastically taken up across women's colleges in the 1920s. The complexity of the various interest groups and the politics involved are such that it would be possible to write extensively about college women's soccer alone. A starting place for those wishing to do so would be Shawn Ladda's thesis, which broadly looks at the history from the mid-1970s until the mid-1990s. The concluding comments in particular set a research agenda which focuses upon the need to collect and commemorate, particularly oral testimony. I couldn't agree more.[73]

Though records in some of the college archives are incomplete, much of the early documentation regarding sporting activity comes from these elite institutions. As Tony Collins has argued, there was sometimes variance around rules, competition and practices that it is unwise to overlook from the vantage of the relatively fixed codification we understand today.[74] For example, there are indications that the mix of field hockey and soccer in early intercollegiate team games in the 1920s had rules which used either the corner kick and eighteen-yard box of Association football or an adaptation of field hockey rules for taking corners in which defensive players would stand behind the end line while attacking players would stand behind an arc, and, once the ball was struck, players could enter the semicircle. In the end, the host institution decided which rule to adopt. There were other variations of this, from allowing women to use their arms rather than chesting the ball, to preventing heading and reinforcing the use of leather shoes rather than boots, some of which appear made for reasons of appropriateness for women and others because of familiarity with a particular set of rules.

In 1924, soccer started at Smith under the Athletic Association, which oversaw interhouse and interclass sporting events. The following year, soccer was listed in the course catalogue as an option for fulfilling Physical Education hours, which were required for first-year and sophomore students but available as electives for juniors and seniors. In 1932 the first annual (all-male) faculty-versus-all-Smith soccer game was held; the students won 2–0. As the Soccer Record Book documents, the sport's popularity at Smith grew over time.[75] In the 1930s, Mount Holyoke had a faculty team in soccer-speedball, though the precise rules are unclear. In a less-is-more way of recording this, Mildred Howard tells us that 'soccer had for some time been played on Pageant Field below the amphitheatre. An Important event was the faculty-student game which was usually won by the faculty [sic].'76 The same document notes that in 1939, three field hockey/soccer fields were constructed on campus. A history of the PE Department notes 'speedball substituted for soccer' in 1934 but also notes the soccer field construction above the upper lake in 1939. Whatever the rules, the heartfelt description of playing the game by Margaret Broadbent does give a good idea of what taking soccer at school was like, and it is recognizable in form to the game as it is played today:

> Soccer certainly is a puffing sport. I was playing forward and because the half-back did not seem to be doing much, I thought that maybe the forward was supposed to do some guarding. Therefore I wore myself out racing up and down the field chasing my forward opponent. It was terrible. I like soccer though, now.[77]

That was perhaps fortunate, as a letter in the same month reports, 'We are required to take some Fall sport. I've got soccer Mon; Tues and Wednesday [sic] at four and, yes, today I donned my bright red gym outfit after lunch and wore it to my organ lesson and Psych [sic] classes (absolute necessity). They certainly are trim and attractive.'[78] In that sense, the element of privacy afforded by a lack of intercollegiate competition may well have enabled experimentation with composite or hybrid games, played in gym outfits, which appear to have been mainly based on association football rules.

However, the effect of this amateur ethos on limiting competitive activities for women was considerable. Proponents favoured the organization of 'play days', designed at once to enable two or more institutions to participate but in which all teams were mixed with players from all attending colleges. The infantilized title is perhaps less significant than the emphasis on team play, collaboration and healthy recreation rather than on the overexertion which representative competition might bring. An even more polite form of direct/indirect athletic event came with telegraphic competition, where each college would perform at, say, bowling or swimming over an agreed set of criteria and then would compare results with other participants by telegraph. The competitiveness and commercial aspects of men's intercollegiate sport were therefore contrasted with 'A sport for every girl and a girl in every sport.' It was not just that it was unladylike to compete but that it was morally superior to resist focussing on better performers. This reticence was to last until the 1960s and was reinforced. By example, the National Amateur Athletic Federation (NAAF) in 1923 adopted a resolution that amounts to 'sport for all and not the few.' That this tradition was by and large not wider public knowledge is indicated by a writer in favour of the British style of sport in a 1930s article assessing changing trends:

> Soccer has had a fast and steady increase quite uninterrupted by the Depression. But the fastest growing ball game is softball, a game officially less than one year

old ... A manufacturer who is forced to keep his eye on the ball lists these as the ten fastest growing sports in the United States at the present time:

1. Softball
2. Badminton
3. Soccer
4. Squash games
5. Archery
6. Polo and horses
7. Ping–pong
8. Trap shooting
9. Horseshoes
10. Tennis

Notice that in each sport in the list above except soccer women participate actively. One explanation of the growth of playing sports in this country over the past five or ten years is the increased participation of women who thirty years ago played few games, and those indifferently.[79]

In contrast, the *Smith Sports Book—Soccer (1924–1979)* has the following train-ing rules which, apart from the lack of studded (or cleated) boots and some sturdy underwear, do not look too out of place today:

> Leather shoes must be worn with light sole and flat heel, no sneakers.
> Middies and bloomers are also worn.
> Running-minimum of 5 minutes preferably on grass except on practice days-should be taken in the morning.
> Sleep-8 hours beginning not later than 11 pm.
> 5 minute daily rest recommended, relax completely.
> 6 glasses of water between meals.
> Coffee at breakfast only, no tea at night.
> Eat moderately, discretion on game days.
> Nothing between meals except fruit, milk drinks, plain ice cream.[80]

Cubberly, writing for Spaldings Athletic Library in the 1930s and advocating soccer as a female appropriate sport, stressed the same cheap flexibility that had made the game popular in a variety of settings for very different participants:

1. It is easy to learn and to coach;
2. It has health values;
3. It is not dangerous for girls;
4. It is an inexpensive sport;
5. It is a team game and involves sportsmanship.[81]

There is much to support his view from very different sources. The notable exception to this educational base for women's football was the establishment of the welfare programme, in the 1930s, of the International Ladies Garment Workers (ILGWU), including sports such as baseball, basketball, bowling and soccer.[82] At the height of its power, in the 1930s and 1940s, it was one of the most numerically important (with more than 250,000 members in fifty-two cities) and progressive unions in the United States and was supported by Eleanor Roosevelt. Another community league was established in 1951 by Father Craig of St. Matthew's Parish of North St. Louis. The Craig Club Girls Soccer League consisted of four teams and played for two seasons. This early but limited growth of association football on college campuses, at high schools and in working-class organized leagues is a key element of the current mass participation in the United States as games for children, particularly school sports, become the recreation of young adults and perhaps the competitive athletic choice of more working women than has hitherto been discussed. Issues of resource, including the time and space to play, train, prepare and socialize, may be solved more easily in these environments.

College competition in that late 1950s and early 1960s hosted by Canadian institutions focussed upon Bishops University, Mc Donald University and Mc Gill University, competing against Johnson State College, Castleton State College and Lyndon State College in the US. Though for reasons very different from those that affected the situation in England, there seems to have been a period of early activity followed by what could be described as a decline or a stasis in growth and then a rapid increase in interest during the 1970s and after. It remains to be debated more widely whether this pattern is seen as primarily a discontinuous one, but it would seem that there is a need for more research rather than assuming that it is. Whatever position on this is taken, the pattern does broadly appear in the English, US and Australian case studies and more briefly in the case of China. Since the 1970s, there has been a United States version of the 'fastest-growing-game-for-females' argument that runs along the lines that football became the second favourite participatory team sport in the US behind basketball and in front of baseball by some way (though not if baseball and softball are combined for all age groups), especially in youth cohorts.[83] Without wishing to tie all women's athletic achievement to Title IX, this legislation has been a major factor in the growth of women's college soccer. Although its implementation was delayed for years and has been contested since, it has resulted in a significant increase in the number of young women in athletic programs, though it has caused problems for women coaches. This has not been a straightforward process, however, and the myths around masculinities and femininities in sport are enduring; as commentators have memorably said, 'Sport is a very prominent social institution in almost every society because it combines the characteristics found in any institution with a unique appeal ... sport may be integrative at the higher political levels, it has not been so at the interpersonal levels of gender and race. The inequality that characterizes society's relations of gender and race is found in sport as well.'[84]

Nevertheless, since the 1970s, Association Football in the United States has emerged as a female-appropriate game in that it is physical yet not necessarily involving violent body contact, athletically demanding but not requiring exceptional size, bulk, or upper-body strength. It now stands as an acceptable outdoor female team sport which is often used to 'balance' male collegiate American football programmes. Title IX, whatever its intention, in a direct way addressed two of the most damaging stereotypes of the place of sport in our societies. The principle of Title IX was to question a financial assumption, made before 1972, that women are not interested in or able to have careers in sport so that therefore what opportunities there are should not be wasted on individuals likely to give up sport for marriage and a family.[85] Critics of statistical proportionality quite rightly show that some institutions have withdrawn male minority varsity sports, while others have taken the regressive step of cutting entire men's (and women's) programmes. To use this reactionary retrenchment as the most fundamental critique of the principles at stake is to miss the point by a country mile. The abandonment of individual and programmatic provision is the choice of institutions and administrators, not the purpose of Title IX.

When women's soccer became a varsity rather than an intramural sport, the process of change appears to have been specific to the institution and subject to considerable negotiation. Consequently, college soccer programs for women began to be established from the mid-1960s and combined over a period of time with the increased entrance of girls into recreational sports initiatives, which in turn provided the potential talent for the new college teams. Around the mid-1960s, Castleton State College, in Castleton, Vermont, had a varsity soccer team, for example. There isn't space here to equivocate about when and how individual institutions gave or witheld varsity status. What seems to have happened are two main processes of attaining varsity status which remain to be developed and debated by future researchers in developing a more thorough understanding of women's college representative teams.

At one end of the continuum, individual football enthusiasts formed club and intramural teams which attracted more players and became increasingly serious in their preparation to a point at which it discomfitted the institution *not* to award varsity status. At the other end of the scale, much less in evidence from the colleges researched here, college administrations provided chances for varsity play in soccer as one of many other opportunities and, as such, pre empted and possibly fostered student interest. At Brown, for example, archive accounts suggest that the transition seemed relatively easy, fairly speedy and brought considerable success. After several unofficial seasons, the women's soccer team, coached by Dom Starsia since 1973, won two of five games in its first varsity season in 1975. The 1976 team finished 7–1, losing only to Yale, and the 1977 team, the first coached by Phil Pincince, improved on that with a 13–1 season and lost only to Lake Champlain College in the final round of the Castleton State Tournament. Brown hosted the first women's Ivy championship in 1978 and came in second, Harvard beating Brown to win the first Eastern Regional championship in 1979. Pincince's teams won the Ivy League championship in 1980 and every year from 1982 through 1990, tying with Princeton in 1982 and with Cornell in 1987.[86]

This relatively smooth transition also seems to be the case at Smith. The Smith Soccer File in the Dunn papers at Smith contains correspondence between 1985 and 1991. Two letters are to Dunn thanking her for her support of soccer at Smith. There is a memo from Dunn regarding Smith's participation in the NCAA Women's Division III National Collegiate Soccer Championship, followed by a letter of congratulations to the varsity players regarding their win in that event and also a letter of congratulations to the soccer team coach for being named coach of the year in 1986.[87] However, Penn State, which now competes in the Big Ten, took more than ten years to change women's soccer from club to varsity level. At one point it was orphaned within the school as the Sports Clubs Office longer provided adequate support and the Athletic Department hadn't yet adopted the club. The team had to fund-raise to travel throughout Pennsylvania and the Northeast, with little money for food or lodging. In this time the team competed against varsities with full staffs and administrative assistance but had no paid coach and no scholarships. Title IX was useful in cases like this, in pressing for opportunities where a demonstrable need and interest were made evident by students and staff looking to challenge themselves in an increasingly competitive environment.

By 1981, there were between 50 and 100 college programmes in women's soccer, plus club teams, and around that time Betty Ellis became the first female official hired by the North American Soccer League. In 1983, Jan Smisek became the first woman to be awarded a coaching licence with the United States Soccer Federation (USSF). The University of North Carolina (UNC), coached by Anson Dorrance, immediately took a commanding position in the women's college game: The 1981 tournament had been held by the Association for Intercollegiate Athletics for women (AIAW), and 1982 saw a takeover of national collegiate competition by the National College Athletic Association (NCAA), along with other changes in women's sport. North Carolina and the University of Connecticut are the only two teams to have been invited to the tournament every year since its inception. Of the first twenty NCAA championships, sixteen were won by UNC, including nine consecutive years, from 1986 to 1994.

By 1982, collegiate women's football had entered the yearbooks of the National Collegiate Athletic Association. With a 29 per cent increase in the number of NCAA member institutions sponsoring women's intercollegiate varsity programmes in 1983, the largest percentage increase since the transition from the Association for Intercollegiate Athletics for Women to the NCAA, the scale of interest became apparent. In 1981 there were 521 men's college teams and 77 women's. By 1990 the figure for women's team was up to 318; nearly 40 per cent of the total. Teams for men also grew in number, from 521 to 569, and were found at 69 per cent of institutions. Unusually, by 1999, there were 790 women's teams in the NCAA and only 719 men's. Women now had a choice of almost 80 per cent of colleges, while the percentage of schools offering men's teams remained steady at 70 per cent. This growth affected all divisions, not just the smaller colleges, and, while the number of NCAA colleges had grown to more than 1,000 during this time, many programs were not in full compliance with Title IX, even by 2000. As women's college soccer grew, through the 1990s, tournaments steadily grew in size, culminating in the 2001 expansion of the Division I tournament to sixty-four women's teams, compared to thirty-two for the men. Leading centres emerged, such as Central Florida, George Mason, Connecticut, Santa Clara, Notre Dame, Portland, UCLA and Penn State, in addition to North Carolina.

However, the Knight Commission, *Keeping Faith with the Student Athlete: A New Model for Intercollegiate Athletics* (1991) sought to address some of the most fundamental abuses of the intercollegiate model.[88] Though these wider concerns remain, they appear not to affect women's soccer to the same degree as other sports.[89] The situation is complicated because of the various types and size of colleges, constituent members of a range of organizations including the NCAA, the National Association of Intercollegiate Athletics (NAIA) and the National Junior College Athletic Association (NJCAA). Outside educational institutions, there appears to have been a rise in the number of organized soccer leagues for children, including the American Youth Soccer Organization (AYSO), United States Youth Soccer Association (USYSA) and the Soccer Association for Youth (SAY), alongside the pastime recreational element. Elsewhere, the development was evident in a wider growth at youth, high school and college levels. By 1980, the growth in youth soccer was already dramatic, with almost 900,000 youngsters participating. At the high school level, participant growth was no less dramatic. In 1976, barely 10,000 girls played in high school, less than 10 per cent of the total. By 1990, this had changed; girls constituted a little more than a third of the total 122,000 youth participants. The increase in the number of girls playing in organized and competitive leagues is most significant in North America, therefore, because it combines mass participation with a means of identifying and developing elite potential which may enable an individual to go on to a college scholarship. So, as the brief historical summary indicates, there was an established tradition of women's participation in soccer well before Title IX, but the form and volume of female play has changed considerably in the past three decades. However, this is not an isolated trend. For example, one of the questions raised by the co-ed tradition is whether soccer is part of a growing social movement that sees the joint involvement of men and women in sporting activities.[90]

Because the competition structure at the intercollegiate level is roughly determined by a balance of teams, this attempt at operational equivalence may predominate over the geographical proximity of teams, so that, in previous seasons, New Jersey has been incorporated into the Central region. Until around 1995, the competition regions could be defined as Northeast, South, West and Central. There are, and have been, a number of general and specialist organizations that have had an interest in intercollegiate athletics, women's sport and soccer which have helped to form the current shape of the varsity intercollegiate participation. Within intercollegiate athletics, for example, there were several governing organizations to which a college or university selected membership depending on the institution's ethos, and the three active organizations have already been referred to earlier as the NAIA, the NCAA and the NJCAA. From 1971 to 1982, the Association of Intercollegiate Athletics for Women (AIAW) had as its aim specifically the purpose of promoting and administering women's athletics. In 1982, its remit passed to NCAA, founded in 1905 to govern men's intercollegiate activities, but there remains divided opinion about how enthusiastically this agenda has been embraced. Some of the smaller institutions especially see their interests better served by the NAIA. There are then a range of organizations solely interested in soccer, not necessarily solely for women. The Intercollegiate Soccer Association of America (ISAA) was founded in 1922 to promote intercollegiate competition, the National Soccer Coaches Association of America (NSCAA) represents all levels of coaches founded in 1941 and the first established organization for intercollegiate women's soccer that has so far been identified was founded in 1978 as the New England Women's Intercollegiate Soccer Association (NEWISA).

Given the enormous success of the Women's National Team at the dawn of the twenty-first century, the team had very modest beginnings. Nor has that success been easily won or steadily supported. Unlike the European examples, rather belatedly women finally made their mark in the club scene, with older women wanting to continue playing after college in women's clubs and leagues becoming a major part of the United States Amateur Soccer Association (USASA). It was not until 1985 that the first women's national squad was formed. In 1985 the United States Olympic Committee and USSF hosted the first Olympic festival for women's football, in Louisiana. Regional players were sent to this festival, where a national team was selected; the roster included Enos, Boyer, Orrison, Bender and Wyant, for example. There was little practice time, few resources and basic travel conditions. The press didn't even notice. The season consisted of a trip to Jesolo, Italy, where the US played four games, losing to England and Italy but obtaining a draw with Denmark. However, there were some signs of the history to be made later as the first goal scored by the US team was by a young collegian from University of Central Florida named Michelle Akers-Stahl. This team disbanded after that series, to be reformed the following year with Anson Dorrance as National Team coach. The more professional coaching regimen, combined with improved selection of talented players, including many from North Carolina, saw a victory in 1986 at the first North America championship with a 2–0 win over Canada. Joining Akers-Stahl were April Heinrichs and the NCAA's Debbie Belkin. The improvement at the elite level was dramatic, and in the same year the first NCAA Division III women's soccer championship was held in New York, with the University of Rochester as victors.

In 1987, the USA Women's National Team really became recognizable as the force that it was in 1999. Joy (Fawcett) Biefield, Kristine Lilly, and Carin Jennings joined, as did the youngest woman to play for the US national team, a fifteen-year-old named Mariel 'Mia' Hamm. The schedule was more challenging, too, with tours of Taiwan and China plus their first wins against future elite opponents China and Norway. The year 1988 saw the international debuts of Julie Foudy and Shannon Higgins, but the lack of a full-time team with regular practice took its toll. Once again, the team was together only briefly in preparation for competitions in China and Italy. European and Asian continental championships had proved a mild incentive; there was limited official interest in the unendorsed women's championships, with the exception of WINS and other US-based tournaments called internationals, as discussed in the Introduction. The United States National Team outlook was very much focused on officially-sanctioned tournaments, which, as we've seen, became a feature of the sport only in the 1990s. However, for domestic participation, 1988 saw the first NCAA Division II championship in Florida, the establishment of an USSF under-twenty women's national team that would prove to be vital in developing the squad in the next decade, and the inaugural award of the Herman Trophy to the best female Division I player. In 1989 and 1990, the women's team, like the men's squad, was hastily assembled for tournaments or friendlies with little practice time. With no overarching purpose, the teams lost focus and were disheartened by the lack of success at tournament levels.

During this lean time for the national team, the main story to hit the headlines in 1990 showed how highly skilled female players continued to meet with profound cynicism in the US, as elsewhere. Natasha Dennis of the Lewisville Blaze team made national headlines after playing so well that two irate parents on the opposing team questioned her sex. The goalie was only nine when she was asked to prove she was a girl. This harassment extended to asking her to go to the bathroom with a designated 'objective' parent who would verify her sex. The episode seems to tell us rather more about the masculine anxieties of the fathers than the gender of the players, but it does show how persistent and widespread the Victorian idea of sports as inherently, in this case biologically, male.[91]

FIFA's first women's world championship, held in Guangzhou, China, in 1991, proved to be the stage for which the US team, in particular Michelle Akers, had been waiting for. A 2–1 victory over Norway in front of 65,000 fans saw captain April Heinrichs lift the trophy. Carin Jennings Gabarra was named most valuable player, and Michelle Akers set Golden Boot records.[92] The USSF underwent major changes after they successfully landed World Cup 1994 and began in earnest to establish a full-time men's team to prepare for the big event. But the women were left behind. A key gap in the women's soccer competition calendar was filled that year by the United States Interregional Soccer League (USISL). The USISL provided a base of support with their Division 3 outdoor league, acting as a farm system for the A-League. Seeing themselves as the foundation supporting the top levels, the USISL established the W-League, a national amateur league that would provide playing time for the top players and which continues today. Although many of the top National squad remained with their colleges or the USSF full-time, the

W-League would sign many of the remaining top players in the country and several international stars, while allowing active college players an outlet to gain additional exposure and continue their careers. They played a brief exhibition schedule in 1994 and launched in 1995 with nineteen teams spread nationwide in a very successful debut. The importance of the W-League is such that several of the former WUSA players moved to play there after the 2003 demise of the professional franchise.

In 1993 the International Olympic Committee voted to admit soccer as an official sport for women in 1996. Following on from their 1991 world championship victory, plus the 1994 men's soccer World Cup, at the Olympic Games in 1996 the American women's team began to capture the attention of the American public; even the smaller women's crowds of between 16,000 and 20,000 were respectable. The crowds built throughout the competition, culminating in more than 76,000 for the final. NBC initially planned to give no coverage at all to the women's competition, but the live support of 65,000 at the world championship final in 1991 and 76,000 in 1996 allowed the organizers of the US-hosted World Cup in 1999 to draw upon an established fan base to fill the Rose Bowl.

After the Cup, the premier players used their new clout to press for a more generous contract. Initially the USSF balked, and the players organized their own unofficial tour, playing in indoor stadiums. They received the lion's share of revenue, and this led to considerable friction with the USSF, but it was the only way they saw to receive proper compensation. Ultimately, the pressure helped, and they received a much better compensation package, although the walkout was lengthy and the US had to compete in the Australian Cup in January 2000 without star players. The team was also facing the fact that many of its veteran stars were approaching retirement, as the team struggled to develop its next generation of stars. But many of the players were determined to hang on until the 2000 Olympics. In the very well-attended autumn Victory tour playing major opponents, averaging more than 34,000 fans per game, the fans did not leave disappointed, as the US registered five consecutive victories.

There had been calls for the establishment of a professional women's league to be in place before the 1999 World Cup, and soon a group was organizing what would be the National Soccer Alliance for 1998. They received commitments from a number of major World Cup veterans, but financing fell through and the effort collapsed. People felt it would be better to make an attempt after the Cup with more solid financial footing. For now, the W-League would suffice, although the West Coast teams broke away and joined with top amateur clubs to form the Women's Premier Soccer League. For a brief time there was the danger that two leagues would be formed, one headed by John Hendricks, CEO of Discovery Corporation, and another proposed by Major League Soccer. MLS already had a going operation, but the Hendricks proposal was backed by $40 million from major media companies. Hendricks was able to get sanctioning for his Women's United Soccer Association, with a partnership agreement between WUSA and MLS promising to work to the benefit of both parties. Eight cities were awarded franchises, spanning the country. Nearly the entire national team was signed by the league, and, in the draft, world stars, the cream of W-League talent, and college drafts filled the squads. WUSA started off well and improved rapidly through the inaugural season. Attendance was predicted at 4,000 to 6,000 per game but averaged close to 8,000, yet TV ratings did not meet expectations.

Women's involvement is therefore central to the divergent interpretations of American soccer. From an international vantage point, the state of women's soccer in the US generates envy as considerable participation sits alongside elite success. It would seem that a nondiscriminatory public policy and the absence of male resistance have opened soccer pitches to women at college level. Yet, in spite of mass participation and elite success, women's football remains separate and unequal in terms of resources, participation and prestige. The perceived 'feminization', Sugden proposes, 'supports the view of soccer as a game for second-rate athletes unable to contend with the masculine rigors of the home-grown variety of football ... as long as soccer is viewed as a game for foreigners, rich white kids and women, its chances of becoming established as a mainstream professional sport there are minimal.'[93] However, the situation is more subtle than that if we also look at the participatory elements. Mixed football, for example, or, to use the local term, co-ed soccer, is a recent and unusual aspect of the American case study. Although there is some evidence that adult women and men are playing soccer together in a structured and sustained manner in other countries, they have not been otherwise covered in detail by these case studies. Co-ed soccer is popular across the USA, with the oldest league established in 1981. The United States Adult Soccer Association, USASA, established the COED CUP in 1999, and there are now an Open and an Over-Thirty division.

Henry and Comeaux's study of 130 players in eight teams during the 2003 autumn season identified the general organization of soccer, but formal adjustments had been made regarding team composition and scoring.[94] It doesn't appear to follow the common-sense logic that men play mixed sport to play down whereas women play up, and so there is not a 'feminization' of the sport in a straightforward sense. It does highlight the view that male players can be rough, fast and aggressive and many female players enjoyed access to a style of play not always perceived to be available in single-sex competition. While male participants in co-ed play were sometimes aware of gender divisions, more often, lower levels of athleticism were attributed across the sexes to balance, physical fitness and skill rather than to gender. The results challenge the thesis of 'American exceptionalism', and more research into the meaning of play for participants would help historical surveys such as this case study to come alive.

The success of the Women's National Team and its relationship to the growth of intercollegiate women's football is an area of considerable interest. Of course the symbolic success of the team since the inception of a FIFA Women's World Cup in 1991 as well as in the 1996 Atlanta Olympic Games has had a wider impact on grassroots and professional levels of the sport, too. The establishment of Women's United Soccer Association (WUSA) was arguably possible because Women's World Cup 1999 presented the Women's National Team to the American public as the best international players in a world competition in which they were central, both to the staging of the competition and in creating spectacle. If, since 1996, Major League Soccer has struggled with the question of imported and native male players, the Women's National Team appeared to symbolize All-American values. However, the question of using foreign players again made WUSA a risky prospect as financial problems due to startup costs began to worsen and the foreign draft was expanded. Decisions were founded on football qualities, rather than on links with possible audiences. With the decline of WUSA at the same time as Germany's victory in the much smaller venues of the 2003 World Cup together with the retirement of the remaining '91ers in 2004, the stigmatization of football as a foreign sport for elites, ethnic groups, children and women seems to have been at least partially reaffirmed.

Also worrying in the current atmosphere, Title IX and other equity programmes remain under threat now and have faced major setbacks in the past.[95] Because some of these problems have been highlighted by the Knight Foundation Commission, the NCAA formed the Gender Equity Committee, and the chair, James Whalen, President of Ithaca College, summarized some of the major problems: an attitude that women are not interested in competing, don't have sporting ability, the 'turf problem' (which relates to protection of field space and resources for male programmes) and the availability of supporting money. The question of how quickly intercollegiate teams funded to varsity status is in one sense crucial because of the principle of a right to resources, which is a world-wide problem with regard to women in sport and is nowhere more evident than in football:

> That the obligatory linking of the U.S. women's soccer team and Title IX is more a political assertion than a historical truth is shown by the fact that the American women were winning long before the summer of 1999 and nobody bothered to say it was because of Title IX. As editorial writer David Tell has noted, in 1991 the US women demolished the Norwegian national team to win the first ever Women's World Cup soccer championship. But no one—not a single sports writer, editorial writer, politician or spokesperson for a women's group—laid their victory at the feet of a federal law. What was different in 1999 was the political setting ... Women's soccer put a positive face on what some were beginning to understand was a law with a significant downside.[96]

As my discussion with Lauren Gregg and the dealings of the Women's National Team with US Soccer around the time of the 1991 and the 1999 World Cup competitions show, those who have been inside that part of social history view Title IX as highly significant, even if it is not in the simplistic terms of cause and effect used here. Of course, there were also heroic amounts of hard work, athletic preparation and political negotiation, but, as consideration of the process of club and intramural to varsity status has shown, Title IX provided a principle above the level of individual institutions to which women athletes and faculty members who felt unsupported by administrators could appeal. There is no need to directly attribute responsibility because the situation is more subtle, not least in the way that institutions have responded in less than constructive engagements with the progressive elements of proportionality.

As someone who has been critical of statistical measures of involvement as the primary measure of progress, I use considerable caution in considering the figures for intercollegiate US sport. With a variety of interest and affiliation, there appears to have been increasing organization of networks in the 1970s that helped to foster interest and provide some external impetus for change, whatever the approach of individual institutions. The New England Intercollegiate Women's Soccer Association (NEWISA) was formed in 1978; an Ivy League tournament was won by Harvard in the same year; and in 1979 the University of North Carolina (UNC) created a varsity team which has arguably dominated women's college soccer. However, the growth was as uncertain and unsteady as other women's sport participation. Clubs have been awarded then demoted from varsity status, and some institutions took more than a decade to upgrade, most notably Indiana University and Penn State in 1993 and 1994, respectively. Penn State was taken to a Title IX hearing, which noted, in 1988, that, although a women's soccer club had existed since 1977, the institution was not in violation, as the overall opportunities for women were sufficient.

The emerging national network of club, intramural and intercollegiate games was fostered by key individuals determined to increase recognition, not least in response to AIAW regulations issued in 1977. These rules stipulated that at least 20 per cent of membership must offer varsity-level competition over at least five regions before a national championship in a given sport could be held. The Interim Soccer Committee included Anson Dorrance of UNC, who personally sent out questionnaires in order to network to fulfill the criteria, and the first national tournament took place in 1980.[97] In 1981, AIAW and United States Soccer Federation sanctioned a Scandinavian tour by forty-three female players from twenty-one colleges, thus beginning to establish an All-American dimension to the women's game which persists today in the prominence of college players in the Women's National Team. Significant for the organization of women's sport was the absorption of the AIAW by the NCAA in 1982 and the decline in the number of women in leadership positions in women's athletics. While in the next decade women's opportunities increased, men's gains almost equalled them, and at the same time more coaching positions for men were created by the growth women's soccer. This is obviously not something to be understood simply, as the history so far has shown how significant male individuals have helped the sport and women coaches, educationalists and administrators have hindered its progress. However, the NCAA provides reasons to be cautiously optimistic in that its annual reports highlight an overall growth in the number of institutions sponsoring varsity soccer for women. An NCAA Participation Study of 1993 found that 69.5 per cent of collegiate athletes were men; 70 per cent of scholarship money goes to men athletes; 77 per cent of athletic operating budgets goes to men's athletics and 83 per cent of recruiting money is spent on men's athletics. This led to the establishment of a Gender Equity Task Force, but the outcome is indistinct. Does equity mean in proportion to female undergraduate enrollment at a given institution (thereby tying the issue to wider educational entitlement); does an opportunity have to exist before a student can demonstrate an interest; finally, should interest lead demand for programme expansion before resource allocated on strictly numeric/financial ratios? Given the large rosters for American football, its dominance in intercollegiate sport and its construction as a male-only code at college level, the dilemmas remain. Even with cases pending and with Title IX itself under threat from the Bush administration, as a team sport requiring about twenty players for a squad, women's soccer looks to remain a considerable presence at collegiate level.

It has been perhaps been unsurprising given the other case studies that historically the development of pockets of interest appears to have been fairly geographically random and dependent upon individual and small-group interest; whether player or administrative. Until the 1970s, this may have been relatively more sexually segregated in the women's colleges. Outside of those environments and later, women have been helped by male coaches and administrators pioneering or defending women's right to play. A considerable area for future research is the disparity in the number of white women and the number of women from ethnic minority groups emerging from this system. Given that the issue of race and ethnicity is a key feature of American history it is perhaps the matter, leading to a view of a lack of success for soccer as a sport.[98] This is especially so when the stereotype of association football is that of a game for elites, women, children and ethnic groups. It is evidently not a sport for many women from nonwhite backgrounds.

In view of the sport's relative underdevelopment until the 1990s, it seems that another old chestnut which survives as a stereotype around women's football is that it is a sign of modernity, a sport of a rapidly approaching future, perhaps, even, of progress.[99] Not always attractive traits to those who value tradition, the status quo and nostalgia. The rapid increase in the number of women playing soccer in the United States should not hide the context which makes the story of that situation, made up of both those who would and those who think they shouldn't. The constructedness of the stereotype ought equally not to detract from an understanding of the determined reconstruction of privilege and dominance in apparently more democratic moments in the history of women and sport. Women's World Cup 1999 was perhaps the first time that women were included in that moment which linked them to their sporting public when, according to Eric Hobsbawm, 'The imagined community of millions seems more real as a team of eleven named people.'[100] The fall from popularity of the Women's National Team four short years later also says something about the sporting culture and how it wishes to represent itself. It isn't, after all, only a game.

## Notes

1.  *Time* magazine covers around the time of Women's World Cup 1999. ABC News called them 'the heiresses of the women's movement' and the Denver *Post* 'the revenge of the soccer moms'. See also Jere Longman, *The Girls of Summer: The U.S. Women's Soccer Team and How It Changed the World* (New York: Harper Paperbacks, 2001). For a view of the broader political context of the 'soccer mom' see Susan J. Carroll, 'The Disempowerment of the Gender Gap: Soccer Moms and the 1996 Elections', *Political Science and Politics,* 32, no. 1 (March 1999): 7–11.
2.  T. Wilson, 'The Contribution of an Athletic Programme to High School Girls', *Teacher's College Journal* (September 1938): 107.
3.  J. Tunis, 'Changing Trends in Sport', *Harper's Monthly Magazine,* 170 (December 1934–May 1935), p. 86.
4.  Brandi Chastain, *It's Not about the Bra: Play Hard, Play Fair, and Put the Fun Back into Competitive Sports* (New York: Harper Collins, 2004) and the related Web site itsnotaboutthebra.com. Both refer to her front-page picture as the US team won the 1999 final without shirt and in black sports bra. A number of the US National Team published books, most notably Mia Hamm, *Go for the Goal: A Champion's Guide to Winning in Soccer and Life* (New York: Harper, 1999) and the children's illustrated book (with Carol Thompson) *Winners Never Quit!* (New York: Harper Collins, 2004). See also Lauren Gregg, *The Champion Within: Training for Excellence* (Burlington: JTC Sports, 1999).
5.  Jessica Gavora, *Tilting the Playing Field: Schools, Sport, Sex and Title IX* (San Francisco: Encounter Books, 2002), p. 5, while disagreeing fundamentally with Gavora's analysis of the significance of Title IX, she makes some useful points about the narratives around the success of the Women's National Team in 1999.
6.  See for example Ernestine Miller, *Making Her Mark: Firsts and Milestones in Women's Sports* (New York: Contemporary Books, 2002), pp. 254–267; Shawn Ladda, *The History of Intercollegiate Women's Soccer in the United States,* unpublished D.Ed. dissertation, Columbia University, New York, 1995. I am grateful to Shawn Ladda for leads on some of the US colleges in this chapter and to the archivists who assisted with the research.
7.  US Soccer Foundation, *Soccer in the USA 2002–2003* (Chicago: US Soccer Foundation), p. 5. The criterion is all females who have played the game at least once during the previous year, which is unsatisfactory but widely used. The figure for American males was approaching 10,400. See also US Soccer Foundation, *Annual Report 2005.* For a wider context of sports participation in relation to children's leisure, 'Children today tend to get outdoor exercise by appointment. Soccer participation has been unchanged in the past decade—about 28% of kids age 7 to 11 play the sport. Soccer leagues and

soccer camps are in full bloom this summer, although non-organized soccer games are uncommon.' Dennis Cauchon, 'Childhood Pastimes Are Increasingly Moving Indoors', *USA Today,* 12 July 2005, p. 5.

8. The Equal Rights Amendment passed the US Senate and then the House of Representatives, and, on March 22, 1972, the proposal was sent to the States for ratification with a seven-year deadline on the process. For an overview see R.W. Francis, Chair, ERA Task Force, National Council of Women's Organizations, at http://www.equalrightsamendment.org/era.htm, accessed June 2005.

9. See http://www.ed.gov An institution is in compliance with the three-part test if it has met any one of the following three parts of it: the percentage of male and female athletes is substantially proportionate to the percentage of male and female students enrolled at the school; or the school has a history and continuing practice of expanding participation opportunities for the underrepresented sex; or the school is fully and effectively accommodating the interests and abilities of the underrepresented sex. In March 2005, new federal guidelines were released that created an alternative way for colleges to be in compliance with the 1972 antidiscrimination law. Schools may now use an e-mail survey to show that they are in fulfilment of the requirements with Title IX. Insufficient interest among female students qualifies as compliance under Title IX's third prong.

10. R. Vivian Acosta and Linda Jean Carpenter, *Women in Intercollegiate Sport: A Longitudinal, National Study Twenty-Seven-Year Update: 1977–2004,* available at www.womenssportfoundtion.org, posted 8 June 2004.

11. Gavora, *Tilting the Playing Field,* p. 5 (my insertion in parentheses).

12. Mark Zeigler, 'Cup of Trouble', *San Diego Union-Tribune,* 19 September 2003.

13. In December 2004 Maribel Dominguez reportedly signed for Mexican men's side Celaya. In 2003 Italian side Perugia announced it had made an offer to the German World Cup winner Birgit Prinz. The club had already pursued Sweden's Hannah Ljungberg, which would have made her the first female player in Series A.

14. A. Markovits and S. Hellerman, 'Women's Soccer in the United States: Yet Another American "Exceptionalism"', in F. Hong and J.A. Mangan (eds), *Soccer, Women and Sexual Liberation: Kicking Off a New Era* (London: Frank Cass, 2004), p. 14. See also A. Markovits and S. Hellerman, *Offside: Soccer and American Exceptionalism* (Princeton, NJ: Princeton University Press, 2001), pp. 7–9; A. Markovits and S. Hellerman, 'The "Olympianization" of Soccer in the United States: From Marginalization in America's "Sports Space" to Recognition as a Quadrennial Event in American Mainstream Culture', *American Behavioural Scientist,* 46, no. 11 (July 2003): 1533–1549. First raised by Andrei Markovits in his comparative work on sport and, in particular, football, the term was originally developed in the German sociologist Werner Sombart's 1906 work *Warum gibt es in den Vereinigten Staaten keinen Sozialismus?* (Tübingen: Mohr, 1906).

Several English translations exist, including *Why Is There No Socialism in the United States* (New York: Sharpe, 1976).

15. Stephen H. Hardy, 'Entrepreneurs, Organizations and the Sports Marketplace', *The New American Sport History* (Urbana and Chicago: University of Illinois Press, 1996), p. 344. As the essay contends, the shift in perspective from social history to include aspects of business and economic history helps to focus on the production and distribution of games as cultural institutions.

16. Markovits and Hellerman, 'Women's Soccer in the United States', p. 14.

17. Mark Salisbury, *American Attitudes toward Soccer,* available at http://www.sover.net, accessed September 2005. At the same time the marginalization of the women's game is replicated here as in other scenarios, for example, in the online essay *The History of Soccer in The United States,* to little more than one paragraph. Colin Jose, *An Overview of American Soccer History,* US Soccer Archives, available at http://www.sover.net and updated by Dave Litterer, *An Overview of American Soccer History,* available at http://www.sover.net, which has improved detail on women's participation, although the treatment remains relatively brief.

18. A. Tomlinson and J. Sugden, *Hosts and Champions: Soccer Cultures, National Identities and the USA World Cup* (Aldershot: Arena, 1994), p. 4. In *FIFA and the Contest for World Football: Who Rules the People's Game?* Sugden and Tomlinson analyzed the role of gatekeepers effective in maintaining existing hierarchies at FIFA in 1998. The analysis of ongoing systems of patronage has been valuable for this study, but I would argue that more notice is taken of the relatively small alterations to include women than the endurance of exclusion. For example, in 1994 the decision by the FIFA Executive Committee to double the number of members on the Women's Football Committee from seven to fourteen was made not in the spirit of increased gender representation but to increase geographical representation. Though the women's committee in 2006 is predominantly female, it remains a moot point whether this will eventually lead to increased gender representation across all FIFA committees. This is complicated by the multifaceted nature of international sports organizations, as women are more evident as administrative appointees than elected representatives.

19. Pierre Lanfranchi and Matthew Taylor, *Moving with the Ball* (Oxford: Berg, 2001), p. 144; Steve Holroyd, 'The First Professional Soccer League in the United States: The American League of Professional Football (ALPF)', US Soccer Archives, http://www.sover.net/, accessed August 2005.

20. Lanfranchi and Taylor, *Moving with the Ball,* pp. 145–146.

21. Colin Jose, *American Soccer League 1921–31: The Golden Years of American Soccer* (Lanham, MD: Scarecrow Press, 1998). See also US Soccer History Archives, http://www.sover.net, as this is a large historiography that describes particularly the relationship between competing and overlapping leagues.

22. R. Todd Jewell and David J. Molina, 'An Evaluation of the Relationship between Hispanics and Major League Soccer', *Journal of Sports Economics,* 6, no. 2 (2005): 160–177; Sandra Collins, 'National Sports and Other Myths: The Failure of US Soccer', *Soccer and Society Special Edition: Making It Happen: Fringe Nations in World Soccer Celebrating World Cup 2006,* 7, no. 2–3 (April 2006): 353–363; for a popular view see Andrea Canales, 'MLS All-Stars Earn Some Respect', available at http://soccernet.espn.go.com/columns, accessed 6 August 2006.

23. D. Andrews, R. Pitter, D. Zwick and D. Ambrose, 'Soccer's Racial Frontier: Sport and the Suburbanisation of Contemporary America', in G. Armstrong and R. Giulianotti (eds), *Entering the Field: New Perspectives on World Football* (Oxford: Berg, 1997); D. Andrews, 'Contextualising Suburban Soccer: Consumer Culture, Lifestyle Differentiation and Suburban America', in G. Finn and R. Giulianotti (eds), *Football Culture: Local Contests, Global Visions* (London: Routledge, 2000).

24. Markovits and Hellerman, 'Women's Soccer in the United States', p. 27.

25. Ibid., p. 14.

26. See for example M. Leigh and T. Bonin, 'The Pioneering Role of Madame Alice Milliat and the FSFI [Fédération Sportive Féminine Internationale] in Establishing International Track and Field Competition for Women', *Journal of Sports History,* 4, no. 1 (1977): 72–83. Alice Milliat promoted football as part of the activities of the Fédération Sportive Féminine Internationale, but this was outside the Olympic movement. The 1994 Congress of Unity stipulated the inclusion into the Olympic Charter of an explicit reference to 'the promotion of women's advancement in sport at all levels: The IOC strongly encourages, by appropriate means, the promotion of women in sport at all levels and in all structures, particularly in the executive bodies of national and international sports organisations with a view to the strict application of the principle of equality between men and women.' International Olympic Committee, *The Promotion of Women in the Olympic Movement,* Lausanne, 2000, p. 3. There remain statistical imbalances in participation as well as administrative inequities; for example, in Sydney 2000, women competed in twenty-five sports and made up roughly 38 per cent of the 10,382 athletes. In Greece 2004, women competed in twenty-six sports and made up roughly 41 per cent of the athletes (4,306), whereas men made up 59 per cent (6,262): *IOC Report Women Participation at the Games of the XXVIIIe Olympiad Athens 2004,* Dept of International Cooperation and Competition, February 2005, p. 8. Women's football reports a 25 per cent increase in the number of participating players since the Sydney competition.

27. At the increased ten-team tournament in Greece in 2004, participants were Australia, Brazil, China, Germany, Greece, Japan, Mexico, Nigeria, Sweden and the USA. The men's event involved sixteen teams.

28. Mario Rimati, in Roger Le Grove Rogers, ed, *Women's Soccer World,* 1728 Mulberry St. Montgomery, AL 36106, March/April 1999, gives the figure as 76,481 spectators.

29. NBC initially refused to cover the women's team in the 1996 Summer Olympic Games, suggesting that Americans equally disdain women's sports and any version of soccer. The 1999 victory over Brazil at Stanford University attracted the largest soccer ratings ever for ESPN, a total of 2.9 million homes, breaking the previous record of 2.7 million homes for the United States's upset victory over Colombia during the Men's World Cup in 1994.

30. The foundation was created with the express intention to support projects that will assist soccer in becoming a preeminent sport in the United States. The US Soccer Foundation has a simple mission statement that guides a wide range of initiatives: 'To enhance, assist and grow the sport of soccer in the United States'. See http://www.ussoccerfoundation.org/, accessed January 2006.

31. Philadelphia Charge, Washington Freedom, San Diego Spirit, New York Power, Atlanta Beat, Bay Area Cyber Rays, Carolina Tempest and Boston Breakers.

32. Lauren Gregg, National Team player, the first woman full-time national coach to the Under-Twenties team and assistant coach of the Women's National Team, VP of Player Personnel for Women's United Soccer Association, personal communication, 31 October 2001.

33. It succeeded in drawing media crowds of around 40 million, earning the Women's National Team *Sports Illustrated* 1999 Sportsmen of the Year Award and winning ESPN's Team of the Year award.

34. Nike named the largest building on its corporate campus after Hamm in 1999. She received other accolades, sporting and otherwise, including being named to People Magazine's '50 Most Beautiful People' list in 1997 and winning ESPN's 'Espy' award for Female Athlete of the Year and Soccer Player of 1999.

35. These included founding the Mia Hamm Foundation in partnership with Nike, Mattel and Gatorade. The foundation is dedicated to raising funds and awareness for research for bone marrow diseases (Hamm's brother Garrett died in 1997) and to encouraging and empowering girls and women who participate in sports.

36. Barbara Allen, Chief Executive, Women's United Soccer Association (WUSA), personal communication, 5 October 2001.

37. 'Attendance at Women's World Cup games has fallen drastically from 1999, when the event was also held in the United States. But this year, soccer officials say, figures do not tell the story': Frank Litsky, SOCCER; 'Organizers Encouraged by Attendance Numbers', *New York Times,* 2 October 2003 Final, Section D, p. 6; Michelle Akers, 'Germany Had USA's Number', *USA Today,* 8 October 2003.

38. Women's Soccer Initiative Inc. (WSII), a not-for-profit entity dedicated to the relaunch of women's professional soccer in the United States, was started in

December 2004. Tonya Antonucci was named Chief Executive Officer to lead the relaunch efforts, but without success to date. The US Soccer Foundation and the US Soccer Federation, soccer's governing body for the United States, agreed to donate a combined $100,000 to support the first phase of business planning, research and market identification. '"Our partnership with these two organizations is of tremendous value to us as we build a disciplined, long-term business plan," said Tonya Antonucci, CEO of WSII. "Not only are they providing us necessary financial backing at this time, but they also offer support as we construct our plan and build momentum in the marketplace to capitalize the league".' US Soccer Foundation, *Annual Report 2005,* p. 18.

39. Nathan Abrams, 'Inhibited but Not "Crowded Out": The Strange Fate of Soccer in the United States', *International Journal of the History of Sport,* 12, no. 3 (December 1995): 1–17.

40. T. Henry Fowler, 'A Phase of Modern College Life', *Harper's New Monthly Magazine,* 92 (December 1895–May 1896), p. 688. 'Inter Collegiate Athletics, particularly inter collegiate football, constitutes the significant phase of modern college life that has of late been most prominenetly before the public.'

41. M. Ann Hall, 'The Game of Choice: Girls' and Women's Soccer in Canada', *Soccer and Society,* 4, no. 2–3 (2003): 30–46, has teams in Blairmore, Calgary, Hamilton and Hillcrest in the 1920s.

42. Christiane Eisenberg, Pierre Lanfranchi, Tony Mason and Alfred Wahl, *100 Years of Football: The FIFA Centennial Book* (London: Weidenfeld and Nicholson, 2004), p. 54.

43. Linda Hirshman and Jane Larson, *Hard Bargains: The Politics of Sex* (Oxford and New York: Oxford University Press, 1998), p. 165. Hirshman and Larson give an overview of the economic reforms and social attitudes which affected women's bargaining power in intimate relationships and identify the beginning of the sexual revolution of the 1960s and 1970s with a new sexual openness evident from the 1920s. Though there is no indexed reference to sport, the argument is related to professional sport; see p. 292.

44. However, the term 'New Woman' was rather vague and embraced considerable numbers of women who were in some way opposed to the existing social order and whose contradictory views covered legislative acts, public policy and private relationships in addition to cultural and popular discourses. For example, the Married Women's Property Acts removed the strictures of coverture and liberalized divorce which Hirshman and Larson argue extended the earlier ideals of sexual purity to the poor and working classes while the companionate ideal became a hallmark of middle-class marriage.

45. See for example M.A. Wensel, 'The Diary of Julia Colt Butler, 1889–1890', *Journal of the Rutgers University Libraries,* 46 (1984): 47–57. Julia Colt Butler's diary from 28 June 1889 to 8 December 1890 contains detailed information about her social and family visits, games and her interest in such sports as football.

Much of the diary concerns a six-month trip she made with other girls and a chaperone to Europe.

46. William H. Rideing, 'The English at the Seaside', *Harper's New Monthly Magazine,* 63 (June–November 1881), p. 484, contrasts 'the peachy glow and bloom which we admire in the faces of the crowds of supple, active, athletic girls who wear glove-like bodices, and who outnumber all others on the pier' with 'a fragile invalid, a pale girl with a remote look in her eyes'.

47. Barbara Solomon, *In the Company of Educated Women: A History of Women and Higher Education in America* (New Haven, CT: Yale Univerity Press, 1989), p. 62.

48. Mount Holyoke claims to be the first of the Seven Sisters, as in 1861 the three-year curriculum was expanded to four. In 1893 the seminary curriculum was phased out and the name was changed to Mount Holyoke College. The "Seven Sisters" nickname came about when the schools self-organized in 1927 in order to promote private, independent women's colleges, it has been argued to associate them in the public mind with the eight Ivy League institutions. See also Irene Harwarth et al., *Women's Colleges in the United States: History, Issues, and Challenges,* at www.ed.gov/offices/OERI/PLLI, accessed January 2005.

49. Bryn Mawr appears to have been a leader, launching a women's athletic association in 1891, in large part because of the enthusiasm of Martha Carey Thomas, with Vassar specializing in rowing when their association was formed five years later. This healthful regular exercise (as evidenced by an enthusiasm for calisthenics and a few scheduled team games) seemed to answer critics as students' academic performance improved.

50. Kathleen McElroy, 'Somewhere to Run', in Lissa Smith (ed), *Nike Is a Goddess: The History of Women in Sports* (New York: Atlantic Monthly Press, 1998), p. 4. McElroy also makes an excellent point that the various industrial leagues from department stores, insurance companies, railroads and manufacturing trades provided signifcant outlets for women's training, recreation and sport, resisting the 'play day' ethic of female competition.

51. William Blaikie 'The Risks of Athletic Work', *Harper's New Monthly Magazine,* 58 (December 1878–May 1879), p. 923. Blaikie was to publish *How to Get Strong and Stay So* in 1880 to counter the emphasis on athletic training.

52. 'Radcliffe Athletic Association', *The Radcliffe Magazine,* October 1918, p. 51.

53. F. Pierce, 'The Beginning of a Football Game', *The Radcliffe Magazine,* November 1904.

54. H. Frost and H. Cubberley, *Field Hockey and Soccer for Women* (New York: Charles Scribners and Sons, 1923), p. xvii.

55. M. Knighton, 'Development of Soccer for Girls', *American Physical Education Review,* 34 (1929): 372.

56. M. Lee, *A History of Physical Education and Sports in the USA* (New York: John Wiley, 1932), p. 53.

57. 'American Physical Education Association: Preliminary Program of the National Convention, Springfield, Massachusetts, April 11–14, 1923', *Mind and Body,* 30, no. 317 (April 1923): 37–39; 'Applicants for Membership in the American Physical Education Association', *American Physical Education Review,* 28 (February 1923): 70; 'Atlantic City Recreation Congress', *American Physical Education Review,* 28 (February 1923): 69. Kathleen McElroy, 'Somewhere to Run', p. 5, states that Lou Henry Hoover, as the president of the Girl Scouts, chaired the conference of the Women's Division of the National Amateur Athletic Federation (NAAF), also attended by YMCA representatives and interested individuals, which ratified the decision to downplay competition for women's sports, which she describes as 'a moderately succesful fifty-year mission'.

58. 'The Football Playing Women: A Most Unsuitable Game', taken from Scottish Football Association Press cuttings, 6 December 1921.

59. Hall, 'The Game of Choice', p. 31, for a discussion of the press coverage.

60. Some, like Bethlehem Steel, appear to have been more gender-specific employers.

61. Gail Newsham, *In a League of Their Own! Dick, Kerr Ladies Football Club 1917–1965* (Chorley: Pride of Place Publishing, 1994), p. 74; see Newsham's account of the whole tour, pp. 69–79, in which she says they played nine, won four, drew three and lost two; Colin Jose, *The Dick, Kerr Ladies Tour of America,* US Soccer Archives, says they played eight, won three, drew three and lost two accessed August 2006.

62. 'English Girl Teams Play Football for Charity', *Pawtucket Times,* 9 September 1921.

63. 'Sports in Women's Colleges', Mount Holyoke College Archives, 1932, p. 17; 'Athletic Activities at MHC', Mount Holyoke College Archives, 1932, p. 4. My thanks to Autumn Winslow, Archives Assistant at Mount Holyoke, for help with the research.

64. 'A Soccer Award Was Established in 1983/4', Mount Holyoke College Archives, LD 7096.2 RG 18.27.2 Physical Education Series 5; Sports/Activities, Soccer, General, Box 12, folder 3 and 4. The awards was donated by Clara Ludwig of the class of 1937, Director of Admissions 1951–1981, and named for Josephine Fiske, who made a career in physical education at Goucher College, Baltimore, and for Mary Harrington, who was based at the University of Wisconsin.

65. Newsham, *In a League of Their Own!* pp. 74–75.

66. The Federation Sportive Feminine Internationale held the first of four Women's 'Olympic Games' in 1922. It included eleven track and field events and drew more than 2,000 fans. Six countries participated, including the US. Alice Woods, who signed to the team in 1919, had won a race held under Amateur Athletic Association (AAA) rules over 80 yards in 1918, equivalent to a twelve-second 100 yards. Nellie Halstead, who later played centre forward

for Dick, Kerr, won bronze in the 1936 Olympic Games. There is the usual story about Lily Parr kicking an American football on a university campus way over the posts on her first attempt, to the amazement of the chauvinistic coach. Invited to repeat the feat for a wager and to prove it wasn't a fluke, at the second attempt Lily kicked it even higher and further. Apocryphal or not, the idea of Lily Parr (who came from the poorer part of St Helen's and who began work and playing for Dick, Kerr at fourteen) teaching elite young things how to kick a ball has an appeal, though the idea that she once broke a male goalkeeper's arm from a spot kick requires disbelief to be suspended a little higher. Lily was then perhaps the most famous woman football player of the time, and she deserves a thesis, plus more recognition from football authorities.

67. Jose, *The Dick, Kerr Ladies Tour*: 'Paterson, New Jersey on September 24 and Dick, Kerr's were beaten by 6 goals to 3. There followed games against J&P Coats of Pawtucket, New York Centro-Hispano, Washington Stars, New Bedford Whalers, New York Football Club, Fall River Marksmen, and Baltimore Soccer Club. Eight games in all of which the Ladies won three, against New Bedford, New York and Baltimore, tied three against Coats, Washington and Fall River, and were only defeated by Paterson and Centro-Hispano.'

68. 'British Women's Eleven Plays Fine Soccer', *Pawtucket Times*, 25 September 1922.

69. 'Record Crowd to See Women in Soccer Game', *Pawtucket Times*, 28 September 1922.

70. 'Women's Team Plays Coasts to 4 to 4 Tie', *Pawtucket Times*, 7 October 1922.

71. Yale did not admit women as undergraduates until 1969. After 1969, it is possible to review the *Yale Banner*, the yearbook, or the campus newspaper, *The Yale Daily News*, for coverage of women's sports, including soccer. My thanks to Diane E. Kaplan, Head of Public Services Manuscripts and Archives.

72. There are a number of degrees of acceptance which an athletic department may show to a sport. For example, 'club soccer' refers to a student activity, not yet recognized by the athletic department of a given college as a varsity sport. 'Varsity soccer' means that the game has been recognized as an intercollegiate sport and that this status is recognized by the chief executive responsible for athletic policy under three conditions: first, it is administered by the department; second, student athletes have their eligibility reviewed and certified on a regular basis; and three, those student-athletes that qualify receive official varsity awards from the institution.

73. Ladda, *The History of Intercollegiate Soccer*, pp. 202–218.

74. Tony Collins, *Searching for a New Webb Ellis? Some Thoughts on the Historiography of Football*, unpublished paper, British Society of Sports History Conference, Lancaster, September 2006.

75. Smith College, *The Smith Soccer Record Book, 1924–1979,* includes team rosters, rules, regulations, yearly reports and photographs and clippings. With thanks to Deborah Richards and colleagues for their kind help.

76. Mildred Howard, 'History of Physical Education at Mount Holyoke College 1837–1955', Mount Holyoke College Archives, 1955, p. 16, item 41.

77. Margaret Broadbent, LD 7096.6 RG 27, Alumnae Biographical Files for the Broadbent Papers, Mount Holyoke College Archives, 6 October 1934; Janet Owen, 'Sport in Women's Colleges', *New York Herald Tribune,* 1932, p. 17.

78. Margaret Broadbent, LD 7096.6 RG 27, Alumnae Biographical Files for the Broadbent Papers, Mount Holyoke College Archives, 1 October 1934.

79. J. Tunis, 'Changing Trends in Sport', *Harper's Monthly Magazine,* 170 (December 1934–May 1935), p. 85.

80. Smith College Archives, *Smith Sports Book—Soccer (1924–1979),* 1924, unpaginated.

81. H. Cubberley, 'Soccer for Girls', *Spaldings Athletic Library-Soccer for Women* (New York: American Sports Publishing Company, 1932), p. 7. Stephen H. Hardy, 'Entrepreneurs, Organizations and the Sports Marketplace', sees this as part of the three-part commodification of the sport industry, including 'the activity or game form, the service and the goods ... This is no mere cottage industry ... 'guides' (including rules and statistics) for all sports constituted a substantial segment of Albert Spalding's empire, both netting him vast profits and supporting the influence of governing bodies whose rules he published. Sales of this commodity continue to be strong. In 1984 NCAA Publishing alone sold approximately $50,000 worth of rule books for college sports' (pp. 343–344).

82. H. Harris, 'America's Best Union', *Current History,* 48, no. 1 (January 1938): p. 55, cites 260,000 members in fifty-two cities in 1936, though the number of women's football players is unclear.

83. See for example US Soccer Foundation, 'Soccer in the USA, 2002–2003', p. 15, though the question of registered players is a gnarly issue. See also Elise Pettus, 'From the Suburbs to the Sports Arenas', in Lissa Smith (ed), *Nike Is a Goddess: The History of Women in Sports* (New York: Atlantic Monthly Press, 1998), pp. 245–260.

84. J. Frey and S. Eitzen, 'Sport and Society', *Annual Review of Sociology,* 17 (1991): 503.

85. Title IX was followed shortly after by the creation of the Women's Sport Foundation, in 1974. The founders, Billie Jean King, Donna De Varona and Suzy Chaffee, had already established and sustained reputations as elite athletes in tennis, swimming and skiing, respectively. The strategic and activist nature of the Women's Sport Foundation is evident in the blend of training grants, research projects, community-awareness-raising activities and elite endorsement that have marked the organization's history. As has already been mentioned, the Olympic movement is significant for international women's soccer but also

for women's sports in the United States. In 1978 federal legislation was passed making it illegal to discriminate on the basis of sex in programmes offered by the US Olympic Committee or by its member federations.

86. Martha L. Mitchell, *Encyclopedia Brunoniana 1764 until 1993,* Brown College Archives. Mitchell was the former University Archivist. I am indebted to archivist Gayle Lynch for assisting with the research. Also recorded: 'In 1990 the Brown team was ranked 13th in the country. The winning streak ended in 1991, when the team finished below the .500 mark for the first time in the history of women's soccer at Brown. At the end of that season, Pincince's fifteen-year record was 149–67–15 overall and 49–4–4 in the Ivy League, and his team had participated in five NCAA tournaments. Brown has had three four-time All-Ivy choices, Colleen O'Day '86 from 1982 to 1985, Theresa Hirschauer '89 from 1985–1988, and Suzanne Bailey '91 from 1987 to 1990. Two others were named three times, Frances Fusco '83 from 1979 to 1981, and Michelle Mosher '83 from 1980 to 1982.'

87. Smith College Archives, *The Dunn Papers 1985–1991.*

88. Knight Commission, *Final Report of the Knight Commission on Athletics 2001,* available at www.knightcommission.org, accessed January 2006.

89. See James L. Shulman and William G. Bowen, *The Game of Life: College Sports and Educational Values* (Princeton, NJ: Princeton University Press, 2001), for a critique of the 'sport builds character' view.

90. The Miller Lite Report 1985 findings found that between 44 and 60 per cent of the women surveyed competed regularly with and against men in volleyball, swimming, tennis, basketball, and softball.

91. Gary Libman, 'Kicking up a Storm', *Los Angeles Times,* 8 November 1990: 'The goalie was a girl, but parents wanted proof. Others wondered why the issue was even raised.'

92. This included most goals in a World Championship match, with five against Taiwan, the most goals in a season (thirty-nine) and most points in a season (forty-seven). Unsurprisingly, she was also first player named US Soccer Female Athlete of the Year two years consecutively, in 1990 and 1991.

93. Sugden and Tomlinson, *Hosts and Champions,* p. 250.

94. J.M. Henry and H.P. Comeaux, 'Gender Egalitarianism in Co-Ed Sport: A Case Study of American Soccer', *International Review for the Sociology of Sport,* 34, no. 3 (1999): 277–290.

95. The ratification of the Equal Rights Amendment failed by three votes in 1982. The *Grove City v Bell* decision of 1984 found that since athletic programmes did not receive direct federal funding, Title IX did not apply. It was not until the Civil Rights Restoration Act, in 1988, that the interpretation was broadened to include athletic programmes. In 1992 the Court, in *Franklin v Gwinnett County,* ruled that a person can sue for damages if it is proven that opportunities were denied under Title IX.

96. Gavora, *Tilting the Playing Field,* p. 40.

97. I am obliged to Shawn Ladda for this information.

98. Oscar Handlin, *The Uprooted: From the Old World to the New* (Boston: Watts and Co., 1953), p. 3: 'immigrants were American history'. However, we are also dealing with second- and third-generation individuals who were born in the US, so both the particular and group identity are complex, sophisticated and shifting. Despite this, both the qualitative and quantitative indicators point to underrepresentation.

99. Though football has been argued to have been associated with modernity along with other cultural forms during the Victorian era, it remains a key issue today in which the progressivism of various football associations is measured by whether they 'recognize' (i.e., allow) women's football under their activities. For a wider discussion of Englishness and modernity, particularly as it affected the image of football. see Lanfranchi and Taylor, *Moving with the Ball,* pp. 19–23.

100. Eric Hobsbawm, *Nations and Nationalism since 1870: Programme, Myth, Reality* (Cambridge: Cambridge University Press, 1990), p. 143; see also Vic Duke and Liz Crolley, *Football, Nationality and the State* (London: Longman, 1996).

# –2–

# The Iron Roses
## Women's Football in PR China[1]

Football was played in China more than 3,000 years ago, according to annals inscribed on bones and tortoise shells. At that time the game often took the form of dance and was played at rituals praying for rainfall. Women were already on the scene in the Han Dynasty (206 BC–AD 220). A relief in the Qimu Temple, built in AD 123 at the foot of Mt Songshan in Henan Province, vividly portrays a maiden in a graceful long skirt and with her hair coiled high on the head kicking a ball. During the Tang Dynasty (618–907) women's football was confined to the imperial palace as a pastime for the lonesome court maids and concubines. Then it spread among the populace in the Song Dynasty (960–1279) when matches were often held with great solemnities. On a festive occasion a women's squad composed of 153 members, all attired in four-colour costume with a brocade band around the waist, had a three day contest, playing embroidered balls to the accompaniment of a musical band.[2]

Just look at these tomboys—darting all over the field, with boundless energy and courage! Now Shaanxi's Hou Yaqin broke though on the left wing and centred the ball to Sun Cuihuan, who received it and drove threateningly towards the goal ... Vice President Wan Li was voicing a widespread view when he said, 'I see a bright future in women's football for the Chinese women have lofty aspirations.'[3]

In 1991 the Chinese Football Association (CFA) hosted the First Women's World Championship for the M&Ms Cup. The carnival atmosphere in Guangzhou, Foshan, Punyu, Zhongshan and Jiangmen was created by the enthusiastic crowds, which totalled 510,000 overall with 63,000 at the final game, and the celebratory media coverage. However, what one commentator called 'Pigtails Soccer in China' has a longer history which predates modern sport.[4] The official line created by the then-FIFA president, Dr João Havelange, was that Norway first suggested an international tournament at the 1986 Congress in Mexico, which led to the establishment of a women's championship. His message concluded, 'The first big step has been taken, thanks to the efficient Chinese organization and to the twelve teams taking part, winners and losers alike, whose fairness, skill and efforts made this World Championship an unforgettable event.[5] The tournament was indeed a departure for the international federation, but the establishment of an event for women appears to have been a longer process, as is suggested in the Introduction and in the chapter on England.

The experimental nature of the championship is evident in the title: it was not immediately established as a FIFA World Cup, though earlier trial events had already taken place. China had previously been hosts to the FIFA U-17 World Championship (for men) in 1985, and FIFA had piloted an Invitational Tournament in Guangzhou in 1983 in order to assess the interest from a range of parties in a women-only event. There had also been a 1982 National Women's Soccer Invitational with ten participating teams (which saw the Shaanxi squad victorious and that from Gunagdong emerge as the runner-up) held in front of large crowds with the formalities of opening and closing ceremonies. More contentiously, the Asian Ladies Football Confederation (ALFC) had been formed in 1968, founded by the Republic of China (Taipei), Malaysia, Singapore and Hong Kong, where an inaugural Asian Cup Women's Football Tournament was held in 1975 (it was renamed the Women's World Invitational in 1978). When this was criticized, a rather aggrieved letter to FIFA asked:

> You stated in your letter as well as in your press release that FIFA does not recognise ALFC. Is there a clause in FIFA's rules which states that women's football cannot have their own body to organise their own competitions? Nor is there a law in any country which bans women from forming their own sporting associations to take care of their own sporting activities. In hockey, cricket and some other sports, women have their own controlling bodies with the men giving them technical assistance and advice. Why cannot this be so with football? What right has FIFA to insist that ALFC must not be allowed to function on its own?[6]

Another departure in 1991 was that women officials were used extensively for the first time in a FIFA tournament, and there was lengthy consideration given to adapting the laws of the game, including the length of matches and ball size, though these were eventually discarded. Some aspects of the organization of the event have proven to be influential in the long term, for example, the involvement of the multinational confectionary corporation M&Ms/ Mars lent a certain status in that the fact that a conglomerate would underpin the competition helped obtain distribution via TV coverage, including live screening of matches and a documentary of the event. Theo Leenders, M&Ms' Managing Director of world-wide events, was happy to be involved:

> To be a sponsor of a major international football event is always exciting. To be a sponsor of a major sports event in China is particularly fascinating. But to be the main sponsor of a football event in China which will have gone down as a turning point in the history of the world's greatest sport, is nothing less than phenomenal ... For M & Ms, it was a privilege to be so deeply involved in an event which helps to cast away old prejudices.[7]

It helped perhaps that a total of half a million spectators were to be entertained in the name of his company. The following year a FIFA/M&Ms women's football seminar in Zurich sought to develop this commercial focus with three objectives: to 'Implement women's football in the overall contracts with television of the National Associations. Implement women's football in sports prognostic systems (football pools).[8] Use women's matches as curtain-raisers in important events in men's football.'[9]

In spite of this commercial and spectator success, the home nation failed to reach the last four of the competition after losing to Sweden in the quarter-finals in front of 55,000 spectators in Guangzhou. The Chinese Football Association used the opportunity to write a 'state of the game' report which also reads like a wish-list. The structure is detailed as comprising four Departments (Technical, Competition, Foreign Liaison and a General Office), plus ten Committees, one of which is the women's committee.[10] The CFA worked in turn under the National Sports Commission, and its financial status reflected this to the tune of 3.19m RMB received in State support, along with 300,000 to 500,000 RMB per annum in societal support (mainly from player transfer fees), TV revenue and player/club registrations. The CFA report a total of 634 teams at various levels in twenty-two key football regions, with the National Team, Olympic Team, National Youth and National Junior Teams as the spine of the structure, fed from Leagues One and Two, which are made up of players taken from provincial, city, college and youth teams. However, the women's competition had two elements: Women's Football Championship competition and a National Women's Under-Fifteen Youth League competition. There were a number of regional divisions at the national and under-twelve levels, including city and provincial male teams but no women's clubs.[11] The CFA list a number of problems under headings such as competition, technical, coaching, financial; these can generally be characterized as a scarcity of players, scarce and poor quality resources, geographical constraints resulting from the size of the country and low levels of playing and coach education. In order to help, the CFA asked for a First-Division European team to play a series of games and for the organization of a high-level football tournament, sponsored in the amount of $400,000 to $500,000 US, with exemption from any levy to FIFA. In some central respects, China '91 raised more questions than it answered. For example, during the tournament both Denmark and Norway recorded their hundredth international women's match.[12] Why had it taken until 1991 to organize an official World Championship for women? What kinds of competition had preceded the FIFA tournament? Why and how was PR China selected as the first host country?

In 2004 the Asian Football Confederation (AFC) made the decision to introduce two new women's football events to the calendar, the AFC U17 Women's Championship and the AFC Inter-Continental Women's Championship. The role of Asia in developing women's football has been considerable, quite beyond the overview here and deserving a text in its own right. So, for example, outside China women's football developed in, for example, Singapore, Thailand and Taiwan. In addition, Asian teams have had considerable success in FIFA events, for instance in qualifying four teams (DPR Korea, China PR, Republic of Korea and Japan) in the 2003 FIFA Women's World Cup finals in the US. There are also an impressive number of FIFA/AFC tournaments: the AFC Women's Championship (biennial); AFC U19 Women's Championship (biennial); AFC U17 Women's Championship (biennial); AFC Intercontinental Women's Cup (quadrennial); Sea Games (biennial); Asian Games (quadrennial); Olympic Games qualifiers (quadrennial) and FIFA Women's World Cup qualifiers (quadrennial). The extent is perhaps surprising given wider historical forces around the development of association football. The relationships between women, football and society in China are evident in archival records, published documents, including regional publications, and interviews with elite sports women and administrators. Women's current relationship to sport, let alone to football, is complicated by a range of forces that includes the transition to a market economy, the competing demands of national, regional and individual interests, the disparity between urban and rural populations, the 'one-child' policy and the decline of government funding for sport as part of decentralization. The relative balance is obviously specific to each state and region, but cultural forces which prevented the wider development of the female game until the 1970s have broader historical and social resonance.[13] In examining elite sport, Jinxia has said, '"Women hold up half the sky" and "Women can do what men do" are not just popular slogans peddled by Chairman Mao but recent actualities of China's elite sport ... At the 1991, 1996 and 2000 Olympic Games, Chinese female participants outnumbered their male counterparts and played a major part in progressively raising China's position in the medal table.'[14]

Like the United States, China has its own woman football star and a celebrated, if ageing, team based around the '91 event. Sun Wen has won the love of fans with her superb skills (part of the mythology is that she practiced alone on the sports ground in the moonlight before she was selected to the national squad) and her leadership qualities. After joining in 1980, she led the Chinese women's national football side to more than twenty championships in various state, regional and international contests, most notably second place at both the 1996 Olympic Games in Atlanta and the 1999 World Cup Women's Football Competition. In February 2000 the International Olympic Committee awarded the team First Prize for Outstanding Achievement in Women's Sports. An IOC official correspondence reads: 'The Chinese Football Team has made outstanding contribution to the sport of football for the whole world with their brilliant achievements. With their perfect personalities, confidence and unremitting pursuit, these Chinese women football athletes have become examples of all women athletes.' The 1991 squad included a young Sun Wen, while her compatriot Liu Ailing (also to be appointed FIFA ambassador for women's football in 2006) was an already established member of the team, while Li Xiufu, the captain, in midfield and Wu Weiyang, as forward, were both outstanding players of the tournament. Extensive pretournament preparation became established for the dominant forces in women's football, and both PR China and the US learned from this example; in the former case with a ten-match preparation schedule against Germany, Finland and the USA. Of the eighteen players on the squad, six were from Beijing, three from Guangdong, four from Dalian, two from Shanghai, and one each from Changchun, Hebei and Pulima (Japan). If the iron or steel rose implies inspiration, there have also been plenty of thorny issues with which to contend.

Though the women's team have qualified and won trophies at Women's World Cup and Olympic Games (post-1996, when women's football was first included), comparisons of relative achievement are difficult. This was reflected by the technical report of the '91 tournament which had an Ambassador Class (USA, Norway), Medium but Rare (European countries and PR China), and Learning the Hard Way (the rest) as classification groups for qualifying countries. While the thesis may hold in a number of sports, it tells us rather more about the politics of international sports governing bodies and of government policies than about women's attempts to play football, as Jinxia acknowledges. The contribution of women to history-making milestones of various regional and international football bureaucracies is an aspect of this story that is often overlooked, as the 1991 report by the CFA indicates. The records kept by these authorities are a part of the story but hardly the most interesting aspect. Nor is it a dramatic tale; on the contrary, when reading the documentation, the overall tone is one of polite civility, measured tones, rational argument and gradual change. What the documents reveal is a wider community actively engaged in the making of various forms of football for women, not least in the systematic organization of international competition and the formation of women's football administrations.

Limited resources and institutionalized discrimination against women's football players are an evident continuity in the case of PR China as the country looks forward to the Women's World Cup in 2007 and the 'sporting mega-event' of the Beijing Olympiad in 2008.[15] Sue Lopez makes this point in characteristically understated style: 'Women's football has come under the Chinese FA since the mid-1980s, when thee were approximately 300 women players. By 1996 it was estimated by Becky Wang, of the Chinese FA, that there were around 800 women players, mostly students. It is extraordinary, given China's international success, that they achieve this with such a small number of players.'[16] Given that the playing pyramid (which refers to participation by the many from whom the talented few can be selected, the staple strategy of sports development officials in the West) is often seen to originate in China, the numbers of participants in women's football is unexpected. In terms of international success, the women's team does appear to have held up more than half the sky as one of the world's finest until, in recent times, an 8–0 defeat to Germany at the 2004 Olympics and a failure to reach the playoff stages of a FIFA event for the first time saw them slip to sixth place in the rankings. Conversely, a second place at the 2004 FIFA U19 Women's World Championship (Thailand) and at the 2006 U 20 World Cup in Russia indicates possible cause for optimism in the forthcoming major tournaments.[17] Optimism is guarded even so. After 2004 the State General Administration of Sports (SGAS) reported that the runners-up had won 1.2 million yuan ($145,000 US), from which each top player was paid 50,000 yuan ($6,000 US) and each understudy 20,000 yuan ($2,400 US). Although the cash bonus was welcome, the preliminary move to disband the team on its return raises some reservations about the ways in which Chinese women football players can be said to be outperforming their male counterparts other than in collecting trophies. Some commentators believe that the CFA put the team together solely for the purpose of the 2004 World Championship. Had the event not been rescheduled so quickly as an Under-Twenty tournament, for example, young women, like Lou Xiaoxu and Xu Yuan, would have found themselves virtually unemployed because they did not have a local team or because their teams had failed to qualify for the planned Women's Super League. Team captain Sun Yongxia, bitter about the squad's unexpected demise, reportedly said at the feast held in their honour at Yiwu, 'This celebration for us also means dissolution. We would rather stay on this team than receive a celebration banquet.'[18]

In 2005, the German conglomerate Siemens ended its sponsorship of the men's Super League, prompting concern over an upcoming financial crisis and rearrangement of all domestic leagues. With lower fan attendance, the women's Super League became the first target. The CFA had already reduced support over the preceding two years. In 2003 each local association and women's club received 60,000 RMB (about $7,255 US) and 110,000 RMB (about $13,301 US), respectively. In 2004, the allowance for the local associations and clubs was cancelled, the players' monthly pay was reduced to 500 to 1,000 RMB (about $60 to $120 US), the CFA continuing to pay only for the referees plus the opening and closing ceremony to save money to ensure the survival of the men's competition. Xie replaced Yan Shiduo as head of the China Football Association as club owners threatened a boycott over allegations of match-fixing, crooked referees and gambling. They also bemoaned the League's lack of commercial direction, complaining that the centralized sports bureaucracy, traditionally geared toward winning medals at international events like the Olympics, lacked the marketing acumen to run a successful league. The situation is not helped by the CFA's being placed under the jurisdiction of the General Administration of Sports, China's sports ministry, a move that blurred the lines between commercial operations and government mandates. With chaos in the Super League and the departure of the men's team from the qualifying games for the 2006 World Cup, the youth women's team was something of a shining light of Chinese soccer in 2004 and 2006 in spite of this.

Unsurprisingly, most of China's women's soccer clubs are struggling financially. It is not just the playing personnel who face an uncertain present, let alone future. They and their coaches have to spend three or four days taking long-distance trains to play matches in other provinces, although Zhang Jianqiang, the chief of the CFA women's soccer department, had said that the Women's Super League will not be cancelled so close to WWC '07. Wang Haiming, youth coach in 2004, who had campaigned to prolong the team's lifespan, was regarded by some as the likely choice for head coach of the Women's National Team. In another surprise move, the CFA approached Tony Di Cicco, the former head coach of the American women's football team, to take the position on a reported salary in the region of $300,000 US. The eventual appointee, Ma Liangxing, was by no means a newcomer to Chinese women's football when he was reappointed national team boss in December of 2005 after leading the team in 2002 and following the team's disappointing campaign at USA 2003, where they failed to progress to the last four. He is perhaps known as the most successful women's football coach at club level in China, for he has guided Shanghai to nineteen domestic titles. Amidst these changes, China edged out its East Asian rival Korea DPR and the new AFC addition, Australia, to recapture continental glory at the Asian Cup 2006. It was China's first title since 2001 and may well speak to a renaissance, but the situation is complex:

> Football provides a good example of an emerging and widening inequality between men and women in the same sport. Although the Chinese women's football team won silver medals at the 1996 Olympics and the 1999 World Cup it attracted few spectators and received insufficient sponsorship. In sharp contrast to the women's situation, the men's football team has never qualified for the Olympic or World Cup competitions, but enjoyed far more enviable financial rewards and the spotlight of the mass media.[19]

On the one hand the football administration appears to be highly ambitious, but unless men's and women's teams are equally supported by resources, the pattern will revert to a long-established one of women's football teams being disbanded and unfunded regardless of women's achievements at the competitive and elite levels.

This attitude also contravenes development principles outlined in Vision Asia, an initiative set up by the Asian Football Confederation and the world governing body, FIFA. The strategy seeks to improve the sport; in China and India particularly the game is generally in alliance with national associations. Women's football is one of eleven priorities:

> Sixty percent of the world's population resides in our beautiful continent, a huge proportion of the fans that support the world's most popular game. Football is not just a business, and not only a game. It is also a social phenomenon, which has the ability to mould the way people live their lives. Our distinct Asian football culture surpasses all boundaries, whether religious, racial or political—indeed, in Asia we are one united team. AFC member Associations should embark on the following principles of development to ensure a progressive development of the women's game throughout Asia.
> To elevate the image, popularize and promote women's football.
> Strengthen the structure of women's football within National Associations.
> Establishment of competitions at all levels.
> Intensify educational programs and specific development plans for players' training.
> Methodology, coach education, refereeing development and training of administrators.

Creating a strong fan base for women's football.
Exploiting marketing opportunities.[20]

So women's play remains a site of discussion over which local and international officials negotiate. In looking briefly at the longer history of this, we see that the variety of strategies and tactics used by Chinese women to combat the situation with regard to sport and particularly football is related to the broader history of women's role in social and cultural changes affecting the country in the twentieth century.

What then of the broader history of association football and women's place in it in PR China? The social changes that have affected women's sport since the nineteenth century include activism for educational amendment, suffrage, and the movement against foot binding.[21] There seems to be broad consensus regarding the strength of Confucianism, adopted as the state ideology in the second century and which continues to exert a considerable influence.[22] The advent of free love and marriage reforms, in addition to the anti-imperialist and revolutionary movements involved in the transformation of China in 1949, are also significant themes in academic treatments of female access to sport and leisure.[23] Since 1949, crucial issues remain family and child-care reorganization, changes to women's legal rights, and the economic, social and political reform movements of the late decades of the twentieth century.[24] In this sense, a number of economic, cultural and social themes within China position football as futuristic, particularly in large international sports events and, more recently, as it moves into global sports markets. The nickname Iron Roses is a depiction of the feminine but resolute Chinese women players. That resolve is evidently necessary when considering the history of women's sport more broadly and in particular the reasons why the growth of women's football in China mainly appears to be a story of the second half of the twentieth century.

Contested accounts of the history of football before it was modern sport continue to trade. The tradition of forms of female football debatably extend back more than four thousand years, to 2697 BC, in the reign of Huang Ti (the first emperor of China), to frescoes found in Congshan, Henan Province (approximately AD 123) and examples under the Tang and Song dynasties, showing individual courtly illustrations of large teams.[25] A porcelain pillow at the Imperial Palace Museum depicts a girl kicking a ball, and a bronze mirror at the Museum of Chinese History has an engraving, said to be of the Song period (960 BC to AD 1279), when matches were played with great solemnity but also spread to the masses, of a man and woman playing a form of football. In the Ming dynasty (1368–644), a woman named Peng Xiuyun was celebrated as a player who could use feet, head, knees, shoulders and chest. Such skills were also cultivated by concubines; among the best-known is Tian Guifei at Sizong's court, known for her 'exquisite skill'. Women's football seems to have declined in the period 1644–1911, owing to social unrest during the late Qing dynasty. This pattern clearly requires considerably more work, but it may help in our understanding of why China has shared in seeing women's participation as an aspect of modernity, so that female participation appears to have developed later than a manly tradition.

Trade links appear to be part of the history of the structural position of women at a time when modern sport was developing in the late nineteenth and early twentieth centuries.

> Modern sport in China is not an indigenous product. It was a foreign import and developed in a hot-house of modernization. Modern sport came to China as an element of Western culture and accompanied by military force, which directly challenged Chinese traditional culture and patriotism. This provoked conflict and confrontation ... The modernization of China provided a suitable climate for the growth of modern sport and the development of modern sport stimulated the process of modernization of Chinese society at the turn of the twentieth century. It was a reciprocal relationship.[26]

For example, European powers including Britain, Spain, Portugal and Holland had expanded their empires, while, throughout the nineteenth and twentieth centuries, Japan and the United States extended their influence. Specifically, the cases of Britain and the United States indicate a combination of military invasion, political influence, economic exploitation and cultural diffusion. It has been suggested that association football was first played in Hong Kong when it became a colony of Britain following the Opium War of 1840; soldiers, merchants and missionaries played, first among themselves and then against the Chinese. The attitude of the exporters that football was a man's game influenced its introduction to a range of countries and its reception. The Shanghai Athletic Club is known to have played the Engineers in 1879, and the Shanghai Football Club was formed in 1887. The first league was created in Shanghai; although it was initially dominated by British expatriates, members of other nationalities soon joined in, notably the Portuguese. The predominantly 'foreigner-based' Shanghai FA was formally recognized in 1910. Whilst Shanghai was the main centre of football, the game quickly spread to other ports, with leagues in places such as Tientsin (now known as Tianjin), Singapore and Canton. The South China Club (Hong Kong) represented 'China' on a 1923 tour of Australia. The China National Amateur Athletic Federation (which included the Chinese FA) was founded in Nanjing the following year. Several commentators have indicated that the gap between indigenous men's access to association football and that of their peers was more than a chronological issue. Traditional culture emphasized imperial academic examinations as the pinnacle of high masculine status and gentleness as an important sign of refined manners.[27] The modernistic aspects of the game are consequently not solely an aspect of women's participation and also had consequences for definitions of masculinity.

The Opium Wars bought Western missionaries as well as military forces and the advent of girls' schools, which sought to give a basic education in Christianity, literacy and feminine-appropriate life skills, including physical culture. It has been suggested that an impetus to reform, in particular the changes between 1915 and 1921 relating to the New Culture and the May 4 Movement, had an effect, albeit not entirely dramatic, on early forms of women's football in China.[28] Though there was resistance which in other case studies developed out of Eugenics, here it took hold as part of two very different approaches to reform. On the one hand, Christian missionaries thought that better health for girls would mean better health for their children. On the other, national-regeneration activists argued for the need to address women's health because it was women who would be the providers of the next generation of soldiers to fight Western invasion and increasing colonization. In terms of modern sport in the Southeast coastal area, there was some girls' football in the 1920s. In 1924 a women's football eleven was formed at a girls' school in Shanghai; it would appear that, for lack of competition, they played against male opposition.[29] Also founded in 1924, the Chinese Football Association assumed administration of the Chinese domestic soccer leagues and national teams. Seven years later, in 1931, the CFA was affiliated with the Asian Football Confederation. As in other case-study nations, the growth of women's access to various forms of education in the early decades of the twentieth century led to an increase in female domestic and international competitions and also established modern sport as a pastime. In the mid-1930s the middle school attached to Zhongshang University in Guangzhou held an intramural women's football competition with three teams participating; this seems to have been the first female multi-team tournament in China. It also appears that women played intramural games at Xibei University in Nanzhou in the late 1930s.

International political developments have affected Chinese sport and women's place within it more generally.[30] The establishment of New China in 1949, the chaotic early years of the Cultural Revolution in the decade 1966–1976 and economic reform after 1979 are particularly significant. Following the 1949 Communist establishment of a People's Republic, a revived interest in sports culture saw the introduction of football as part of the compulsory physical-education national curriculum in school for boys. Guandong Province, with its proximity to Hong Kong, also began to develop as a centre for football, and there appears to be evidence of mixed football as an extracurricular activity in school. The Football Federation was reformed in 1951, and the initial League Championship (for the first time a 'national event') was played. China withdrew from FIFA in 1958 because it objected to the acceptance of Taiwan as a member, but the proliferation of international matches continued (237 between 1958 and 1961).[31] This period of apparent progress ended with the decade of the Cultural Revolution and continued until the death of Mao, in 1976. With the support of the FIFA executive Henry Fok, China was allowed to enter the Asian Games in 1974, while further promptings allowed FIFA member countries to play the Chinese. From 1977 the country welcomed a number of international guest teams from twenty-nine countries, with forty-seven nations hosting the Chinese. These included Pele's New York Cosmos and West Bromwich Albion. China had rejoined

FIFA by 1980, and was immediately involved in the World Cup, Olympic and Asian Cup qualifying matches. A World Women's Invitational Tournament had taken place in 1978 and was scheduled for two weeks as part of the 'glorious' October national festivities in Taipei, Taiching and Kaosiung, with participating teams from Europe, America, Asia and Oceania 'in celebration of the 70th anniversary of the Republic of China'.[32] Fan Hong suggests that 'these developments did not interest China, particularly since Taiwan was a member of the Association. The Communist China would not participate in organisations in which Taiwan was involved.' The National Women's Soccer Invitational in Beijing in 1982 set this tournament in a context of both the wider Chinas (PR, Hong Kong, Macao, Chinese Taipei and Singapore) and the development of association football.[33]

> No game played at the 80,000 Workers' Stadium in Beijing had aroused so much joviality and so many encouraging cheers as did the final match between Shaanxi and Guangdong. The spectators had not expected much of the girls ... How could they present anything spectacular in a pitch where so many footballers of the national and international calibre—including Pelé who visited China in 1977—had left their foot-prints? The good showing did come as a delightful surprise to the big crowds in the stands and to the bigger TV audience as well. Thanks to the generous support given by overseas Chinese and compatriots in Hong Kong and Macao, the game is gaining wider and wider popularity among the women.[34]

During this period the men's national team was perceived as being far more impor-tant than the domestic clubs. By the mid-1980s, the financial and social rewards involved in elite sports were sufficient to attract large numbers once more in what some attacked as trophyism—sport as a state-sponsored and consequently a central-ized activity. In 1981 eleven teams from five provinces participated in a women's football invitational in PR China held in Chuxiang, Yunnan Province (referred to at the time as an autonomous prefecture of the Yi nationality in southwest China), with sixty girls in regular training, and the following year the aforementioned Invitational attracted twenty-seven teams; this number increased to thirty-five three years later. Teams were also recorded in Liaoning, Jilin, Shanghai, Tianjin and Hebei. The first Guangzhou tournament was held in 1983, and the following year a second Xian International Women's Football Tournament took place. This seems to be where the idea of PR China as the 'cradle' of women's football comes from, as does the official team nickname as a municipal women's tournament took place in Xian, the capital, in 1979, which was won by the Shaanxi Iron and Steel Works, whose leadership had promoted the sport for girls and boys. This development combined school-based and work teams to produce a professional squad of twelve players. The Jilin team was said to have been composed entirely of Korean nationals who had played against boys in another 'homeland of football', Meixian County. 'Of the eighteen members of Guangdong's provincial team, runners-up in the recent national tournament, eleven came from the Huqiao Middle School established for the children of returned overseas Chinese.'[35] By 1986, an increased international schedule saw a tour to Europe, two invitational tournaments and the inaugural Asian Cup Championship. Domestically, an All-China under-sixteen competition was contested, followed two year later by an undergraduate championship for eight teams at Penglai County, Shandong Province.

Also a significant factor in the late development for women's football and the medalism of the Iron Roses in the 1990s was China's participation in the Olympic Games. China's men first entered the Olympic Football Tournament in Berlin in 1936. It is unsurprising that the women's competition didn't attract central support or funding, though the Olympic strategy of 1985 appeared to benefit women athletes who were considered more likely to excel internationally. Specifically, male competitors were provided for sports teams, including football. This undoubtedly assisted in preparation for major tournaments; in this China has been extremely influential in the intensive preparation for women's football, as national teams from Norway, the US and, more recently, Germany have indicated. In view of a lack of Olympic competition, the Chinese Sports Ministry included women's football as a competitive activity in the Sixth National Games in 1987 but discontinued it for the next year as it wasn't an Olympic sport. However, there were already established international links both with the ALFC, which had tournaments since 1974 in the Asian Women's Football Championships, with victory in 1984, and with the Asian Women's Football Cup. The 1983 Guangzhou invitational included Singapore, Japan and six Chinese teams (Liaoning, Guangdong, Jiling, Chanching, Shaanxi and Guanxi).[36] It was reprised again as a FIFA invitational sponsored by Huo Yingdong of Hong Kong with twelve countries and Norway as title winners. Also in 1988 the Chinese team was victorious at the World High School championship in Belgium, the Asian Cup seven times, the Asian Games three times and the 1993 World Student Games.

The independent status of the National Sports Bureau in 1998 indicates a degree of prominence of sport in Chinese society; particularly the elite-oriented programmes, intended to ensure success at the 2008 Olympic Games and other international events, such as Women's World Cup 2007. Market values and centralized interests are likely to continue to converge on this approach. What is less clear is the role of the centralized talent identification systems, the balance between urban and rural participants and the future of women's sport as the state planning system, which supported female engagement, is gradually replaced by commercial marketing. Thus, Chinese women's elite success in football is a product of many factors, which include the use of state planning to enact a form of 'equal but different' equality and political and economic reform in an era of male dominance in global sport. The CFA, for example, sent a teenage male team to Germany because of its better football environment. The so-called '08 Stars will live, train and play there before supposedly carrying greater hopes back to Beijing for the 2008 Olympics. Fans may be skeptical about the German incubating program, but they have reasons to prefer the chances for the women's team, even with the differential treatment shown to male and female youth squads. There have also been very precise practices within sports administration and training which have continuities from the early 1950s, such as early talent screening, identification and specialization of young athletes from school to the national team, and for years, football has been the most watched, if not played, sport in the world's most populated country.

The 'Steel Roses', a powerhouse in the women's game in the late 1980s and early 1990s, have seen a recent loss of form. They went out in the group stages at the 2000 Sydney Olympics and in the quarter finals of the 2003 World Cup. They have also lost regional dominance to North Korea, winners of the Asian Women's Champion-ship in 2001 and 2003 and of the 2002 Asian Games. China's victory at the Olympic qualifiers, where they beat Japan 1–0 thanks to a Li Jie penalty, seemed to signal a re-vival in fortunes, but their humiliating loss to Germany showed that the current team lack experience. Furthermore, traditional culture reinforced the view of women's physical and social inferiority to men, in spite of isolated incidents of women's teams being formed and sustained over a period of time.[37] What is particularly interesting in terms of trying to depict the shape of female participation in football in China in the early 1980s is that the traditional Communist sports system and market-oriented reform combined to produce a degree of professionalism relatively early on. For example, Sun Wen was picked out by a coach as a child athlete, as was Liu Ailing, but Gao Hong was selected after being told to play for a factory and then a provin-cial team. Because of geographical and transport issues, it is perhaps unsurprising that cities such as Beijing, Tianjin, Dalain, Datong, Guangzhou (Canton), Shanghai and Changchun dominated the representation among the thirty or so teams formed during the peak of popularity, but there were provincial squads too in Guangdong, Yunnan, Liaoning and Yanbian.[38] Of course, more remains to be uncovered about this participation.

These elite women athletes share with their counterparts in the US, Britain and Australia the difficulties of their relative positions in the international sports market. While the professionalization of the women's team in the 1980s and increasingly in the 1990s brought increased respect and support, the move toward a market-based economy has impressed upon the Chinese FA that the pinnacle of success on the international stage is the World Cup, not a feminized subbrand. Since the move to-wards a market economy, aspects of the centralized system continue to exert a hold on women's football at the same time that they create new problems. In an era of entrepreneurial development, the State has increasingly seen football as a sport likely to appeal to a large domestic and foreign audience and consequently also capable of attracting sponsors and commercial partners. There had been a long-standing part-ner for the women's team because of the Chinese FA's disinclination to financially support the squad; the FA was not above benefitting from allowing administration costs to be paid by the Guangzhou Qixing Pharmaceutical Company, to the tune of one-third of the £15,000-a-year deal, however. Without State support from 1987 until 1994, the remaining £10,000 a year sustained the women's team players in difficult circumstances. Nevertheless, these women 'professionals' share in the difficulties caused by football and women's football because, as we have seen, they suffered sparse and challenging conditions as successful full-time athletes, while the less successful men's squad received money from the government and from the governing body. This clear discrimination in financial support and respect for elite athletes has repercussions now because the women's team finds it hard to obtain viable sponsorship. Women footballers may have brought credit to China in representing their nation, but lack of financial assistance and the current situation over the youth teams make future predictions for women's football difficult, even if such activities are one of the key eleven themes in Vision Asia. It will be interesting to see the allocation of resources and the justification for that division of money and support for the men's and women's teams at the elite level. Given the practice of allocating to underperforming men's national teams, not just more than their successful counterparts but in some cases up to 200 per cent more in wages plus incentives, it seems something of an understatement to say that overt discrimination is evident and, to some extent, accepted and expected.[39] Will this stoic response continue? Can discriminatory practices in sport be justified by economies of scale in an exceptional market?

One of the most interesting aspects of the source documentation that became available during this project was the role of the Asian Ladies' Football Confederation in the 1970s and 1980s in lobbying various football bureaucracies over the authority to administer the sport. The relationships between the Asian Ladies Football Confederation, the Asian Football Confederation and FIFA is a particularly apposite one because it raises some legal questions in addition to acting as comparator for other examples of international development. Though the Asian Ladies' Football Association was formed six years earlier, the tension arose when at an international tournament in 1974 and again in 1975 the organization entered into a well-reported media argument about the legality of FIFA's insistence that the ALFC would not be recognized in its own right.

As you already know, the ALFC was formed sometime in 1968 with the sole intention of promoting women's football in Asia ... Tun Sharifah Rodziah, wife of our former Prime Minister Tunku Abdul Rahman, was elected its first President, with Mrs Veronica Chiu of Hong Kong as Vice President and Mr Wong Lee of Malaysia as Secretary ... In August 1975 Mrs Chiu organised the first Asian Cup Women's Football tournament in Hong Kong. She spent HK$60,000 from her own pocket to sponsor the tournament. Since then more and more countries in Asia formed women's football teams and joined ALFC as affiliated members. The Republic of China (Taipei) organised the 2nd Asian Cup in 1977; India organised the 3rd Asian Cup at Calicut in 1979; and this year Hong Kong again organised the 4th Asian Cup. Some time in 1975, ALFC wrote to FIFA seeking affiliation, but FIFA refused to accept us, stating that ALFC must come under AFC. But AFC also refused to accept us. We were 'nobody's child', hence we had to stand on our own and fend for ourselves. Through our own hard work and dedication, we achieved popularity and success. All these years of our existence, nobody bothered about us. Suddenly now FIFA insists the women must come under the men's control with so much hue and cry.[40]

And so it went on. After the 1975 tournament, in which Australia, Hong Kong, Malaysia, New Zealand, Singapore and Thailand had taken part (with New Zealand beating Thailand in the final), the ALFC proposed a women's World Cup Tournament in Hong Kong in 1977, to be sponsored the by the Ladies' associations there. The sixteen-team event was planned under men's World Cup rules, and teams were to play under national flags. An Asian All-Stars team had been selected for a European tour in August 1976, but it is unclear whether either a full or modified visit took place. It wasn't a World Cup, but 40,000 saw the final game in that year's tournament, in which Thailand lost to Taiwan.

Having repeatedly tried to affiliate, the ALFC suffered the same fate as women in AFC countries who had tried to align themselves with national associations.

The Asian Football confederation (AFC) will do everything in their power to stop the formation of an international women's football federation ... AFC President Datuk Hamzah Abu Samah said: Some of our affiliates control the women's FA in their countries. We have informed them to advise their WFAs not to support the motion for the formation of an international body outside the jurisdiction of FIFA ... Datuk Hamzah who is also the president of the FA of Malaysia (FAM) said that his association were in a dilemma because they had no control over their women counterparts. 'Only last Sunday the FAM turned down the women's application for affiliation. Now we are in no position to influence their decision on the formation of the international body ... We at FAM consider football unladylike and are against them playing it at competition level. However in view of the AFC recommendation we will have to reassess our stance.'[41]

The press reports and correspondence indicate that the acknowledgement of the 1981 Taipei tournament and the creation of FIFA-sponsored First World Invitational Soccer Tournament in 1983 were intended as a direct replacement for the biennial ALFC Cup as the AFC committee suggested. Though very concerned about the respectability of the ALFC, lack of interest on behalf of FIFA and constituent associations meant that relatively autonomous developments such as this proved the market for women's football. Nor was this a one-way process, as less than a month later,

The Football Association of Malasia (FAM) decided at their Council meeting not to grant affilation to women's football. 'Although we have been directed by FIFA to get women's football affiliated to the FAM, we have decided to join the Arab countries and go our own way' said FAM president Datuk Seri Hamzah Abu Samah yesterday. We don't want to be seen encouraging women's football. But they are free to do what they like.[42]

The 1981 tournament in Hong Kong included a Mulan Girls Soccer Team, led by Pao Teh-Ming and nine delegates supervising a team of sixteen. The whole issue rumbled on for another two years with several telexes along the lines of 'Pls adv whether we should encourage, support or help the promotion of 1st World Cup Women's Football Tournament organized by the Hong Kong Ladies' Football Association which is not our affiliate', plus warning letters to the associations of Japan, the Philippines and other ALFC member countries. It was evident that a woman's international federation would have required a change to FIFA statutes and the principle of one national association in each country, even where this is not observed. Eventually, with much polite negotiation, which Mr Blatter seems to have coordinated during Havelange's tour of Asia in 1981, the matter was subsequently deferred until Autumn 1983. As the introductory chapter indicates, this delaying tactic was to be a repeated strategy.

On the one hand the establishment of this foundation challenged the work of national and international football authorities in the region, but on the other it also allowed for a relatively rapid development of the Asian international calendar of female fixtures once the independent administrations had been absorbed into central bureaucracies after a good deal of negotiation. There had been sufficient work done by administrators in various Asian countries in the 1970s (most notably in Taiwan, Malaysia, Thailand and Singapore) so that by the time of China's 'open door' policies later that decade, there was sufficient momentum behind the women's football community in the region to see the creation of several 'invitational' tournaments that anticipated FIFA-supported international competition by some years. By extension, the scale and frequency of these tournaments increasingly began to create external pressure on national and international football administrations, which had undertaken to oversee all aspects of the game but whose conservative and inward-looking attitudes led them to conclude that there was no 'market' for international female events. This combined with international invitational events elsewhere (as we've seen for instance in England, Italy, Mexico and the United States) to eventually require more than piecemeal responses to each.

There remains a great deal of variation in female participation across regions as well as in individual nations. Regions that have euphemistically been classified as having 'potential' in West Asia include Bahrain, Jordan, and Qatar; in Central South Asia, Iran and Bangladesh, Uzbekistan and India are classed similarly. Those that are classified as 'emerging' amongst the Association of Southeast Asian Nations (ASEAN) include Malaysia, Philippines, Myanmar, Indonesia and Singapore, as well as the Eastern nations Hong Kong and Guam. Developing ASEAN countries include Thailand and Vietnam, in addition to their Eastern colleagues Chinese Taipei and Korea Republic. Those with a mature tradition are considered to be China PR, DPR Korea and Japan, and there is some support for this because of PR China, DPR Korea and Japan's qualification to the 1999 FIFA Women's World Cup in USA and since there is a clear indication of sustained improvement.[43] As of 2005 there were twenty women referees and thirty-two FIFA assistant referees registered in the FIFA list.

It has been suggested that, 'If western scholars want to write satisfactory Chinese sports history, they should be aware of Chinese informed perspectives; employ meticulous scholarship, have appropriate language skills and a satisfactory understanding of Chinese culture and history.'[44] While agreeing that the quality of an interpretation is crucially linked with the evidence, historical or otherwise, I have taken a two-part approach to this subject: part of the approach has been chronological and part has been thematic in order to refer to important dates and events but also to consider the social, political and cultural forces shaping women's football. In referring briefly to some of these events I intend not to take a rather superficial approach to topics about which other academics have debated in terms of evidence and interpretation but to give sufficient attention to the narrower focus of women's football where it seemed that the majority of original material could lend a productive interpretation to that already in the public domain. There is a lack of literature on Chinese football. Furthermore, the few texts available on women's sport in China, both in Chinese and in English, provide very brief analyses of the social, cultural, political and historical aspects. Clearly, questions about Chinese women's participation in football remain unanswered. How did modern football for women evolve in China, and who were the stakeholders? What factors have determined its development on the international stage, and how will men's football affect female participation? In particular, studying the history of generations of women players through their own words would be an important approach but is more than a brief visit would allow. In acknowledging this limitation, the judgement has been made to provide logical connection with themes sustained throughout and to use sources available in English and Chinese to address this analysis to an international audience.

The technical report of the first FIFA World Championship identified a three-tier model for women's participation across the globe at that time. The first group was composed of mainly European national associations which already held regular championships; the second group included the US and China as examples of national associations without regular championships but with an established representative squad; the third group comprised those countries without a regular championship and without support from a national association (this was taken to imply that there was no national women's squad, but in several countries there was a representative team in place, often selected on a trial system).[45] In these countries, the national association was effectively ignoring the FIFA stipulation to act as overseer of all aspects of the game. This is telling regarding not only the ideology of sport and gender order but also the organizational framework and structures of sporting federations, which, we are told, are acting for the good of the game. It's also disappointing to note that when the 2007 Women's World Cup takes place in China, a number of representative teams are likely to have been prevented from participating because of a lack of financial or resource support by their national association. In 2006 Peter Velappan retired from

AFC after thirty years: women from countries whose teams don't make regional or final competitions for Women's World Cups and those on teams from countries like PR China that do make it and are still discarded after major tournaments, will find his confidence as hollow now as ALFC officials did in the 1970s and 1980s.

> FIFA and AFC are very concerned with the recent initiative to form a World Women's Football Federation. As you know, it is most undesirable as women's football activities can well be served by the various National Associations. In fact it is to the great advantage of women that they should be under the control of the national associations who are in most cases well established to provide the support and guidance for the game to develop.[46]

## Notes

1. F. Hong and J.A. Mangan use the term 'Iron Roses', for example, 'Will the Iron Roses Bloom Forever? Women's Football in China: Changes and Challenges', in F. Hong and J.A. Mangan, *Soccer, Women and Liberation: Kicking Off a New Era* (London: Frank Cass, 2004), pp. 47–66. However, FIFA regularly refers to the team as the 'Steel Roses', for example, 'Women's football has long been regarded as China's strongest footballing suit, with the Steel Roses having won silver in the 1996 Atlanta Olympic Football Tournament and finished runners-up at USA 1999,' in FIFA Women's World Cup China 2007, 'Sun Lends Weight to LOC Efforts' http://www.fifa.com/, 22 November 2006. The team is also referred to as the 'Forceful Roses' and the youth team the 'Steel Rosebuds'.
2. Unattributed author (possibly Qiu Zhenqi): 'Women's Football in Ancient China', National Women's Soccer Invitational brochure, Beijing: China, 1982, p. 17.
3. Qiu Zhenqi, 'Women's Soccer Has a Bright Future', National Women's Soccer Invitational brochure, Beijing: China, 1982, p. 16.
4. Shan Zhongcheng, 'Pigtails' Soccer in China', National Women's Soccer Invitational brochure, Beijing: China, 1982, p. 20.
5. Dr Joao Havelange, *China '91: 1st FIFA World Championship for Women's Football for the M&Ms Cup*, FIFA, Zurich, 1991, p. 3.
6. Charlie Pereira, ALFC General Secretary, 'Women's Football in Asia', 10 February 1976, FIFA Correspondence Files, Zurich.
7. Theo Leenders, *China '91: 1st FIFA World Championship for Women's Football for the M&Ms Cup*, FIFA, Zurich, 1991, p. 4.
8. A form of paper-based gambling in which the outcome of matches is guessed and entered on a form that is issued weekly.
9. FIFA/M&Ms Women's Football Seminar, Conclusions, Section C. Promotion, 23 October 1992, FIFA, Zurich.

10. The following information is mainly taken from a CFA document, *Football in China: Present Problems and Future Prospects,* 16 November 1991, Peking, China.

11. China PR Team Statement, *China '91: 1st FIFA World Championship for Women's Football for the M&Ms Cup,* FIFA, Zurich, 1991.

12. Anorak fact: the Norwegian defender Gunn Nyborg had played in each of the 100 matches and received a special award to mark the occasion at the banquet closing the final against the US team.

13. Peter Velappan, Secretary of the Asian Football Confederation, used metaphors of infancy to describe women's football and cited cultural factors as primary before indicating that state football associations are responsible for the progress of the women's game. The AFC history of women's football fact sheet has women's football as a 'novelty' in the 1960s.

14. Dong Jinxia, *Women, Sport and Society in Modern China: Holding up More Than Half the Sky* (London: Frank Cass, 2003), p. 1.

15. See for example Paul Close, David Askew and Xu Xin, *The Beijing Olympiad: The Political Economy of a Sporting Mega-Event* (London and New York: Routledge, 2006).

16. Sue Lopez, *Women on the Ball: A Guide to Women's Football* (London: Scarlet Press, 1997), p. 117.

17. AFC Player of the Year Awards proved a triumph for youth as China's eighteen-year-old Ma Xiaoxu won the women's event in 2006.

18. 'Li Xiao 8 Ch-ch-changes in Chinese Women's Football', available at http://www.china.org.cn, 8 December 2004.

19. Dong Jinxia, *Women Sport and Society in Modern China,* p. 132. The point also seems to apply elsewhere: 'the women's volleyball team of the 1980s was in the same predicament as the women's football team. It fell from being world Champion in 1986 to seventh place at the 1992 Olympic Games because differential rewards were unattractive to young female athletes, who chose other sports.'

20. Mohamed bin Hammam, AFC President, *AFC Vision Asia: Building the Future Brochure 2002–2012,* 2003, p. 2. This strategy was launched in 2003 with the tagline '45 footballing nations 3.7 billion potential consumers'. The eight member national football associations selected as pilots for the Vision Asia development programmes are Bangladesh, PR China, Hong Kong, India, Indonesia, Jordan, Vietnam and Yemen.

21. See Susan Brownell and Jeffrey Wasserstrom (eds), *Chinese Femininities/ Chinese Masculinities: A Reader* (Berkeley: University of California Press, 2002) for an introductory overview of key themes and events.

22. Fan Hong, *Footbinding, Feminism and Freedom: The Liberation of Women's Bodies in Modern China* (London: Frank Cass, 1997); Dong Jinxia, 'Ascending Then Descending? Women's Soccer in Modern China', *Soccer and Society,* 3, no. 2 (2002): 1–18.

23.  See Mayfair Mei-Hui Yang, *Spaces of Their Own. Women's Public Sphere in Transnational China* (Minneapolis: University of Minnesota Press, 1999) for a discussion of the transnational sphere (including the mainland China, Taiwan, Hong Kong, and Chinese communities abroad in a number of public domains), especially ch. 8.
24.  For an overview of this see Fan Hong, *Footbinding, Feminism and Freedom;* Dong Jinxia, *Women Sport and Society in Modern China,* for more extensive coverage of women's football compared to other sports; Susan Brownell, *Training the Body for China: Sport and the Moral Order of the People's Republic* (Chicago and London: University of Chicago Press, 1995); though it has no indexed reference to football, Part 4 deals specifically with Western sports.
25.  A summary of these dates is given at China PR Team Statement, *China '91: 1st FIFA World Championship for Women's Football for the M&Ms Cup,* FIFA, Zurich, 1991. See also General Wego W.K. Chang, President, ROCFA, 'Welcome Speech', *World Women's Invitational Tournament 1981,* Taipei, 11 October 1981, pp. 12–13; 'Women's Football in Ancient China', National Women's Soccer Invitational brochure, Beijing, China, 1982.
26.  Fan Hong and Tan Hua, 'Sport in China: Conflict between Tradition and Modernity, 1840s to 1930s', *International Journal of the History of Sport,* 19, no. 2–3 (2002): 189.
27.  See also Susan Brownell's *Training the Body for China.*
28.  For more detailed discussion of women's sport see Fan Hong, *Footbinding, Feminism and Freedom*; for a more detailed discussion of the effect on elite sport see Dong Jinxia, *Women Sport and Society.*
29.  Fan Hong, 'Will the Iron Roses Bloom Forever', p. 48, has this as an overtly radical symbol of sexual liberation and says translation of the English *The Rules of Women's Football* into Chinese took place, but it isn't clear who the author of this was, other than possibly H. Frost and H. Cubberley, *Field Hockey and Soccer for Women,* New York: Charles Scribners and Sons, 1923), referred to in Chapter 1.
30.  This combined with civil wars (1927–1837) and (1945–1949); the Anti-Japanese War (1937–1945); the Korean War (early 1950s); and the Great Leap Forward (1958–1960). The Marriage Law and Land Law of 1950 protected a woman's right to own and inherit property and to her own status within the household. A new emphasis on education, and specifically the campaign to improve literacy, saw a dramatic increase in the number of teaching institutions but also in the numbers of women in mainstream and higher education. So the scale and speed of change appear to have accelerated in this decade, though, of course, more privately-held material may yet be unearthed to give us details about the era before. However sudden the improvement, a combination of the effects of the Great Leap Forward, three years of natural disasters, and the Cultural Revolution meant that in the 1960s, most of the gains made by women athletes

were lost, though some parents encouraged their children to take up elite sport as a means of escaping fighting and field labour.

31. Christiane Eisenberg, Pierre Lanfranchi, Tony Mason and Alfred Wahl, *100 Years of Football: The FIFA Centennial Book* (London: Weidenfeld and Nicholson, 2004), p. 284: 'claiming that FIFA was "controlled by imperialistic elements". It was not until 1979 that the People's Republic of China could once again be accepted as a member and then only after the Taiwan Association, which had acted faultlessly over many years, had been renamed Chinese Taibei Football Association.' Spelling as the original.

32. Chang, 'Welcome Speech', *World Women's Invitational Tournament 1981,* pp. 12–13.

33. Hong and Mangan, 'Will the Iron Roses Bloom Forever', p. 48.

34. Qiu Zhenqi, 'Women's Soccer Has a Bright Future', p. 16.

35. Ibid.

36. *Results Sheet: Final Standing 1983 Guangzhou International Women's Football Invitational Tournament.* Japan came third, Singapore eighth. The Chinese teams are listed in rank order otherwise.

37. For a more detailed discussion of women's football teams before 1949 see Hong and Mangan, 'Will the Iron Roses Bloom Forever'.

38. Datin Teoh Chye Hin, Vice President, ALFC, 'Re: Women's Football in Asia', 28 October 1981.

39. See http://www.fifa.com/en/mens/statistics/index/0,2548,All-Mar-2005,00.html, accessed 6 March 2005. For further details see the analysis of the peaks and troughs of team rankings at the web site address.

40. Datin Teoh Chye Hin, Vice President, ALFC, 'Re: Women's Football in Asia', 28 October 1981, FIFA Correspondence Files, Zurich.

41. Chandra Segar, 'AFC Want Total Control over the Women', *The Star,* 31 August 1981.

42. Unattributed author, 'FAM Say No to Women's Soccer Control', *The Star,* 20 September 1981.

43. For a full list of the classification see Vision Asia Women's Football Web site, http://www.the-afc.com/uploaded/administration/23_english.pdf, accessed 5 April 2005.

44. Fan Hong, 'Two Roads to China: The Inadequate and the Adequate (Review Essay)', *International Journal of the History of Sport,* 18, no. 2 (June 2001): 162.

45. For example, Scotland has had a representative squad since the 1970s, and both Rose Reilly and Edna Nellis had played professionally in Italy, but the Scottish FA recognized women's football only in 1998.

46. Peter Verlappan, General Secretary, Asian Football Confederation, 'Women's Football in Asia', letter to Datin Teoh Chye Hin, 28 September 1981. For further details of whether and when teams were recognized see Sue Lopez, *Women on the Ball.*

**Figure 1** Festival of Britain Programme, 21 July 1951, Corinthian versus Lancashire Ladies at Barrow. The range of civic interest, sponsorship, patronage and sporting entertainment combined to raise funds for one of a number of charities.

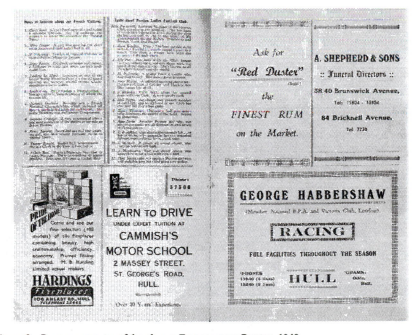

**Figure 2** Programme notes of the players France versus Preston, 1948.

**Figure 3** Stoke versus Dick, Kerr's Ladies Programme cover, 1923, including pen pictures of the players and an appeal on behalf of Alice Kell, the Dick, Kerr captain, promoting the sporting and health benefits of women's football.

**Figure 4** London team, circa 1917. Photograph courtesy of Jane Ebbage, showing the chaperone, the trainer and sponsors.

**Figure 5** Liverpool Ladies Football Team (date unknown but believed to have been circa World War I). Courtesy of Ann Berry, whose grandmother is seated front row far right. W.E.D is written on the football, but it would seem, on the basis of a comparison of this uniform with that shown in Pathé newsreel coverage of the 14 February 1921 match at Anfield (gate 25,000), that the image predates the considerable popularity of women's football on Merseyside, including Boxing Day 1920 at Goodison Park (gate estimated at 50,000 plus).

FEMINA SPORT CLUB OF PARIS    THE CHAMPION TEAM OF FRANCE

**Figure 6** Femina postcard. There are potentially many more images of this kind in the hands of post-card collectors. They show that munitions football was not the only form of women's participation in the early phase of interest and that women's work and leisure, rather than charitable fundraising, influenced the formation of teams. The uniform has also become more standardized; both French and English women wore a recognizable football strip at this time.

**Figures 7 and 8** Stoke Ladies playing Femina in Barcelona 1923. Photographs courtesy of Peter Bridgett. The player with the outstretched leg is E Carroll, the coalman's daughter. These privately-held photographs are very rare in that they show the women in action and something of the crowd.

RAILWAY BENEVOLENT INSTITUTION.       LEEDS, *April 6th, 1921.*

**Figure 9**   Railway Benevolent Institution, Leeds, 6 April 1921, Dick, Kerr versus the French team in front of a crowd of 27,000, raising £1,700 for the charity. This image is notable for being one of the few postcards which shows the very large crowds and because it documents the amount raised at a not particularly important match. That month alone, Dick, Kerr also played at Stoke, Standish, Bradford, Rotherham, Kilmarnock, Bury, Bolton, New Brighton, Rochdale and Barrow, in that order, in a year when they played sixty-seven games in total in front of crowds conservatively estimated at 900,000 spectators. Photograph courtesy of Winnie Bourke, daughter of Alice Mills, shown here in the striped shirt in the foreground, who became Mrs Alice Lambert after moving to the US following the Dick, Kerr tour.

# –3–

# A Grass Ceiling
## Women's Football in England

A Woman's Football Team is to startle the 'World of Pas-time'—with evolutions anything but ladylike, I venture to think, albeit Lady Florence Dixie is President of the British Ladies Football Club. I have every admiration for Lady Florence Dixie. I have read with admiration her lively narrative of her stirring adventures in the southernmost part of South America (including a plucky 'header' into the straits of Magellan), and have been greatly interested in many of her movements in England. But surely Lady Florence cannot be aware of the rough and tumble horseplay of the football field when she writes: 'I cannot conceive of a game more calculated to improve the physique of women than football.' The exercise football affords might surely be acquired more becomingly by girls in the gymnasia which are multiplying all over the kingdom. We don't want even the newest of the 'New Women' utterly unsexed by indulgence in such unwomanly games as football.

Now for some fashions which are really ladylike and becoming. The pretty little toque [hat] sketched is of bronze green velvet.[1]

A *Times* article covering the North-versus-South fixture of the British Ladies Football Club at Crouch End in March 1895, to which this excerpt refers, called the events 'Irksome'.[2] Traditional views of the 'unsexing' and potentially corrupting nature of some games, specifically football, have shaped the image of the woman player as an irritating and unwelcome aspect of modernity. Construction of this convention of Association football as a manly sport which honour requires to be kept amongst men has been a long-term project of the sports' authorities against which to judge more recent attempts since the 1990s to deconstruct it. The establishment of the Football Association (1863), the Football League (1888) and the club (both professional and amateur) have tended, by and large, to exclude female players by either formal or informal means. However, there are moments when women players, teams and associations have been both the focus of male support and bureaucratic concern. Fortunately, there is an increasing amount of evidence in the public domain which suggests a need to revisit the historiography of women's involvement in Association football in England. These include sources in the archives of sports federations and those available to wider audiences, like the Pathé newsreel collection and the North West Film Archive. In accepting the most frequently expressed critique of *A Game for Rough Girls,* namely that it was skewed toward contemporary events, I discuss in this chapter some of the earlier episodes in more depth. The social and cultural milieu of the ensuing twenty-game British Ladies tour, for instance, saw Lady Florence linked to the major moral scandal that year; provoking public concern over what was decent and what was unnatural behaviour, likely to corrupt the young. The first of three trials involving her father, the Marquess of Queensbury, her younger brother, Lord Alfred 'Bosie' Douglas and Oscar Wilde began in April and concluded in May with Wilde's two-year sentence for gross indecency. At the final trial at the Old Bailey, Wilde reportedly said, 'The ages live in history through their anachronisms.' A view with much to support it in view of women's place in sport, particularly football, in the twenty-first century.

Sociologists and historians have become interested in what life is like for women in football, both as a participatory and as a spectator sport. Aspects of this, albeit very recent, literature focus upon the experiences of playing, spectating, supporting, organizing or coaching, for example, and identify discrete groups of players to do so.[3] Emphasising the micro study of the female player doesn't necessarily present women at play (or in support and so forth) as a disjunctive experience, but there is potential for it to do so. It tends toward a dislocation from the players' other multiple and changing identities when playing (or supporting and so on) and when not. Politically, this seems to fit with the notion of women's involvement as an irregular aspect of modernistic sport (titles such as 'The Image Problem in Women's Football' being a case in point). In trying to avoid the feminist taboo of depicting a universal woman player, studies have tended to identify groups of black or Asian, gay or straight players at elite or competitive levels. Methodologically, academia chances possible exoticism of women football players unless we can combine historically-sensitive sociology with sociocultural history in the literature. An emphasis on recent groups, or types, may overlook the preceding development of women playing football and their impact upon a wider sports culture and history. Looking both at the macro level in terms of how the sport came to be codified, organized and perpetuated and at individual examples of women's play before the 1990s, it is possible to find that the players' experience may not always accord with our current view. Most of what follows is small-scale and brief compared with the weight of tradition reinforced economically, geographically, politically, legally and in myth-making by male participation in what became the national game. Nevertheless, the evidence indicates that the processes were more open (in chronological terms and as multiple and shifting identities) than has so far been discussed.[4]

Wilde was not a football man. The construction of masculinity, like the process of codification in sport, particularly in football, sought to demark what was acceptable and what was not. The homophobia around the game is another aspect of its gendered history still to be fully treated. As a means of preventing undesirable behaviour, for example, it is thought that games were gradually introduced at Harrow and other public schools as a way of disciplining boys' spare time and to foster staff-pupil relations in the mid-nineteenth century.[5] In the eventual establishment of the Football Association in 1863, the need for a uniform set of rules predominated.[6] Three elements of this manly image commonly highlighted in the popularization of football require to be addressed. The first of these is the process of codification, which enabled the Football Association, 'not a very powerful organisation in the 1860s and 1870s', to reinforce a degree of agreement over games which had been 'governed by a mixed bag of local and traditional regulations' even if through a fairly gradual process involving much compromise.[7] This led to the creation effectively of a national infrastructure of regional football associations in the 1870s, supplemented by the foundation of the Scottish FA in 1873 and that of Wales in 1876. A second element appears to have been football as a manly sport but one less violent than rugby; no small matter for working-class participants who could not afford time off due to sporting injuries.[8] The third and most significant factor is argued to be 'the invention of competitive cup football which changed the nature of the game'.[9] The FA Challenge Cup Competition was first held in 1871 and its popularity as a working man's sport is seen to have spread when Blackburn Olympic defeated the Old Etonians in 1883. The role of the FA secretary, the sports journalist Charles Alcock, in promoting both the game and the competition helped to provide a focal point for local rivalry and gambling. As football became a national game, it also came to be seen as appropriate for working-class boys, first as an extracurricular activity, then as representative sport following the establishment of the South London Schools Football Association in 1885.[10] At its founding, in 1904, the English Schools Football Association (ESFA) had as its primary objective 'The mental, moral and physical development and improvement of schoolboys through the medium of Association Football'.[11] However, semantics aside, the Department of Education agreed, in 1906, that games could be added to the curriculum of state elementary schools for girls, and we see some evidence of school-based girls' football. There are examples of working-class girls' teams in 1905–1906 where a Reading boys' side had won the English Schools Challenge Cup. Otherwise, it's difficult to overlook another legacy: that, as a nonschool sport, football for girls has been seen as exceptional and outside the mainstream.

The FA was not particularly progressive in their outlook, in spite of the perceived modernity of the game they were promoting, and so outlawing, suspensions and disqualifications became commonplace methods of including some individuals or activities and excluding others. After seeing off the threat of a breakaway British Football Association in 1885 by accepting the principle of professionalism, the model of one body to oversee all Association football was established and, to an extent, remains today at national and global level. The Football League Championship followed in 1888, and, with the practice of home and away fixtures, football's popularity became extensive. It is a system which has proven to be enduring and much replicated across a variety of sports at both the professional and the amateur levels. This brief summary raises sports-specific questions and more general questions as to why women's grounds are not a part of the human geography of England, as well as how and why women's teams and women's clubs have been formed largely outside these structures.

If there was a good deal of popular support for working-class football teams at this time, there was little spare leisure time for working women in the rapidly industrializing urban Britain. The wider development of football as a spectator-supported event relied on a well-documented increase in leisure, and the Saturday half-day provided a gap for it to become match-day. In the meantime, the working-class female's 'double day' meant long shifts at the factory, mill or store before she could engage in home-based activities designed to support the household. In the context of this lack of nondomestic leisure time for both working- and middle-class women, it is hardly surprising that we have a view that football teams were run by youngish men for young men.[12] There remains considerable contention over whether the sport was spread 'top down' by the public school-educated schoolmasters and missionary workers or 'bottom up' as part of what has been called 'the proletarianization' of the game by working-class men.[13] There are a range of sources in both the public and the private domains to support interpretation along this continuum.

However, 'football facts' about which there is much common sense (when was the word 'soccer' first used, what was the first football club) are in the process of continually being refined.[14] Conceivably also, for a variety of reasons, which might include a lack of record, a view that sport was an essentially transitory activity, part of high day or holiday celebration, or just because it was humdrum, we know very little of the involvement of girls and women. As sport, a public form of entertainment and leisure before 1895 and until 1993, when the FA formally took control of women's football, we know only a little. The world of working-class pastimes, marked by transient escapes including traditional town and country fairs, music hall, the 'day out' and, later, cinema, in addition to sport, hobbies and other leisure and recreation activities, is another contentious area. Interpretation varies considerably over this growing historiography regarding whether activities were primarily indicative of gender difference or dominated by class concerns.[15] Specifically with regard to this study, we have some evidence of working-class male support for female football play, though at the present time of a fragmentary nature.

The establishment of the British Ladies Football Club, in 1894, could be seen as in some ways unsurprising. It was one of several, what might be called, special-interest groups that formed sporting links. Though the topic of women's access to various sports has been covered in greater depth and to better effect elsewhere, it is worth making the point of how arbitrary judgements over individual sports seem to have been, with hockey and cricket approved by some, lacrosse by others, or combinations of gymnastics and team games for middle-class girls. We know that there were high school girls' football teams formed at Brighton in 1894 and Nottingham in 1895, for example. The first match of the BLFC doesn't appear in the FA minute books for that year, which are characterized by the FA historian David Barber in dry style as 'not big on discussion'.[16] The media did show some interest, though perhaps predictably the *Athletic News* and other sporting press overlooked the event, which is reported to have drawn a crowd of between 7,000 and 10,000 spectators with the consensus toward the higher figure, even in the less enthusiastic articles. If the FA Cup Final had attracted a crowd approaching 37,000 the previous year and the FA Amateur Cup final 3,500, this was a pretty respectable gate, particularly for an inaugural event of a similar size to Dick, Kerr's first game in 1917 (when at least some of the money went to charity rather than the organizers and participants). It may be that they were inspired in 1887 by the formation of the first women's cricket club, White Heather (it survived to 1957) and in 1890 by two professional teams known collectively as the Original English Lady Cricketers, which toured for two years, after their manager had put an advertisement in the newspaper and before he absconded with the proceeds. The White Heather club was formed by noblewomen as a form of country-house cricket, and the number of members rose from eight to fifty in four years. The alliance of Lady Dixie and the organization of Honeyball appears to have amalgamated upper-class patronage with a degree of commercial acumen and a relatively mild form of feminism.

The *Penny Illustrated* newspaper coverage of this game is piquant in its enthusiasm for the 'President' of the club diving into the Straits of Magellan but concerned about her colleagues' physical welfare during a game of football in an article entitled 'Home, Sweet Home'. There's no indication that Florence herself intended to play. The illustrations of the game are among the first representations of 'feisty' women players made shapely by belted tunics, knee-length breeches, shinpads over stockings and what look like boots with slightly elevated heels. Long hair is roughly kept under woollen hats. While two players could be passing the ball, one is face down on the ground in a pose that could only be described as flattened, and the distant 'keeper has a silhouette and stance reminiscent of a ballet dancer'. The rather less fragile illustration of a player which opens the article resembles the photographic images of the Secretary of the BLFC, Nettie Honeyball, taken at the time and now on show at the National Football Museum. Honeyball's shorts are more like culottes and less brief; the whole appearance more sturdy than the illustrations and appears to support the reports of players' average weight at about ten stone (140 pounds), 'a fairly heavy team'. If this article appeared a month before the game, do the images tell us that women's (practice or competitive) matches using these sports uniforms had already taken place since the BLFC had been formed or that there had been some kind of preview of the photograph and a little imagination on behalf of the illustrator? An interview with Nettie Honeyball on 2 March indicates that there had been opportunity, between the announcement of the organization in that newspaper in January of the same year and her related letter of rebuke, to watch the team practice. Had the illustrator done so, he would have found a club of fifty members of whom thirty were players who had responded to advertisements such as the appeal referred to later in the Programme. The class background is unclear, but it appears that players did not have to pay entrance fees or subscriptions but incurred 'a good deal' of expense which they hoped to recoup at the forthcoming match. The reprimand followed a comment of the *Graphic* writer that the players did not like practising in the cold. It had a grain of truth but seems to be less about the inclement weather than its effect of the training surface. John Bailey, in *The Great Women's Match of 1895*, cites

Our ground is a shockingly bad one. It lies just underneath the Alexandra Park racecourse, it is a clayey soil, and I have never know it free from water ... We have one young lady who comes from Woolwich who can kick like a Corinthian. But some are not so expert at moving about like others. We find that the girls who have gone in for cycling are the most nimble ... We are being coached by the centre-half of Tottenham Hotspurs and we practise regularly at Hornsey.[17]

The link with cycling is an important one because much of the frisson of interest on behalf of the newspaper reporters (and presumably some of the crowd) related to female bodies as public entertainment, with the women wearing split skirts, bloomers or, as they were reported, knickerbockers. The *Daily Graphic* at least felt 'The dresses of the ladies—North, red shirts and blue knickerbockers, and South, light blue and dark blue—were details which it seems more important to specify than any point in the play.'[18] This still-evident tradition of playing in basically male sports wear, albeit rather looser versions, appears to indicate a regard for female modesty; the use of breeches, stockings and tunics represents a feminized version but not greatly so. The hats and complete coverage of flesh may indicate a degree of modesty, but the look is recognizably suitable, if not exactly pleasurable, for playing football. This question of modest female athlete-as-public-entertainer in combination with the upper-class patronage of Lady Florence Dixie and the middle-class Nettie Honeyball raises questions about who the players were and why they played. In the Programme for the first match there is a polite appeal: 'Ladies desirous of joining the above Club should apply to Miss Nettie J Honeyball, 'Ellesmere' 27 Weston Park, Crouch End N'.[19] It is a difficult line of enquiry to pursue because match reports give little or nothing in the way of individual comment other than that referred to earlier. Presumably the local residence of Honeyball contributed to the ease of arranging the fixture, though the reference to 'Frequent trains from Moorgate Street, Broad Street, King's Cross and intermediate stations to Hornsey' indicates a wish to draw a crowd from the capital at large. A crowd of 10,000 at the first match suggests that it was intended as both a commercial venture and a political point; not so much in the needy sense that Sheila Fletcher calls 'Me too' feminism but more perhaps in the sense of 'why not me too?'[20]

When the first game took place, on 23 March 1895, *The Times* has it as a note at the bottom of a column entitled Midland Challenge Cup and could hardly be less interested:

Ladies' Football—A match, under Association rules between teams of ladies was played at Nightingale Lane, Hornsey, on Saturday, the title of the game being North v South.

Great curiosity was aroused, and the ground was thronged by some 7,000 people. The football was of a very harmless nature, and its novelty soon grew irksome to many of the spectators. The North won by seven goals to one.[21]

Having a North versus South (of London) competition was perhaps too vague to replicate the partisan spectator experience developed after the inauguration of the Football Association Challenge Cup and the creation of the Football League. Here maybe Lady Florence's lack of expertise showed. The Ladies Match was preceded by Crouch End versus 3rd Grenadier Guards, and admission for both was set at 1s (covered stand 1s extra). The professional women cricketers had been paid sixpence a game, were not allowed to play under their own names and had been accompanied by a chaperone. The double bill makes it difficult to know how many of the crowd had paid a not insubstantial sum primarily to see the women's match. However, it is more likely because of the question of the respectability of the ensuing tour in the Midlands, the North and in Scotland that it became beset by difficulty, including pitch invasions. Bury, Brighton, Doncaster and Edinburgh were major local events, although most significant appears to have been the Newcastle fixture, with a crowd approaching 8,000 and with the more sympathetic reporting from the radical *Manchester Guardian* and the liberal *Westminster Gazette*. It isn't clear how or even if players were paid nor the extent of expenses. Players such as Miss Obree seem to have played under their own name, but nicknames were awarded. A popular player referred to as 'Tommy' seems to be an amalgam of two people from the articles, a Miss Gilbert and Daisy Allen, who were both small and lithe.[22] Ambiguous use of pronouns went beyond the tomboy stereotype; the goalkeeper Mrs Graham was also singled out for recognition but was referred to throughout as an outstanding player, even for a married lady. Though the tour seems to have ended the involvement of the BLFC by the end of 1896, the sport for women neither took the next step in becoming an established network nor ceased to be played at all. It also set a tradition for newspapers to become quite contrary in their coverage of women's events. For the researcher, there are glimpses of new and corroborating evidence amidst a considerable silence on the subject. For example, rather gallantly concerned about the propriety of the event, the reporters also chide the level of skill. It wasn't those making the coarse and ribald remarks who were behaving disrespectfully—that was taken pretty much as inevitable—but those who would put themselves at risk of provoking such responses who degraded all those present.

Writing more than fifty years later, Geoffrey Green, in *A History of the Football Association*, provides an uncompromising analysis on the matter of a woman's place:

There now remain a few subjects upon which the FA have taken a definite stand from the beginning and remained unwavering in their attitude towards them. Among these may be counted Women's football, Greyhound racing, Betting and Rough Play ... This in truth has not been a subject ever to bring about a crisis within the Association, yet it represents but one of the many items upon which the FA has had to keep a watchful eye.[23]

There is both a wistfulness about this analysis written in the middle of the twentieth century and a contemporaneity. The 'definite stand' seems to be a question of respectability around whether women's involvement would bring ignominy to the game. To risk men's love of the sport made ridiculous by women's participation, a predicament: the FA wished neither to oversee female play nor to risk to be seen *not* to govern all aspects of the code. On 25 August 1902 the question of women's football became sufficiently an issue for official FA comment when the Council issued instructions to its affiliated associations not to permit matches against 'Lady teams'.[24] However limiting a lack of Association-backed and school-based development has been for the history of women's football, the idea of female players continued to pass into popular culture, for example, with *The Collegettes* ('Book and Lyrics by Edgar Smith. Music by Maurice Levy') at the Aldwych Theatre in February 1909. Set at a high school (perhaps like Brighton, Nottingham or one of the North American women's colleges) the play appeared on a double bill with *Philopoena* (subtitled 'A Farrago of Fun, Fancy, and Foolishness in Two Acts' to little effect so far as the critic was concerned) by the same authors, with which it compared favourably but only marginally so:

> These two pieces are much better suited to the ingenuous atmosphere of Binghampton or Peoria than to the more sophisticated air of London and there could only be one excuse which would justify their importation into a country where the native product is so vastly superior—namely, that they gave Miss Dressler a better opportunity than the music halls provided ... The second piece, *The Collegettes,* is more coherent and deals with the cultivation of a ladies' football team in order to defeat a neighbouring college whose inhabitants are succinctly described as "doxology-shouters." Incidentally, there are lectures on the disadvantages of a superior education as a training for life.[25]

Marie Dressler, a Canadian star comedienne on the Broadway and Vaudeville circuit, played Philopoena Gesler in the first play and Tilly Buttin in the second.[26] The isolated nature of the examples supports Green's view that, exasperating as the female player may have been, a crisis in the manly nature of the sport did not apparently develop until shortly after World War One. During this time, the balance of mercantile and charitable interest was one of several areas which caused a certain amount of consternation and required something of a drastic response.

During the era before World War One, two elements of Association football's relationship with commercial enterprise were to be significant for women's involvement, or lack of it. The first of these was to be detrimental to the long-term future of the women's game as football was being popularized abroad by expats and emigrants who would play against local opposition if they could find no other. The very

Britishness of the game (including the Laws of the Game in English) appears to have spread the standard and reinforced a gentlemanly sportsmanship even if ideas of the dissemination of the sport by the British are subject to contention. However, games were not just for affluent individuals; new or distinct social groups played for a variety of reasons, including social integration, modernity and available leisure.

The second element was to prove rather more valuable for an early growth of women's football because commercialism led to spectatorship as an increasingly popular activity. As Tony Mason, Wray Vamplew and others have shown, football as both spectacle and activity had become the passion of the British urban working classes by the outbreak of war in 1914. The first women's game on film in the ITN collection concerns two women's sides playing at Ilford, London. It was recorded on 1 January 1914 but may have been anywhere in the period 1914–1918.[27] It hasn't been possible to corroborate this dating so far from other sources, and the teams are not recorded as works' sides though there is another film, also with a 1 January 1919 dating, showing a game between Handley Page Girls and the Ladies' Sterling Football Club, Ilford, Essex. In what appears to be the earlier example, there is a fair-size crowd, a child performs the kickoff and there is much good-humoured encouragement all round. One team plays in a recognizable football strip with various head coverings, and the other players are in gymslips with mobcaps (looking incongruously more mature and certainly taller than their opponents). The football crowd at the game appears to be mainly, though not exclusively, male, although there is the occasional highly fashionable woman dignitary or celebrity, as well as female chaperones and off-field assistance. What became evident around the time of the rise in what Ali Melling called 'munitionettes football' is that employers of working-class women used football in some similar ways that it was used for working men; namely to motivate workers to identify with the workplace and as a relatively healthful form of cheaply-facilitated recreation to encourage employees to act as representatives of the company outside working hours.[28] As a kind of stealth advertisement and benevolent activity, football was preferable to less moral and more physically risky leisure pursuits likely to impact on output. With the level of surveillance provided by a team manager and a coach plus a (usually older female) chaperone, the women players were encouraged to think of themselves in workplace terms of solidarity and mutuality but also as working and playing for 'our boys'. Perhaps now the term 'munitionettes' needs to be revisited, as there appear to be a wider range of occupational teams in addition to other kinds of clubs from representative to women's-interest groups.

What remains to be addressed, however, is the players' receptiveness to the cultural and social values that such supervisory arrangements sought to reinforce. The debates around the period reflect concerns over female health as the result of warwork, the blurring of gender identities as jobs, fashion, labour and leisure changed, bringing struggles over what was 'natural' for women. Much of this was motivated by a concern for the physical fitness of the race and women as mothers to be. In the light of concerns about the 'sexless gymnast' and in particular the unfeminine, possibly sterilizing, effects of strenuous exercise on women who were thought to have a limited amount of energy, much of it nervous, the enthusiasm of women football players seems to have caused much surprise amongst elites, even while occasioning little amongst working-class organizers.[29] The combination of work outside the home and regular training, though perhaps initiated by welfare workers, meant that that football took off as an enjoyable entertainment and relaxation. Women had blocks of identifiable leisure that had been 'earned' in public, sufficient colleagues to form teams and access to resources like pitches that would otherwise not have been made available. Work and leisure for female football players like those to become famous as the representatives of W. B. Dick and John Kerr Tramway and Light Railway Equipment Ltd (Dick, Kerr Ladies) were fused.

Some employers capitalized on this realization of the morale-boosting qualities of the game for women employees, and in this respect the management of Dick, Kerr Ladies, led by Alfred Frankland, were particularly astute in understanding the supporter mentality. As a form of ambient marketing of the company's products, very quickly the team were being portrayed as variously 'the best', the 'world champions' and the 'world-famous' women's team. Regional pride had, of course, been developing for a much longer period, with a music-hall song commemorating Preston North End as first champions of the Football League and of the FA Challenge Cup in 1889.[30] From the outset, Dick, Kerr were keen to attract large paying crowds, though the question of how and where to stage was matches continually reappraised. There would be no commercial cartel, no independent property or grounds and no league structure, nor even a fixed programme of games. This appears to be a large gulf in the organization and purpose of women's involvement in Association football. In looking to answer Alfred Gibson and William Pickford's question in *Association Football and the Men Who Made It*, 'Is sport a pursuit of profits? Or is it a commercial undertaking which places a premium on winning and providing pleasure for its followers?' women's football in the period 1917–1921 was rather more the latter than the former.[31]

Though the Pathé newsreels may be contested as primarily 'documentary' or 'feature', thereby having elements of fictional composition, they make a point that this largely unremembered aspect of sport passed into popular culture sufficiently to be reproduced and presented as what might now be seen as infotainment.[32] In this way, the moving image is itself a valuable source, though admittedly it is at least a second-hand, mediated construction of events that occurred more than eighty years ago. Established by Charles Pathé in London in 1902, by 1910 the company were producing a biweekly newsreel, the Pathé Gazette. After World War One they were producing various Cinemagazines including *Eve's Film Review*, covering entertainment, culture and women's issues.[33] The records are of moderate quality and very brief; most lasting a few minutes. Even so, not only did the women players draw large crowds at games hosted on Football League and Association-affiliated grounds consistently over at least a four-year period, but also the newsreels ensured that they were seen to do so by a larger audience. If, as Wray Vamplew notes in *Pay Up and Play the Game*, First Division matches in the League were averaging crowds of 23,000 by 1913 in the fastest-growing and most commercial spectator sport in the country, the enthusiasm for 'following' football extended to the Dick, Kerr and other matches from 1917 to 1921 and, it could be argued, beyond.[34] As part of a growing civic culture and identity, places where women's teams were conspicuously popular (the South, London, the Midlands and the North East) were industrial and commercial centres made up of urban settlements with good transport links and populations with some collective spare time in which to spend a share of their disposable incomes.

Jeff Hill has explored how the mediated nature of much sport is best characterized as processes that shape how people understand society and the relations of power within it.[35] It has been claimed that the cinema is often seen as primarily a female and juvenile pursuit (though not particularly so).[36] A study of the thoughts of those different audiences would make an appealing exploration of an historical situation which may contest the generally unfavourable view of women's play as wartime exception. This is not to say that the local and national press, including some coverage in the sporting papers, are any less valuable as sources, despite the fact that that the assumed readership may have dictated editorial policy (whomever and however consumed the final product). What was the social, cultural, economic and political environment which produced these films and their use? Put simply, for those men in work, able to have some surplus money to spend on leisure pursuits, what made them choose to spend a portion of it to watch women's football matches? What would the audiences in the cinema (many of whom had likely paid less than the minimum entrance price to attend a match) have thought of the sporting spectacle and of its topicality?[37] These issues are worth returning to later in looking at the chronology of development of Association football as a code. This period of popularity ended with the 1921 Football Association ban on women from Football League grounds and affiliated Association clubs. If this sanction reflected an insiders' view of sport, the moving image raises ambiguities about public support for women's football, the manner of its representation and audience receptiveness to it as live and mediated spectacle.

There has been a sustained popular and academic consideration of the Dick, Kerr team in the period 1917–1921 in Gail Newsham's *In a League of Their Own*, Barbara Jacobs's *Dick, Kerr's Ladies* and in Ali Melling's writing, so at the risk of overemphasizing their significance, I will concentrate on the filmic evidence, which does focus primarily on them while also giving indications of other teams presented to a wider audience.[38] The film and press sources reported that Grace Sibbert, who worked at the Dick, Kerr factory while her husband was fighting in France, organized the first match proper, held on Christmas Day 1917. In front of a reported crowd of 10,000 at Preston North End, playing against Arundel Coulthard Foundry, the game raised in excess of £600 for wounded soldiers at the Moor Park military hospital. Though amongst the best-known then as now, the 'Dickless Kerrs' (as they were unofficially nicknamed by some onlookers) were unlikely to have been the first of the women's teams to form during the war.[39] For instance, *The Times* has a tiny note in the Personal column regarding a Ladies Football Match which took place on 8 September 1917 at Maryport, raising £26 for the Serbian Relief Fund, which was patronized by Her Majesty the Queen and presided over by the Bishop of London.[40] While there may have been primarily works teams formed in 1917, including Lyons Tea Houses, Leys Light Engineering and Ediswan Radio, there were also Bath and Plymouth representative teams as well as women's-interest groups such as the more middle-class Atalanta and working-class miners' wives who played against single women in matches. The variety suggests that women's football was more developed in Britain than anywhere else at this time.

Teams up to the 1921 ban included Aberdeen, Arundel Coulthard Foundry, Barrow, Belfast, Birmingham City, Bolton, Cardiff, Coventry, Edinburgh, Glasgow, Heywood Ladies, Lancaster, Llanely, Newport, Newcastle, Renfrew, Rutherglen, St. Helens, Swansea and Whitehaven, in addition to munitions sides like Bennets of London along with one-offs like Harry Weldon's Rest of Britain.[41] It has been only too easy to overlook the ways in which the women's teams were woven into social history. In 1921, among the Harvey Nichols and Selfridges advertisements plus various news items ('£40,000 Necklace Missing after New Year's Eve Party', 'Collision in the Thames Four Men Missing') there is a piece on Bath City Ladies' forthcoming match in Manchester 'in aid of the unemployed ex servicemen of that city'.[42] So, combined with the match programmes, films and the postcards (such as the really useful example issued 6 April 1921 for the Railway Benevolent Institution in Leeds which indicates a very large crowd for the home team game against Dick, Kerr), the media coverage does show a degree of public awareness of the players, if little was reported in the sports pages.

The structures of patronage and favour already in place in the sporting press by the time that women played football in large numbers during the period 1914–1921 no doubt played a large part in its failure to find support. The most sustained article to appear on the sports pages in 1920, entitled 'Ladies at Football England v France by a Special Correspondent', bears this out. Just how special our guide is difficult to convey without substantial coverage, but suffice it to say that a pretty frisky digression lasts two-thirds of the article. When we do get to The Game (which neglects to mention it was played in front of at least 25,000 spectators for the National Association of Discharged and Disabled Soldiers and Sailors, presumably because of the distraction of the writer), it is both businesslike and condescending.

It was a hard, sporting game, and it was treated by both teams as a sport and not a spectacle. Both looked to enjoy it, and exhibited quite enough skill to disappoint those who had come to laugh. Most of their mistakes would have passed unnoticed if they had been a scratch team of men making no pretensions to science. Indeed the science spoiled it—for it was the science of a different but not necessarily a better game. Two or three of the English players in the centre were obviously familiar with good football.[43]

The national, regional and local media reportage gives cause for reservation in seeing women's football in this early phase as somehow belonging either to wartime mores or to restricted sporting cultures. The mediatization of these events arguably placed them as a small but growing element in a transformed national leisure market with regularities in finance, organization and presentation. A distinctive public image emerged. Not a national cartel comprised of local semiautonomous sporting clubs like the Football League perhaps, the women's teams were sports entertainers whose performance was used ostensibly to respond to fluctuating economic circumstances, usually for regionally specific charities. That is, women's football didn't take the same league structure or network of male football, but there are discernible archetypes in the way that it structured itself, and a lack of centralized control also meant a degree of discretion about the distribution of funds. As the manager of the Original English Lady Cricketers had shown, touring female sporting spectacle also entailed a degree of economic freedom for those who facilitated their play. Three examples of matches recorded by Pathé newsreels give this balance of production, consumption and exchange.

The first is a match played at night on 16 December 1920 at Deepdale with a white football under searchlights in aid of local unemployed ex-servicemen. Though less than two minutes long, the film shows packed terraces and supporters waving their hats in the stands. Gail Newsham has Bob Crompton of Blackburn Rovers kicking off, Bob Holmes a member of the 'Old Invincibles' whitewashing the footballs and Winston Churchill authorizing the hardware.[44] The teams run out and perform the usual prekick off routine, the effect of which, under the artificial light, is quite eerie. The size of the crowd is unclear but the overall mood of a hazy modernity unmistakable. This is not the only use of technology; in 1924 a game was played 'at night by means of a new system of lighting invented by Siemens and the English Electric Lamp Company' and the event was repeated in 1927.[45] So the organizers of the 4–0 victory over the Rest of England who raised 'in excess of' £600 and were entertained to supper in the canteen of the Dick, Kerr works in 1920 were willing to use novel means of presenting female players to a paying audience as part of the display. It also shows that the players were apparently quite pragmatic about raising funds for returning out-of-work ex-forces personnel keen to take back jobs in traditional industries, which would mean that by 1923 Dick, Kerr players would have to find alternative employment.

The large crowds raise queries about motivation and enthusiasm and how accurate the coverage of the newspapers was. To put it bluntly, if the women's games had been poor events and a spectator had chanced an attendance out of charitable altruism, it's unlikely that that he would have returned. The games were neither the only sporting events available nor the lone means of raising money for charity.

Would being seen at a women's match by friends and neighbours provide something to talk about at the same time as enhancing an individual's reputation for charitable community support? Was it perceived as a less selfish way of getting sporting entertainment, or was it viewed as an aspect of civic and local pride or combinations of these? Some commentators have used the image of the larger-than-life landlady, popular on postcards at the time, to suggest that part of Dick, Kerr's success lies in the tradition of strong women in a maternally centred Northern culture. This seems to go too far in overlooking the discretion working-class men had in spending their free time and money. It also raises the question of whether this evaluation depends too heavily on postwar myths of masculinity.

The second film relates more to the rapid development of women's football as sport and spectacle following a match on Boxing Day at Goodison Park in 1920 that drew a reputed crowd of 55,000. That match between Dick, Kerr and St Helens had used a local rivalry to raise in the region of £3115 for former servicemen and had been kicked off by Ella Retford. A vivacious comedienne and popular pantomime Principal Boy (later a character film actress), Retford had also made songs like 'She's a Lassie from Lancashire', 'Yorkshire', 'We're All North Country Lads and Lassies' and 'She's a Girl up North' music-hall hits.[46] A January game at Old Trafford against Bath Ladies two weeks later drew a crowd of 35,000 who saw a fourteen-year-old football prodigy, Lily Parr, score four goals in her debut. On 17 February 1921 a well-known comedian appearing in pantomime on Merseyside gave his name to Dick, Kerr's opposition, and 'Harry Weldon's Team of Lady Internationals' competed in aid of unemployed ex-servicemen, Liverpool hospitals and the Variety Artistes Benevolent Funds. A reported crowd of 25,000 produced £1,500 in declared gate receipts. Entertaining sports performance in the broad sense was not looked approvingly at by the Football Association, though it would appear that the whole thing took place in an atmosphere of athletic goodwill and propriety. Harry Weldon's mock boxers and variety artistes mean that the publicity was not exactly confined to the sporting contest.

The third match, kicked off by 'le gentleman boxeur' Georges Carpentier, was a glamorous November tie in Hull 1921. 'Gorgeous George' had fought, and lost, the world heavyweight championship against Jack Dempsey in July of that year in front of a crowd of 80,000 in a $1 million event in the US.[47] Carpentier is shown being photographed and filmed.[48] Some discussion has taken place as to the identity of the camerawoman involved, with John Adderley suggesting that technique indicates her to have been a novice.[49] While happy to give credit to the progressive politics of the working man, that the crowds of male supporters had somehow become allergic to the opportunity to take charge of a technological gadget and had decided to volunteer a female neophyte as sole operator tests belief. Perhaps we'll have to agree that she was working towards proficiency in a professional context until such time as her identity can be clarified.

Very popular in this country at the time, Carpentier made an appearance at this Yorkshire Ladies v Dick, Kerr match that may well have raised the gate at this game and helped to increase the receipts. It would be useful to have a programme to find out what cause the game was played for and how much was charged. It would be even more intriguing to know who had the idea of inviting Carpentier, what the arrangements were and who made them. As possibly the last mediated match before the ban (though, as has been said, not the last Pathé coverage of women's football), it also raises questions about where the organizers of female games for large, paying live audiences thought the spectacle would develop. The images of celebrities such as Retford and Carpentier seem to be rather wholesome and hardworking ideas of glamour: his fame conceivably more A-list than hers (if such a list had existed then). Nevertheless, they were popular with the public in ways that may already have been slightly nostalgic in 1921 as Carpentier's popularity had already been superseded by the Dempsey-style heavyweight and Retford's variety-hall act increasingly gave way to overseas tours. What isn't in question was the ability of women's football, in variously constituted forms, to draw paying crowds from among the working class who had limited time and less expendable income to spend on a competing range of leisure pursuits. Those in the contemporary situation, say *Radio 5 Live* phone-in participants, who rehash stereotypes about female athletes being incapable of providing entertaining sporting display are more chauvinistic than their grandfathers or great grandfathers, who, it appears, appreciated good football that just happened to have been played by women.

Another lingering mystery is the question of money. Without wishing to enter into discussions of appropriation, there are a number of issues around the raising of funds and their use which are unclear. First, does the financial situation help to explain the timing in the popularity of women's teams? There remains some debate about the decision not to suspend play at the outbreak of hostilities, which meant that for the 1914–1915 season both the FA Cup competition and the Football League tournament were brought to a full conclusion.[50] In 1915 Sheffield played Chelsea in the 'Khaki Cup Final' where Lord Derby, in presenting the trophy, is reported to have said, 'You have played with one another and against one another for the Cup; play with one another for England now.' The patriotism of the people's game was questioned as the nostalgic charge that football had become a business rather than a sport became a frequently made one.[51] It would be overstating the case to see the suspension of the Football League as equating to an absence of male professional football for supporters to attend, which seems to be part of the rationale for dismissing the women's game as a wartime aberration. In effect, professional football continued under regional tournaments of varying sizes such as the Midlands, London and Lancashire leagues. In 1916, in order to swell the coffers of the war effort, football, among other pastimes, became subject to a supposedly temporary Entertainments Tax. The effect of this was to raise the minimum admission price from the 6d set in 1890 (boys under fourteen and women excepted) for Football League Games (more for grandstand seats and Cup ties) to 9d in 1917 to cover the Entertainment Tax. This was to rise to 1 shilling in 1921. There was to be no provision for the unemployed to attend matches outside these minimum admission fees, and clubs who tried to do this were warned against it. It is notoriously difficult to make conclusions about the size of reported crowds because of the cash economy on which most football clubs operated as a way of underpaying tax. It would be very useful, but difficult, to know for each game whether women's football matches became popular in the 1917–1921 period when charging the same admission prices or whether a different pricing system was used. Programmes exist and show a variety of prices, from 2d to 9d, but it is unclear whether the programme also served as an entry ticket or whether the cost of this souvenir was a customary addition to the admission fee. Not only are the figures available in the public domain contradictory as sources; they don't add up in terms of the number of spectators reported and the amounts raised (if tried with variations of 6d, 9d or 1s per head). Special trams were put on for some male matches to encourage female supporters, but whether there were similar concessionary arrangements, including a reduced paid fee to enter the gate at women's games, is unsolved.[52] To further complicate matters, the convention of the celebrity kickoff frequently resulted in the ball being autographed and raffled, with programme buyers pointedly reminded: 'Have YOU bought your ticket for the Autographed Ball? Price 3d each. Programme Price 3d.' There are also advertisements for the various local goods and services. What did A. Welsh Limited, 'the progressive Gent's Outfitter'; Asbestos Sports, Outfits 'For Every British sport'; L. Rapstone, 'For Antique Furniture of all Descriptions'; S. P. Wood Ltd, 'that Nice Chap next door'; Hardaker and Sons, Removals and Storage 'Motor Vans to all Parts' and Northern Clothing Co., 'Macs and Rainwear for Men, Women and Children' pay to sponsor Preston versus the French team in Hull? Was the money for sponsorship or expenses?

Does the orthodoxy of charitable purpose of the games therefore raise more related questions than the seemingly clear rationale for their creation disguises? For example, were the motivations of organizers primarily altruistic, or was a tax loophole exploited? The War Charities Act, in 1916, ruled that where the takings of an entertainment, without any charge for expenses, were to be devoted to charity, exemption from the Entertainment Tax could be made by Customs and Excise. It took until 26 March 1918 for the FA, in conjunction with the Football League, to register the Football National War Fund to aid association players and others who had rendered service to the game and their dependents who needed assistance because of the War or other causes. Given that estimates refer to half a million players and spectators joining His Majesty's Forces by the end of 1914, this covered a range of the population. A consensus view is that women's football from 1917 raised money for a range of good causes more than to pay players' or organizers' expenses. The soccer-by-searchlight game of 1920 involving Dick, Kerr's 4–0 victory over St Helens Ladies is reported to have raised in excess of £600 with 22,000 supporters, which would equate to at least 12d (1 shilling) per person, whatever the constitution of the crowd. How great were the players' expenses compared to other necessary costs? Was there any transparency in the accounting systems? Does this explain why the unregulated, uncoordinated nature of women's football continued in this form for the following three decades? In short, was charitable purpose honoured more in execution or in the breach?

It is possible of course to overstate the economic and symbolic dimension of women's football. It did not compare to the emblematic commercialism of the Football League, betting (including the Pools from the 1930s), the sporting press, cigarette cards, and the establishment of a home for the FA Cup final in 1923 at Wembley. On an international scale, by 1924 FIFA had more than forty members, making it the largest sporting federation in national association representation and athlete numbers. It would be a considerable overstatement to argue any form of direct competition, though money does seem involved in defending a manly image for the game. [53] The ban was perhaps a form of safeguard in that whatever revenue streams were available through performing football for a paying public were to be defended as under FA and League jurisdiction under the twin principles of enclosure of grounds and the right to charge a paying audience to enter.

A very sympathetic reading of the minute books might conclude that the Football Association viewed women's teams in much the same way as other 'scratch' teams. Consider the reinforcement of the general rules, for example, in Council minutes of July 1921:

> Item 19. Scratch Team Matches Rule 28. The attention of the Council was drawn to certain matches having been played during the past season without permission. It was decided to call to attention the following provision, and to require clubs to observe the Rule:- Two scratch teams shall not play against each other when gate money is taken without the permission of this Association or of the affiliated association or Associations concerned. [54]

With no formally constituted women's alliance, there may well have been anxiety that, unlike the other special interest affiliates to the Football Association, women's football was developing outside and beyond the immediate control of the sports' governing bodies and was achieving a degree of commercial success in raising gate money, wherever it was eventually directed. The Council minutes of 10 October 1921 detail this expressly with regard to women, although apparently more concerned with fiscal than biological matters: 'The Council decided that Clubs must not permit matches between ladies' teams to be played on their grounds unless sanction for such matches is first obtained from The Football Association. It will be a condition of any application granted that the club on whose ground the match is played shall be responsible for the receipts and payments, and a statement of the account must be sent to the Association showing how the whole of the receipts are applied.' This was a recurring theme in the minutes of the FA Emergency Committee for the remainder of the year, for instance, regarding a match between Dick, Kerr and South of England: 'Permission given for the match to be played on the ground of Bristol City FC upon the condition that the club be responsible for the receipts and payments, a statement of Account to be sent to the Association showing how the whole of the receipts are applied [*sic*].'[55] In the minutes for the following session of the same committee, item 55 concerns a 'Ladies Football Match, Ediswan v. Lyons 27 October 1921. The explanation and apology of the Tottenham Hotspur Club for having allowed the match to be played on their ground before permission had been obtained, was accepted.' Meanwhile, the Emergency Committee minutes dated 29 November to 12 December 1921 details at item 60 Plymouth versus Seaton: 'Winchester FC censured for having permitted the match to be played on their ground without first having obtained permission. The Club also ordered to pay a local approved charity the amount received as their share of the gate receipts.'

Whether this indicates the relative strength of Tottenham as against Winchester, the issue could not eventually be resolved on a case-by-case basis. It appears that the continuing success of the women's game caused the FA to regulate by default rather than desire. As a crudely effective blanket strategy, the Consultative Committee had adopted the following resolution on Women's Football Matches by 5 December 1921:

> Complaints having been made as to football being played by women, the Council feel impelled to express their strong opinion that the game of football is quite unsuitable for females and ought not to be encouraged.
>
> Complaints have also been made as to the conditions under which some of these matches have been arranged and played, and the appropriation of the receipts to other than charitable objects. The Council are further of opinion that an excessive proportion of the receipts are absorbed in expenses and an inadequate percentage devoted to charitable objects.
>
> For these reasons the Council request the clubs belonging to the Association to refuse the use of their Grounds for such matches.[56]

It seems to imply that perception of uncharitable misuse of the money raised would taint the remainder of football and in particular its own exemptions from the Entertainment Tax. In terms of the unsuitability of the game, only one brief item reached the newspapers in that year before the ruling which seems related. Doris Smith, age fourteen, had fallen and fractured her leg at a practice match to select a Lincoln team to meet a Yorkshire club.[57] The ruling was reported verbatim with little by the way of commentary in *The Times* the following day, in contrast to the *Athletic News* which treated the expulsion of women as something of a cathartic opportunity:

> Some time ago the Association declined to recognise women players or accept the duty of governing them. At that time no reason was given. Now it is clear that their objection arises because 'the game of football is quite unsuitable for females.' There is no ambiguity

about this expression of opinion, which will be approved by the majority of people who are interested in sports and pastimes, and without reserve by the general community who disapprove of the forward movement of women. Women who freely take part in sports and pastimes abound by the thousand, but those who have gone to the extreme of football are an insignificant minority. It is impossible to forbid their participation in the game, and neither the fiat of the Association nor the thunders of their critics will stop women who want to play.

The greatest influence is public disapproval. Most of those who have seen this type of match have come to the conclusion that football for girls and young women is unseemly, and that the games are often travesties of the sport. Let us, however, ask why games are played? Primarily for mental refreshment, for bodily invigoration, and for amusement. For these purposes any sport or pastime must be possible within the physical strength of the organs of the body. Football, played as it was intended to be, was not designed for the average woman. It is a game for strong men and for the development of masculinity. That women would invade the football arena was never contemplated, as such violent exercise is not adapted to the physique of the sex.[58]

Two particularly noteworthy phrases from this excerpt, subtitled 'Recreation—Not Fatigue', have contributed to the legacy of this attitude in contemporary England and more widely. The first is the influence of public disapproval, which remains a general problem for women's sports, particularly those involving contact, high risk and/or strength. The view that women would engage in pursuits contrary to their own best interests and, by extension, would need to be prevented from doing so is evident in a case brought more than fifty years later, after the ban was lifted, in 1972. Theresa Bennett, age twelve in 1978, was prevented from playing for her local mixed football team, Muskham United, by legal ruling brought by the FA, even though she had been selected on merit and 'had run rings around the boys'. Though Theresa had been playing mixed football for some time, the attitude of the court depended upon the notion that young women are so intrinsically vulnerable, fragile and physically deficient that the state must protect them from the folly of participation in vigorous competitive athletics. This cultural anachronism linked the idea of separating males and females as necessary for the safety and welfare of the latter in the original 1975 Sex Discrimination Act, particularly Section 44, which differentiated competitive from participative sport. [59]

Nothing in Parts II to IV shall, in relation to any sport, game or other activity of a competitive nature where the physical strength, stamina or physique of the average woman puts her at a disadvantage to the average man, render unlawful any act related to the participation of a person as a competitor in events involving that activity which are confined to competitors of one sex.[60]

The second continuity is reference to an 'insignificant minority' of female players, prompting the need of legal safeguard and the term 'average woman' used as a comparator. In 2006 this was still an issue, as a coach who submitted this heartfelt plea to a House of Commons Select Committee on women's football indicated:

> I have heard all the arguments reference why girls cannot play football against boys from under 12, and I have to say they are outdated based on ignorance and bias. The two female players who play for me are physically strong and mentally tough. They know when they walk onto the pitch they will get no favours and don't expect them. They also know, like all of our male players, if their performances are not good enough, I will have no hesitation in dropping them. Both girls have adapted brilliantly to 11-a-side football, surely not even the ignorant or biased will claim it is a progressive step to move them back into seven-a-side next season. I know for a fact every team we played against last season would love to have Hannah Dale in their squad for next season. It is fairly obvious to me that people who know and truly understand football at grassroots (ie. ourselves and the opposition managers and coaches) who witness these games every week, cannot see why these girls are not allowed to play next season. I can understand and tend to agree with the fact the average male player is better than the average female player. Hannah Dale is no average player. She should be allowed to compete at the highest level her ability takes her. At this moment in time that is against male players. The Germans and Americans have the best female teams in the world. Ask yourself why? They have been allowed to compete at the highest level their abilities took them and that included competing against male players well over the age of 12. All I ask the FA to do is allow these girls to play at their true level, for the sake of the boys in our team, but most of all Hannah and Addi themselves. The FA have done a wonderful job with girls football, but in my opinion girls football is being held back with this outdated rule. The sky should be the limit, unfortunately the German and American girls have wings on their boots and our girls lead weights.[61]

The unsuitability of the average woman for vigorous competition in law and the ruling by the FA over mixed football remain as issues to be reviewed. As the correspondence from the Chair of the committee makes clear, 'We made our recommendations, which included a strong conclusion that the ban on girls playing mixed football after the age of 11 should be lifted. The Government has since responded to our report and we await the decision of the FA. We will monitor the progress and are in regular contact with them. We will therefore ensure that pressure is maintained although at the end of the day, the decision is theirs.'[62] Past ages do indeed live on.

In returning to the earlier events, why was the ban quite so successful? First of all, it appears that there was a transitional phase of two to three years before it really took hold. For example, Stoke Ladies formed shortly after World War One by Arthur Bridgett (of Stoke City, Sunderland, Port Vale, who was capped for England seven times at what was then termed outside left) and his brother, Len, whose four daughters played for the team at various times. In June 1922 the Stoke team won an English Ladies Cup competition by beating Doncaster 3–1 in the final played before more than 2,000 people at the old Cobridge ground. Speaking to Arthur's youngest son, Peter, who claimed the charming distinction of having been one of the worst professional football players ever, I was told that family lore has it that the Stoke team were unbeaten in the five years of their existence. He also had memorabilia from a match the same year at St Andrew's Birmingham against St Helen's which drew a crowd of 40,000. In addition to the tour to Barcelona to play the French Femina team in 1923 that had been, in part, made possible by Arthur's experience with England, there are other colorful tales associated with the team; one player, Daisy Bates, 'daughter of a Hanford collier', later married Stoke City's goalkeeper, Bob Dixon. The team was disbanded in 1923, less, it seems, due to FA pressure than to a new contract for Arthur and development of Len's mercantile interests and not before they met Dick, Kerr on 22 September on the Horsfield Ground Colne, with the local brass band 'playing selections prior to the match and during the interval'. This is an area for considerable further work using local newspapers and oral history. The *Coventry Evening Telegraph* for 20 November 1989, for example, has Coventry City Ladies FC in the 1920s when the then Elizabeth Warren played hockey for Courtaulds, before the football team was formed, playing a few matches on Coventry City's ground and travelling to Stoke and Luton before the team dissolved. Known as Dot, on account of being the smallest member of the team (as the accompanying picture confirms), Elizabeth's sister Nellie was captain and her friend Sally Siddle (known as Vim) played as goalkeeper.

Part of the wider answer seems to be the pragmatism of the women's football teams which were closely involved with their local communities, which, in the 1920s and 1930s faced economic and social hardship. This effectively contained fundraising on smaller grounds but still sought to help alleviate whatever circumstance a women's match coincided with. In the case of some, it is clear that the cause prompted the match; in others, it may have been that the sporting contest bought some legitimacy by collecting funds for a charity which was selected as a secondary event. Against this background, the established infrastructures of the Association and League enabled them to be national institutions able to ride out those same difficulties. Also significant has been the hold over the Laws of the Game by the International Football Association Board (IFAB), which in effect meant that the world-wide rules of the Association code would be overseen by the British associations. The various relations between the FA and FIFA in the years 1904 to 1912 are too complex to detail here, and the issues were not primarily regarding the place of women in the sport. Briefly, against the declared FIFA statutes of recognizing only international states, Scotland, Ireland and Wales were admitted in 1910. The IFAB membership was comprised solely of the four British Associations until the Congress of 1912, when two FIFA members were invited onto the IFAB board. British control of the Laws of the Game as part of the exportation of a manly sport, as exemplified by gentlemanly conduct, was undoubtedly influential (whether the FA were members of

FIFA, had withdrawn on one of a number of occasions or were sanctioned as quasi affiliates, as happened in the next few years).

On a national scale, there was a broader move from 1921 to reinforce prewar patterns of the Association game and to extend the professional competition of the Football League. For example, the twin principles of ground enclosure and the right to charge for admission that related to Association and League football were a repeated concern of the FA, as evidenced by the minute books (if applied somewhat shambolically by some association affiliates) with which the non-League format of the women's games on borrowed sites did not sit easily. In a 1950s analysis of what might be now seen as the spirit of 'for the good of the game', Green wrote:

> Football because of its very popularity, is fraught with many dangers. It has always been, and perhaps always will be, something of a stamping ground for those who see in it an opportunity for commercial enterprise. It is against such temptations that the Association has always adopted a protective attitude, eager to prevent the game being brought into disrepute both by external and internal influences.[63]

The working women who made up the majority of the playing personnel do not appear to have benefited materially above or beyond the wage potential of their occupations at any one time. If the national leisure market which had been established by the end of the nineteenth century regained some of the patterned regularity by 1921, the Football League was also seeking to expand its operations. After the Football League's inaugural season with twelve clubs in the 1888–1889 season, the League had grown to a second division in 1892–1893, and two regional third divisions were added in the 1920–1921 season, bringing the total number of League clubs to eighty-eight.[64] Whether some of those in the women's football community had succumbed to temptation matters less than the protective attitude of the Association and the League officials. It is also worth remembering that by 1921 the Football Association had built up its own charitable activity since the Football National War Fund was set up in 1918. The minute books for the season 1921–1922 have details entitled Proceeds of Practice matches played in August as totalling £20,304 19s 2d from 259 clubs as diverse as Arnold St Mary's to West Ham United.[65] Extended, careful negotiation with the Inland Revenue as to what constituted a benevolent purpose can be seen from the summary in *Athletic News*:

> For years some clubs have been fighting the Inland Revenue officials on the question of deducting the amount due to the Football League Charity funds during war-time football, and the Manchester City Football Club, when the supervisor declined to allow the deductions, gave notice of appeal ... The commissioners held that if the contribution to charity had not been paid, matches could not have been played, and such contributions were therefore paid as a means of earning profits. It therefore followed according to law and decisions on the point, that such contributions were properly deducted by the

club from the income in order to arrive at the profits from which income tax should be charged.[66]

It appears that charitable fundraising was an elastic term that could also entail profit for those League clubs that took part, and it may be that part of the FA's defensive attitude involved benefiting from this pretext. This was not the only revenue stream to be safeguarded. The Rules Revision Committee of the FA, sitting on 23 January 1922, set the following guideline for the Association Challenge Cup Competition and the Amateur Challenge Cup Competition respectively:

Rule 30. For Footnote A substitute the following:

'All members, and also ladies and boys, must be charged for admission to ground, enclosure and stands in matches in all Cup Ties. The minimum admission (except to ladies and boys) to matches in the Qualifying Competition shall be fivepence including Entertainments Tax, and to matches in the Competition Proper, one shilling including Entertainments Tax. The price of admission for ladies and boys shall be mutually agreed between the competing clubs'.

Rules 14 and 31. Delete Rule 31. For the second sentence of rule 14 substitute 'the Club not having an enclosed ground where gate-money may be taken, or whose field of play is less than the minimum allowed by Rule 21, shall play on its opponent's ground'.

Consequently, these principles were being applied to a wide range of competitions and clubs under the control of the Football Association. A well-disposed reading of the situation would perhaps see women's events as one of many between 'scratch' teams and part of a maverick element from which the FA wished to distance itself. In a case of nearly but not quite, the ban for women's teams followed an opportunity for ground-sharing for Dick, Kerr women's team that could have imitated this enclosure and charging model and enabled them to further capitalize on their popularity. For example, at the beginning of 1920, Dick, Kerr and Co Ltd had bought the eighty-three acre Ashton Park site, known locally as 'Lively Polly Corner' after a popular brand of washing powder advertised there. Football Association Emergency Council minutes for the period 21 March to 22 April 1922 show that Dick, Kerr FC were 'informed that if women's football matches are played on its ground, clubs under the jurisdiction of the FA will not be allowed to play theron'.[67] This does seem to have been observed in spite of the company being willing for the team to use the Dick, Kerr name until 1926 (the company had changed its name from Dick, Kerr to English Electric in 1923), when they became Preston Ladies.

While there was broad reinforcement of the principles across the Association's interest, it *is* still clear that special case was made in issuing the ban on all women's games, not least because no substantiating evidence to support a view that there was misuse of funds or scandalous behaviour was brought. The minute books detail individual or scratch teams treated as distinct cases, not as a classification, as was applied to women's football. We know also that the breakaway of the Amateur

Football Association between 1907 and 1914 had given the FA confidence to pursue exclusionary tactics. Public enthusiasm for watching women's football declined but did not die altogether. In an early version of 'football isn't a matter of life and death, it's more important than that', we have:

> Women are as God made them, and those who recognise the relative parts of the scheme of creation will see that there are games suitable for each sex and those which can be adapted to both men and women while preserving the chief characteristic of each ... While considering this problem with every possible desire for the complete emancipation of woman—we believe that is the phrase—there can be no doubt in the mind of any sensible person that football is no more a ladylike recreation than boxing, wrestling, weight-lifting, and other strenuous pursuits ... Without wishing to be either paternal or narrow-minded, we hope that so far as football is concerned women will rest content with being enthusiastic spectators—if they are not playing a game which is for them more rational.[68]

The first film dated after the ban of Dick, Kerr in the Pathé collection is said to be set at the time of transition. *Playing Adam's Game* may have been edited and re-edited, possibly from *Eve's Film Review* and also from *Eve and the Noble Art* as it contains boxing alongside other supposed training activities, including riding bicycles, horseback riding, and playing leapfrog games. The novelty value of a group of young women performing quasi-athletic stunts for the camera is evident, but ambivalence over the exact date and context remain. There was a film made on Ashton Park, in the period before the ban became widespread, in conjunction with a letter written by the captain, Alice Kell, and published in the *Lancashire Daily Post* at the time, detailing the sporting prowess of the players. However, there is some cause for reservation because the hats appear to be a generous cut and some players have loose hair. Later that year the team wore more close-fitting hats before doing away with them altogether.[69] Whatever the Dick, Kerr players' intention in making it, the film also contrasts with other examples in the collection because of the prurient *mise en scene*. Perhaps influenced by the idea of unsuitability, the camera is peeping on the rough and tumble of the team, who conclude the film by sitting in a semicircle on the ground massaging their legs while a female trainer tends to each in turn. The women almost incidentally play a little football as a short closing phase. Whatever the attitude of the person behind the camera, we know that Dick, Kerr players had a rather more serious attitude to their football than this, as recorded by the other films. There is another example, also attributed to 1922, which could show a continued attempt to take on manly sports where the intertitle reads: 'We've heard a lot lately that certain sports are injurious to Eve. What about these boxing girls from Dick, Kerr's famous sports team ...? If the spectators at the Carpentier-Lewis fight had got as excited as these, Olympia would require a new roof.'[70] We see two players in football kit, supposedly boxing with each other whilst others look on and cheer in an overexcited manner. Whether this was intended as public relations for women's sport, caught an informal mood, or the players were flattered to be on camera, the intertitle of the first film sums up the voyeuristic mood: '"Weaker Sex?" said the Captain of the famous Dick, Kerr Women's Team. "Not much weakness about us." Watching their training, we agreed.' If the date is correct, it was the first of many publicity turns in the fifty-year life of the ban orchestrated by Alfred Frankland, including, on occasion, resorting to Shakespeare ('It is excellent to have a giant's strength but it is tyrannous to use it as so'), inviting twenty-one Preston doctors along to women's matches and involving local dignitaries, entertainers and professional sportsmen in fixtures. Whether the flourish was down to generous postmatch hospitality or warmth of feeling, the message was clear:

> The mayor (Ald. J Porter) looking spry after the first stretch of refereeing for ten years, rose and thanked the two managers of the teams, Mr Frankland and Mr Hunt and all the players for the splendid game. Commenting on the 'arrogant and old fashioned outlook of the Football Association' he said how much he appreciated their gesture for coming and playing. 'I should like to say further,' continued the Mayor vigorously, 'personally I hope you people will go ahead and fight the FA which is a narrow, bigoted authority. To one who has been in the game for 30 years I personally resent it'.[71]

The overtly altruistic nature of women's football continued as the spectacle diminished, so it is possible to find Bank Holiday matches 'in aid of the Rhyl War Memorial Hospital' in July 1921 and those between Preston and Manchester in Roundhay Park, Leeds that were part of Coronation celebrations in June 1953.[72] The lack of opportunity to host large crowds on enclosed grounds meant that the spectacle which had been an integral part of women's matches was lost. Without forming their own association, the remaining sixty or so women's teams were consigned to a more peripatetic existence: playing in considerably reduced surroundings, enabling them to raise smaller sums of money in front of fewer people in less controlled environments. It also raises questions as to whether those organizing and playing women's football had sufficient time and common interest to establish a women's association. A second association for women's football, the English Ladies FA, *was* formed, but only twenty-five clubs met in Bradford in 1921. Though the second meeting had sixty clubs, the decision to prevent any club affiliated with the association from playing against nonaffiliated teams effectively ended its appeal in 1922.

Pathé newsreel interest and postcard release did not end with the ban, nor did coverage in the local, national or sporting press. The *Football Special* newspaper available at Colindale Nos. 1–70 ranged from 10 September 1921 to 6 June 1923 and contains a column by 'The Football Girl', who charts the rise and fall of the game, including various women's teams, their support and featured pictures of them. In March 1922, a *Times* report indicates that the degree of civic recognition given to the players was not immediately affected: 'The Lord Mayor and the Lady Mayoress will receive the members of the French Ladies' Football Team at the Mansion House next Tuesday at 3.15.'[73] The following Wednesday, of some twenty-three photographs under the headline 'Royal Ceremony at Waterloo. The Mons Trial', two show the French women's football team. The first more celebratory image has as the subtitle 'French Women Footballers, who are now visiting this country from Paris, being entertained to tea yesterday by the Lord Mayor and Lady Mayoress of London at the Mansion House', and the second, more sombre, 'A French Tribute—Mme. Courand-Morris, the Captain of the Paris women's football team, placing a wreath on the Cenotaph yesterday.'[74] There is also, for example, a celebratory air to the film of 18 September 1922, which shows the women on deck as the SS Montclare of the Canadian Pacific Line undertakes its maiden voyage from Liverpool; the full title reads 'GOOD LUCK GIRLS! Dick, Kerr's Ladies Football Team leave for Canada Tour'. By 1924 many team members had moved to Whittingham Hospital Lunatic Asylum, where the sister of Alfred Frankland was Ward Sister. Florrie Redford, Lily Lee, Jessie Walmsley, Lily Parr, Lizzy Ashcroft, Lydia Ackers and Lily Martin all became nurses and were later joined by other players, who were found jobs, including a young Nancy 'The Canonball' Thompson, who went on to work in mental health after she retired from football. Another article in *The Times* for 12 January 1924 for example has as the twin headlines 'The Loss of the L 24' and 'The Prince of Wales in Paris'. Amidst photographs of these and other events is a centrally placed photograph with the description 'FOOTBALL BY NIGHT—Dick, Kerr Ladies' Association Football team played a charity match at night by means of a new system of lighting invented by Siemens and the English Electric Lamp Company.'[75] Perhaps even more intriguingly, it would seem that Alice Woods had never worked for Dick, Kerrs, that she had played for them while living at home in St Helens. There is much more around the story of Dick, Kerr to be developed and also for related teams; for example, it seems that occasionally St Helen's Ladies played against Billinge men on the Pilkington sports ground in the early 1920s.

There are umpteen Pathé newsreels made during the ban. One reel, for example, shows the Miners Wives' final of November 1926, presumably played in aid of their striking husbands. [76] One, taken in 1931, has the subheading 'Aren't Girls Wonderful? Despite continuous rain and ground ankle deep in mud not a single one retired in vigorous game won by Quaker Girls 3 Darlington, Durham.'[77] This does seem to have been an area of some continued activity for the whole of that decade, as it is possible to find fixtures of store, factory and representative teams as far back as 1930 with crowds of 10,000 spectators. In 1936 the Darlington versus Terry's Chocolate factory game was recorded, and in 1939 for example, York and Stockton ladies football teams played a charity match at Hungdens Lane for the National Union of Railwaymen's Orphans. The fact that women's football remained a problem, albeit less pressing than some others, is reinforced in FA Council minutes of 1936 and 1946, while the council chose to confirm the ban again in 1963.[78] Though seriously affected by rationing during World War Two, around the period 1947 to 1950 there were at least seventeen women's teams (including Barnsley, Blackpool, Bolton, Corinthians, Kent, Lancashire, Manchester, Stoke, Weymouth, Wythenshawe) playing regularly, and international matches were revived. A policy of barring those involved with women's football also continued; for example Referee E Turner was suspended by Kent County Football Association for refusing to quit as the manager and trainer of the Kent Ladies team.

In addition to the other public sources, the memorabilia associated with the games provides links with wider social occasions, such as the Festival of Britain Ladies' Championship, and with the presentation of the players to their sporting public.

### Corinthian Ladies (Manchester)

Claire Mason. Age 16. A very efficient goalkeeper, 'Lofty'. Has a style like Frank Swift.

Jean Collier. Age 17. 'Smiler' uses her head to save her legs. Is a very good and intelligent positional player.

Joan Clarke. Age 18. 'Clarkie' never gets worried, plays an unorthodox style. Is hard to get past.

Irene Hebron. Age 18. 'Legs' is an ardent Denis Compton and Arsenal fan. Is a fine exponent of the sliding tackle.

Muriel Jones. School Teacher and good attacking footballer. Could give lessons to many in this art.

Kathleen Lear. Age 15. Little 'Kathie' is regarded as one of the best ever. She is a schoolgirl champion runner.

Alice Elliott. Age 17. Known as 'Twinkle toes' is very tricky with a splendid shot. She is an ardent player and lives for the game.

Doris Ashley. Age 27. 'Skiper is captain and schemer in chief. Always seems to be where the ball is. Odeon lady footballer of 1950 gold medal award. Played for England and France.

Dorothy Allcock. Age 19. 'Dot' is a very cool headed player and holds her forwards together excellently and yet when occasion arises goes well on her own.

Barbara Large. Age 16. 'Babs' is a box of tricks and has a terrific shot. Can play equally well on either wing.

Edna Broughton. Age 20. 'Nippy' is undoubtedly the best inside left in the game so far as ladies are concerned. Has played for England.[79]

One aspect of this particularly of note relates to the use of space. These women players often had disciplinarian managers and chaperones plus trainers and physios. Their every move was therefore subject to scrutiny in training and play, and they were required to be modest in their behaviour at social functions when representing the team. However, the oral-history accounts of their time on the team buses and the stops made at pubs and so on indicate a protected space for behaviour that might be considered inappropriate in other contexts. There are some wonderful photographs, for example, in Joan Whalley's scrapbook of social and sporting activities, and it would be good to know more about this aspect of the players' experience. The legacy of not having space of their own other than in this rather temporary way has no doubt added to their lack of remembrance.

On an international scale, the Corinthians games from 1957 referred to in the Introduction, in which an England XI played against West Germany in Stuttgart, are also on film and show large crowds. Some of the early conventions of the women's matches are present, such as Bert Trautmann kicking off the game. However, it is worth noting that the description provided is, on the one hand, extremely patronizing and on the other not really representative of what happens on the clip. Whether it has been edited at a later date by an unsympathetic hand or reflects antipathy at the time, it was at least thought to be sufficiently newsworthy to have been recorded. By 1961 primary school teachers were seen to be a useful part of a supposedly more progressive FA policy, but with limits, as 'The instructional committee decided that should LEAs organise courses of instruction for women teachers in primary schools, the FA should provide coaches. Women teachers, however, should not be allowed to qualify under the FA scheme.'[80] The status of football as a profession altered immeasurably following the removal of the maximum wage in 1961 and the eventual abolition of the 'retain and transfer' system from 1963. As stars grew to become media personalities, the 1966 World Cup victory in England no doubt sparked some female interest. For example, the stewardesses of the Queen Mary team played a Royal Exchange team that year which reached national television as the Mayor of Southampton was introduced to the Queen Mary team by the captain Margot Fruauf at Southampton Sports Centre.[81] However, the importance of 1966 shouldn't be overstated. Manchester Corinthians, formed in 1949, had disbanded by the early 1970s. Fodens played since 1955. Stewarton Thistle first played in 1961. The last game of a depleted Preston (Dick, Kerr) came in 1965. EMGALS began in early 1967, the Doncaster Belles in 1969.

With television came new opportunities. 'Opportunity Knocks' was a popular Saturday evening talent show in the 1960s, and the FA Council was sufficiently aware of women's teams and tournaments, such as host Hughie Green's the Butlins' Games and the Deal Tournament organized by Arthur Hobbs, which disregarded the ban. The establishment of the Women's Football Association (WFA) meant that women's play was respectable enough by 1 December 1969 for the FA to rule:

Ladies Football—recommendation to delete decision of council in 1921 (and confirmed by the council of 1963) and that ladies' football no longer be considered to be classed as unaffiliated football and that any ladies' team which wished to affiliate to county Association might be permitted to make such an application - matter to be deferred.[82]

The tentative nature of this phrasing and its deferral are repeated themes: in a letter to the Executive Committee the following year, the WFA asked for closer links, but the response from the Executive Committee in January 1971 noted that the Committee 'did not feel that the time was opportune for any formal association to be established with that association', though they were prepared to give advice on medical and coaching matters.[83] Events effectively overtook the inhospitable home association in July of that year when UEFA decided by a 31–1 majority to recommend that members take control of women's football (the opposing association was, notoriously, Scotland). From there, cautious development, punctuated by the Theresa Bennett appeal in 1978, followed until the FA took control in 1993 and the title WFA was no longer used. The loss of name also implied a loss of ownership as the more democratic aspects of the women's association were changed to regional leagues applying centrally-directed FA policy, and several administrators were lost to the sport as a result of this.

A televised Women's World Cup based in England and backed by Moore, Hurst, Peters and Ramsey sponsored to the tune of £150,000 in 1973 was also declined as financially risky and premature in the development of the sport. The tournament, which Hobbs (who some called 'the father of women's football') tentatively supported and WFA members sympathetic to FA policy opposed, would certainly have presented women's elite play as entertainment potentially to millions of viewers with the backing of national football heroes. However, concern had grown as the result of the 1971 Women's World Cup competition in the Aztec stadium when teams from Mexico, Argentina, Denmark, Italy, the United Kingdom and France had contested matches in front of crowds of at least 40,000. The participation by Chiltern Valley as an England representative team in Mexico had been rewarded with the expulsion of the whole East Midlands Ladies Alliance (of which Chiltern Valley were the champions) from the WFA. Pat Gregory's letter to the FA outlining the proposal from August 1973 to July 1974 initially proposed this as a women's European Competition of four countries (already referred to in the Introductory chapter) and is significant on several counts:

> Should the first competition prove successful I know that Viners would be prepared to consider extending the event to further seasons and to encompass more countries. It might appear that the Women's FA is once again 'running' before it has properly learned to 'walk' but I hope that this will be more accurately discerned as an eagerness to help the sport progress.[84]

Somewhat cautiously, the letter heading has the WFA 'Recognised by The Football Association' and reflects the fact that it wasn't formally affiliated until 31 May 1984.[85] However, the discussion then takes a more interesting turn, and excerpts from Pat Gregory's letter are worth quoting at length.

The main purpose of this letter is, however, to seek clarification of FIFA's regulations governing a World Cup Competition. We have recently been approached by a group of businessmen who wish to put a considerable sum of money at our disposal for the organisation of a World Cup Competition for women. In view of the fact that they anticipated financing the whole project and then, of course, taking any profit which accrued, I sought the advice of The Football Association on this delicate matter. The rules quite clearly state that no match shall be organised for the personal gain of an individual or commercial concern and this would thus seem to block any possibility of the scheme progressing.

Perhaps you could clarify for me the international rules governing the organisation of such a competition. It might even be an idea if you could provide me with a copy of the FIFA rules and Regulations which I am sure would be invaluable help to my Association in the future.

FIFA has until now taken only a passing interest in women's football but I believe the time has come for your Body [*sic*] to take a longer and closer look at this fast-growing sport. There is scarcely a country in Europe which is not experiencing a steady growth in the number of clubs, and I am in correspondence with contacts in Australia, Singapore, South Africa, Canada and the USA. What, if anything, does FIFA plan to do about staging a General Conference of its members who have a specific interest in women's football? Additionally when does FIFA think it can contemplate a competition for women's national teams?[86]

The reply attempted to disassociate the commercial from the regulatory functions of the federation and firmly passes the matter elsewhere. This is somewhat disingenuous as an argument, as topflight football is all about commercial exploitation and Käser was writing during the World Cup competition in West Germany; the letter was set also in the context of the decline in a gentlemanly ethos in elite football as fewer national teams had supported the UEFA amateur cup. What is clear is that just as the level of interest from a paying public in the 1920s for women's football caused concern for the football authorities, so did the degree of commercial appeal fifty years later.

May I inform you that all organisations affiliated directly or indirectly to a National Football Association in membership with FIFA are bound by the existing FIFA Statutes and Regulations. This means that the Football Association alone would be entitled to organise or approve the Women's World Cup. FIFA is strongly opposed to any intervention by business people who try to earn money by organising football competitions for women. You may know that quite a large number of National Associations in membership with FIFA organise Cups and Championships for female football teams.

However, I must insist that those concerned adhere strictly to the existing Regulations as FIFA is interested in the game and not in the commercial exploitation of female football teams. I know that approximately four years ago some businessmen organised a so-called 'World Cup' for female football teams in Mexico, but the main purpose was to earn money and not to promote female football.[87]

The correspondence ends with a polite acknowledgement from Pat Gregory that the response 'was not unexpected as we had anticipated this would be the official view of FIFA'.[88] A favourable analysis of this could see it as part of a policy of shelter developed by FIFA, challenged by the opening of sports borders and the business of football. An unsympathetic view could point out that it did not reflect existing elements of female play; for example, Scotland, one of the later national associations to recognize women's football, had two professional women players and a thriving league system before the football association relented grudgingly to accept the fact. Aspects in the correspondence indicate FIFA's concern about commercialism, whereas the women's football community, albeit in a very diplomatic manner, favoured graded financial viability.

Though the proposal of a World Cup was first written about briefly by Sue Lopez (specifically with regard to how the voting system used by the Football Association used a system incorporating a Scottish representative to turn a majority of approval into one of refusal), it wasn't apparent that FIFA and UEFA had been asked to support the venture extensively until this paper trail was examined. Naturally, what the effect would have been can now only be guessed. Had some kind of sponsorship deal been agreed in 1974, in what ways would development of the women's game as a business be affected today? Were FIFA concerned by the unofficial Women's World Cup in Mexico to the extent that they sought to prevent women's football from exploitation? Were they more concerned to regulate and control women's football, which was attracting commercial interest in several regions in the world? Was a sports development model being employed whereby a mass of participation leads to a degree of commercial play? What Lopez shows is that the episode was a missed opportunity and that the rather short-sighted responses made by the authorities to the women who had managed to secure backing have repercussions to this day. Of course, the more salacious elements of the international showgirl tour and unofficial World Cup in Mexico, together with a certain reputation for women's football which led to games like that between the Grassmoor Golden Girls and Inkersall Frillies played at Chesterfield in July 1975, could have meant an unsavoury commercial future for the game.[89] This proposal, the Italian professional league, and subsequent 'world' cups in the 1970s and 1980s seem to have been relatively innocent competitive events. The response more bureaucratic fear of impropriety than any manifest scandal. A final attempt to plan the event for 1975 met difficulty with FA rules over the 'close' season before being sent away for consideration by committee; effectively stalling the proposal.[90]

At the time British women's teams were involved in extensive international competition, primarily, but not exclusively, involving European clubs. Between April and August 1973 the FA sanctioned thirty-four matches involving foreign clubs, including Amersham Angels versus DVSNE in Holland twice and Bollebygd WFC in England; Birmingham were hosted by Oxabacks TF Damlag and Dingtuna FC, two Swedish sides; Blewbury Ladies had two fixtures with KMVZ of Holland;

Coventry Bantams arranged three matches in France; East Kent Ladies played Rhade and Marl in two separate ties in Germany; Emgals played FC Bavos three times; Evesham North End hosted Metze; Farley United played at DJK Borussia-Scholven in Germany; Kay's Ladies competed with both Halma and FC Bavos in England; Kent Women's League hosted DKF Eintracht Erle 1928 three times; Lodge Park Ladies FC travelled to Eitrach Trier in Germany and Royal Club Arlonaise in Belgium; Neilsen Ladies visited DVC Elisabeth in Holland; Wanderers Ladies FC attended the Royal Gossiles Tournament in Belgium; Wantage and Watford played KMVZ and Helmond 1899, respectively, in Holland.[91] By 1974 there had been a tournament run by Ruelle Ladies in Mallorca that involved Bath, Beccles, Bedworth Ladies, Bletchingley YCFC, Bracknell Bullits, Corinthian Nomads, Coventry Bantams, Feltham United, Fodens and Southampton, as well as games in Belgium, France, Germany and Luxembourg and 'unofficial' tournaments in the US and Hong Kong.[92]

As the Introduction has shown, the 1973–1974 example in England was not the only proposal that could have broken the sport into those new markets that FIFA now wishes the women's game to pursue. It would also have created a World Cup tournament seventeen years before the sports' governing body hosted a world championship for women. Ironically, the 1991 tournament was entitled as contested 'for the M&Ms Cup', by which time FIFA had overcome at least some of their commercial squeamishness. Even if your opinion still tends towards a view of the federations' actions as motivated by recalcitrance rather than malice, the women's football community of the 1970s and 1980s had more ambitious, timely and innovative plans than the bureaucracies created to regulate men's football with which they were obliged to integrate. The significance of external pressure and the activism on behalf of the women's football community is further indicated by a series of meetings around the years 1980, 1981 and 1982 which led directly to the first UEFA tournament for women but more belatedly and indirectly to a Women's World Cup.

In spite of the existing international network, paranoia over commercialization took precedence over whether women's football could support a world-class tournament. A summary of the contradictory attitudes is again worth quoting in full as it shows the thinking behind the decisions reached, in addition to the recommendations themselves.

> It was noted that invitational tournaments were taking place in various parts of the world and details were available to the Committee of a tournament to take place in Taiwan in October 1981. This tournament was by invitation to National associations but was entitled the 'Women's World Invitational Football Tournament'. The group considered it incorrect to use the expression 'World' within the title and that such invitational tournaments should do no more than refer to 'international' tournaments.
>
> There is no one reason why women's football is not developed in certain areas although in many countries it is for religious reasons and therefore any further developments in the foreseeable future are unlikely.

It was the unanimous opinion of the group that a world women's football tournament run by FIFA would be premature at this time. The game is still developing and it appears that in most countries the attraction to the public is still very limited and therefore financial problems would exist.

Another problem is that it would be a world tournament that in no sense would embrace countries from all Confederations as there are many areas without any women's football, as referred to above.[93]

Minutes of the meeting of the 1981 FIFA Technical Committee indicate that the issue of women's football and competitions was discussed by Group A, the English-speaking group, comprised of O. Oyo (Nigeria), Ted Croker (England), E. De Moraes, O. Al-Saad, R. Ruhee and M. Marotzke. The report produced confirms this in its title, Meeting of FIFA Technical Committee 17 and 18, 1981 Group A (English), which then produced a list of recommendations. The first point of analysis is to reinforce that the rather disparaging view of the Football Association towards women's football has had a disproportionately damaging effect at key points. It would overstate the case to say that the 1981 meeting seems to have been one of those points, though Ted Croker was secretary to the FA at the time of the 1973–1974 correspondence, because events forced a change of policy. It may well have been that the Spanish-, French- and Dutch- or German-speaking groups were similarly unenlightened. However, it isn't clear whether the matter was allocated to the English-speaking group because the idea of a Women's World Cup seems to have originated there or because their response in 1974 would dictate the outcome of this discussion. We can make educated assessment of their general attitude nevertheless.

The group believes that tournaments within the Confederations should be encouraged wherever possible and the progress of these tournaments would give a clear indication or [sic] whether or not a world tournament for women, under FIFA's control, would be worthwhile. Such tournaments within the Confederations could be developed within the next few years which would mean that if they are successful a women's world cup would not be unduly delayed.

Although the group was briefed only to discuss women's football, it was impossible to ignore the possible proliferation of world tournaments and the over-expansion that may result. We now have the Olympic Tournament, The World Cup, The World Youth Championship, a possible Under-16 World Tournament and an indoor World Tournament and therefore the development of a women's world tournament must be considered within this total framework. In addition in certain Confederations major tournaments have developed, such as the European Nations' Cup. It should also be noted that within the continental Confederations Club Championships between countries have assumed much greater importance and therefore greater thought must be given to extensions of international competitions.

The group unanimously agreed that women's football should come under the jurisdiction of the National associations. Similarly mixed football, i.e. with men and women in the same team or men's teams against women's teams should not be permitted. This would imply that women should benefit from training and coaching facilities run on a national or local basis within countries.

It was noted that in many countries that the influence of women in administration was proving of considerable value.[94]

Given that the prevention of commercial exploitation had been a prime motivator in 'protecting' the women's game, the idea that 'the attraction to the public is very limited and therefore financial problems would exist' seems to be based on the idea that there was a finite pool of support that 'over-expansion' might risk. Most amusing or annoying, depending on your outlook, is the juxtaposition of the attitude that women players should be kept separate and not be led to infer that they had a right to resources, while the contribution of female administrators had been of 'considerable value'.

The most significant pattern for participation is that in one decade the number of clubs affiliated to the WFA increased sixfold from 44 clubs in 1969 to 300 clubs with 6,000 players in 1979. The 1991–1992 *WFA News* development report says, 'Such is the growing interest in women's soccer that by the end of this next season we could be looking at a total of 500 affiliated clubs' with around 9,000 players. Particular questions are in part raised by the unfashionable status of women's sport and football particularly in the UK. Compared with other leisure activities and those involving physical exercise specifically, team sports such as football, cricket and rugby remain numerically and symbolically minority activities for women and girls even if we accept participation figures of 131,000. Compared to netball, the traditional favourite sport of girls which has 56,000 registered players, football continues to grow at a fantastic rate, since becoming the top female sport in 2002.'[95] The 'fastest growing' tag is part of the PR campaign to try to make the sport seem part of a new cultural trend, as are equally clumsy campaigns about women putting the 'beautiful' into the game used in Euro 2005. Yet, as any Saturday or Sunday demonstrates anywhere in the UK, the participation of the mass of players of whatever age or gender has little to do with spin and lots to do with parks and pitches, enduring the weather, volunteers acting as everything from referee to provider of hot beverages, cyclists or dogwalkers who become spectators for a while plus other ad hoc components too numerous to mention, including travel and family arrangements, the social organization of the weekend and, more recently, fear of paedophiles in youth sport.

It seems that the mass of amateur participation is consequently hard to tackle as an object of research and is itself relatively unfashionable as an academic topic compared to work on elite professional elements, especially the Premiership and moral panics about hooligans. Isolating women's and girls' participation is then, in a sense, a rather convenient way of looking at an aspect of this bigger picture. It also deals with a cohort of players who are systematically given uneven access to resources and for whom the unfashionable nature of their enthusiasm makes the do-it-yourself nature of the organization more pronounced. While developing an uneasiness about using the term 'women's football' as a way of perhaps reinforcing the use of the gender difference of which I'm critical, its continued use here is intended to reflect the way in which women and girls have been identified as a distinct group rather than to support the use of that distinction.

The confused but persistent stereotypes that a female football player is demonstrating masculine tendencies (if she's skilful) and is doomed by biology (if she isn't) is slow to change even in the context of the recent UEFA competition in the North East, which received little media support once England were out of the competition. The contempt shown to English female footballers simultaneously trivializes their sporting accomplishments and insists on the male player as the object of masculine desire. Indeed this seemed to be implicit in the 2005 PR campaign surrounding the UEFA tournament about The Beautiful Game. Thankfully, though, the 'ubiquitous ponytail', a longtime FIFA symbol of women's tournaments, was not uniformly worn by all of England's players (or any other teams) as the cultural and racial reality of the female football population presented itself in a wider mix.

Disparities in the treatment of men and women in sport generally and in football particularly may be relatively innocuous compared to other inequalities that women face, but the very every-dayness of sport in our lives and common-sense ideas of how this developed serves to disguise the anachronism. During the conference surrounding the UEFA championships, the media found it incredible that in football as a professional sport, an industry, an educational specialism and so forth, women's opportunities at the highest level are limited. The questions from journalists centred on the tired use of the average man and woman as comparators, the relative physical weakness of women, their recent interest in team sport and so forth. Emails and texts centred on three issues; the majority suggested that adult mixed play was an equality too far, summed up by one who begged, 'Please leave at least our football women-free' and the (dim)wit who equated it as a sporting spectacle to 'monkey tennis'; a second cohort suggested a partial acceptance of mixed football at junior level with varied age limits and a final (very small) minority supported the idea of women's equity as a concept even if untenable in the present. So, what to conclude about being seen as an out-of-touch academic who was using football to make a political point?[96]

The unease between the theorists of sport and the ordinary players is a tension that there remains some way to go to resolve. Instead, the intention has been to capture some detail of players' experiences and to discuss this difference against the backdrop of surrounding factors which bear upon the creation and understanding of those subjectivities in the history of association football. There was a methodological as well as personal choice in beginning with people in *A Game for Rough Girls* and moving on to documentation and artefact in *A Beautiful Game*. Participant observation at everything from league meetings to tournaments to FIFA symposia to England training camps suggested a transience that informs actions that is crucial to encapsulate as an example of 'history from below'. It hopefully interrogates examples of 'history from above' as represented by the archival material that seems to offer clear answers. As an example, four responses to the relatively straightforward question 'Why do you play football?' indicate the motivations of women players are diverse, but engaged:

> Taking the ball away from a very skilled player—whoever—just to knock them down a notch is good for me because I learned to watch the ball ... but it's not the best. The footwork is good, if I can pull off a skill move, especially in a game and I scored last week with a little reverse pass—I've bored my family with it all week—like this (demonstrates). I got man of the match, well women of the match ... or player of the game ... whatever! Scoring goals is the best because its creative—I just see defence as stopping someone else be creative so it's not as much fun.
>
> (Andrea, 18)

> It's demanding on my body—even if a player is not skilful there are so many of us out there. My game is all about 110% which I know makes me sound like some kind of nerd but I'm running hard! The pace, lots of running around, that's why I like to play! I'm not skilful, I used to do aerobics and stuff ... but chasing that little white ball is so much more fun.
>
> (Maggie, 30)

> I love the patterns. I first used to go and watch Chelsea under Gullit and Vialli—it was all about patterns even if they lost. I'm not so sure now but then definitely and it has affected my game to try and see the patterns forming—not just who has individual skill or a bit of flair. After all it's a team game and some good players hog the ball. I'm looking to pass to space, to change the play. I have a tick list in my head to achieve each game and I want to change the pattern successfully just once. So play-making is my buzz.
>
> (Jas, 25)

> Well, it was a lot more fun when we played for fun, if you see what I mean! Because we got together to play our daughters in a friendly and they were only something like twelve and still playing junior football. So some mums got together and a few female relatives, friends or what-have-you and we played on astroturf just in our trainers ... even though some were lesbian mums, partners, or single parents or marrieds—it was just a laugh because the kids were our focus. Kind of like a joint interest. We liked being a women-only club at that stage because it suited everyone and the politics weren't too ... but now we have some want no men, some want their boyfriends to coach, someone's dad's got a big mouth ... it all got a bit serious and competitive.
>
> (Ronda, 29)

Oral history and ethnographic methods developed to complete *A Game for Rough Girls* helped to inform this project, but, as the focus was on international comparisons, the framework entailed a need to interrogate evidence in documented collections affecting the localized and specific issues.

In the case of the WFA, individuals were key to getting access to the material, as it remains uncollected for academic and wider use for the time being. The new material led to a greater sympathy and understanding of those administrators working in the 1970s and 1980s, as the section on the development of a Women's World Cup indicates. Given the developments in other nations and the wish to be seen as legitimate, it's perhaps more likely that the WFA would be prepared to moderate their ambitions, but this, combined with other factors did lead to something of a stall in female participation mid-1980s and the delay in fostering international competition for women. The material itself, when combined from the different sources, is of sufficient weight to provide new insights into the role of the WFA in international competition. Much remains to be uncovered. In particular, Colin Aldis has lent material from the British Universities sports files from the 1980s onwards, and quite why education has been so slow to support women's football is in need of study itself. In contrast with the representations and perspectives which English society has of women football players, including views of players and administrators, now held in centralized archives such as the National Football Museum, the methodology reflects the topic itself in that still more data remains in private collections. How then may we help academic and generalist researchers of the topic in future to democratize the subject?

Drawing the chapter to a conclusion just as the women's game looked set to take off in the 1980s in some fundamental ways leaves key events in the history of association football for women in this case study and seeks to raise remaining research questions: What constitutes female identity as it relates to women who play Association football Britain? How has the identity of women players been culturally constructed in images, artefacts and texts and through the various processes of self-fashioning? What roles have these objects and processes played in defining women players in society, in how women have been 'pictured' historically and how they are perceived today? What have been the roles played by material culture and representation in defining our understanding of women's football in general?

A notable element of English social life at the end of the twentieth and into the twenty-first centuries has been the use of the Internet. Between mid-1993 and mid-1995, the number of Web servers—the computers that house Web sites—jumped from 130 to 22,000.[97] By 1996, Yahoo counted 873 US history Web sites in an incomplete census; seven years later, an even less complete tally returned almost ten times as many. A search on Google for UK history sites alone in November 2005 returned 8,520,000 sites.[98] These results reveal a deep and wide fascination with history among the Web-browsing public. The final research question of this conclusion therefore is how we can use digital media and computer technology to democratize history—to incorporate multiple voices, reach diverse audiences, and encourage popular participation in presenting and preserving the past of women's participation in association football.

Would it be possible to create a nationwide or even an international network to collect the oral histories and mementos of women football players? Professional archivists complain that many so-called Web sites are not archives at all because they lack 'provenance,' that is, a firm custody of a coherent body of materials since their origin. Instead, their creators have assembled them, sometimes carefully and other times haphazardly, from diverse sources. Whatever the view, one could arguably include almost every type of historical document on women's football, including books and other printed texts, manuscripts, programmes, motion pictures, photographs, prints and sound recordings. The project could exploit two intrinsic advantages of the digital medium: accessibility and searchability. The ability of digital searching to turn up previously hidden riches applies particularly to records that contain large amounts of detailed information with no easy way to find specific pieces of data. The fever to bring the primary sources of the past online that began in the mid-1990s has infected many people who think differently about documents than librarians and archivists. Collections focus on a particular historical topic in order to make documents available online even if those artefacts don't necessarily have a shared 'provenance'. The historical aspects show why there has been no common association in the manner of a traditional archive.[99] Private collections often mix published and unpublished materials in ways that 'official' archives avoid. They have been valuable in unearthing a range of detail such as the names of people and groups in some of the anonymous photos and newsreels still in search of attribution. Put simply, much of the information base for this history lies not in the public but in the private and familial domain. Potentially, this also has implications for other aspects of the National Game as it has been played by amateurs and professionals, the way it has been made and refashioned. Depending on your view of the Internet as fundamentally democratic or as undiscriminating, that submerged world of voluntarism that is so much part of our national sporting life could at least in part be made more evident by this means.

## Notes

1. *Penny Illustrated,* 23 February 1895, p. 10; spelling and punctuation as the original; my parentheses.
2. 'Ladies' Football', *The Times,* 25 March 1895, p. 12.
3. J. Caudwell, 'Women's Football in the United Kingdom: Theorizing Gender and Unpacking the Butch Lesbian Image', *Journal of Sport and Social Issues,* 23, no. 4 (1999): 390–403; J. Caudwell, 'Women's Experiences of Sexuality within Football Contexts: A Particular and Located Footballing Epistemology', *Football Studies,* 5 (2002): 24–45; J. Harris, 'Playing the Man's Game: Sites of Resistance and Incorporation in Women's Football', *World Leisure,* 43 (2001): 22–29; J. Harris, 'The Image Problem in Women's Football', *Journal of Sport and Social Issues,* 29, no. 2 (2005): 184–197; C. Mennesson and J. Clement, 'Homosociability and Homosexuality: The Case of Soccer Played by Women',

*International Review for the Sociology of Sport,* 38, no. 3 (2003): 311–330; S. Scraton, J. Cauldwell and S. Holland, ' "Bend It Like Patel': Centring "Race", Ethnicity and Gender in Feminist Analysis of Women's Football in England', *International Review for the Sociology of Sport,* 40, no. 1 (2005): 71–88.

4. See for example J.M. Henry and H.P. Comeaux, 'Gender Egalitarianism in Co-Ed Sport: A Case Study of American Soccer', *International Review for the Sociology of Sport,* 34, no. 3 (1999): 277–290, for discussions of gendered terms in a mixed team and a critique of 'American exceptionalism'.

5. Geoffrey Green, *A History of the Football Association* (London: Naldrett, 1953); N. Fishwick, *English Football and Society: 1910–1950* (Manchester: Manchester University Press, 1989); J. Walvin, *The People's Game: The History of Football Revisited* (London: Mainstream Publishing, 1994); D. Birley, *Sport and the Making of Britain* (Manchester: Manchester University Press, 1995).

6. T. Mason, *Association Football and English Society 1863–1915* (Brighton: Harvester, 1983); R. Holt, *Sport and the British: A Modern History* (Oxford: Oxford University Press, 1989); D. Russell, *Football and the English: A Social History of Association Football in England 1863–1995* (Preston: Carnegie, 1997).

7. Christiane Eisenberg, Pierre Lanfranchi, Tony Mason and Alfred Wahl, *100 Years of Football: The FIFA Centennial Book* (London: Weidenfeld and Nicholson, 2004), p. 18.

8. For a revisionist view of the role of the public schools in the creation of the modern game subtitled 'The Untold Story' see A. Harvey, *Football: The First Hundred Years* (New York and Oxon: Routledge, 2005).

9. Eisenberg et al., *100 Years of Football,* p. 21.

10. Followed by the English Schools Football Association in 1904 and a national knockout competition from 1905.

11. For seventy years the organisation pursued a consistent policy of schoolboy promotion before a misunderstanding about the wording of the 1975 Sex Discrimination Act led administrators to consult legal experts about whether mixed football was required by law. Goodger and Auden letter to English Schools FA, for example, suggests: 'It does occur to me, that there must be in existence and English Schools Football Association for schoolgirls, and I wonder if they are a registered charity.' I am indebted to Chief Executive John Read, who provided information from English Schools FA files, 16 July 2001.

12. This is a literature of some contention especially of bifurcation of codes, status rivalry and the civilizing process; see, for example, the debate in Eric Dunning, 'Something of a Curate's Egg: Comments on Adrian Harvey's "An Epoch in the Annals of National Sport"', *International Journal of the History of Sport,* 18, no. 4 (December 2001): 88–94; Adrian Harvey, 'An Epoch in the Annals of National Sport: Football in Sheffield and the Creation of Modern Soccer and Rugby', *International Journal of the History of Sport,* 18, no. 4 (December 2001): 95–116; Graham Curry, 'The Trinity Connection: An Analysis of the

Role of Members of Cambridge University in the Development of Football in the Mid Nineteenth Century', *The Sports Historian,* 2, no. 22 (2002): 46–68; Tony Collins, 'History, Sociology and the "Civilising Process"', *Sport in History,* 25, no. 2 (August 2005): 289–306; and Graham Curry, Eric Dunning and Kenneth Sheard, 'Sociological versus Empiricist History: Some Comments on Tony Collins's 'History, Sociology and the "Civilising Process"', *Sport in History,* 26, no. 1 (April 2006): 110–123.

13.  J. Roberts, '"The Best Football Team, the Best Platoon": The Role of the Football in the Proletarianization of the British Expeditionary Force 1914–1918', *Sport in History,* 26, no. 1 (April 2006): 26–46.

14.  The OED attributes 'socca' to E.C. Dowson in 1889, and John Hutchinson, 'Football in Edinburgh from 1880', British Society of Sports History Annual Conference, St Martin's College, Lancaster, September 2006, unpublished paper, discusses a gentleman's football club in Edinburgh from the 1820s to 1840s which had recently come to light.

15.  J. Mangan and R. Park (eds), *From 'Fair Sex' to Feminism: Sport and the Socialization of Women in the Industrial and Post-Industrial Eras* (London: Frank Cass, 1987); K. McCrone, *Playing the Game: Sport and the Physical Emancipation of English Women 1870–1914* (Lexington: University Press of Kentucky, 1988); P. Vertinsky, *The Eternally Wounded Woman: Women, Exercise and Doctors in the Late Nineteenth Century* (Manchester: Manchester University Press, 1990); A. Guttman, *Women's Sports: A History* (New York: Columbia University Press, 1991); S. Scraton, *Shaping up to Womanhood* (Bucks: Open University Press, 1992); J. Hargreaves, *Sporting Females: Critical Issues in the History and Sociology of Women's Sport* (London: Routledge, 1994); M. Polley, *Moving the Goal Posts: A History of Sport and Society since 1945* (London: Routledge, 1998); J. Hargreaves, *Heroines of Sport: The Politics of Difference and Identity* (London: Routledge, 2000).

16.  I could find three references which mention women in the 1895 Minute Book: two from the Emergency Committee minutes of 14 January to 4 February, one of which indicates consent given to a 'Match between Preston North End v. Blackburn Rovers for a benefit match in aid of the Widows and Orphans of Fleetwood Fishermen who lost their lives in gale of 22nd December' (*sic*) and another consents to a benefit match at 'Hull on 14th February for Widows and Orphans of Shipwrecked Fishermen'. The third is from the Emergency Committee of 5 April to 2 May 1895 under 'Other Decisions', where 'Miss A Matthews told that there was no objection to benefit matches for J. Gordon, of Preston North End F.C. if clubs or clubs take it up.'

17.  John Bailey, 'The Great Women's Match of 1895', *Soccer History* Issue 7 (Spring 2004): 36.

18.  Ibid.

19.  British Ladies Football Club programme, London, Mizen Printers, 23 March 1895.

20. Sheila Fletcher, *Women First: The Female Tradition in Engish Physical Education 1880–1980* (London and New Hampshire: Athlone Press, 1984), p. 1. The term is Eleanor Rathbone's; she asked whether were women 'to behave for ever like a little girl running behind her big brother and calling out, "Me too?" ', in Ray Strachey (ed), *Our Freedom and Its Results* (London, 1936), p. 57.
21. 'Ladies Football', *The Times,* 25 March 1895, p.12.
22. The tradition of the tomboy has elements dating back to the sixteenth century: 'A rude, boisterous, or forward boy; a bold or immodest woman; a girl who behaves like a spirited or boisterous boy; a wild romping girl; a hoyden': OED, at http://dictionary.oed.com/, accessed January 2006.
23. Green, *A History of the Football Association,* p. 534.
24. Again the context of this ruling is not clear, as the FA Minute Book for 1902 was missing from the collection at the time of my visits in 2005 and 2006.
25. *The Times,* 1 March 1909, ten reviews. Doxology, as a liturgical formula of praise to God, perhaps characterzed one college's effort in depicting a local rivalry of competing feminities and the football-playing collegettes as relatively avant-garde in their behaviour.
26. In 1910, she was to have a hit with 'Tillie's Nightmare', which Mack Sennett adapted to film as *Tillie's Punctured Romance* (1914), with Charles Chaplin.
27. REF: BP010114189045, 'Can Girls Play Soccer? Well—Ilford Representatives Give Good Display', London: Pathé PLC, 1 January 1914, at http://www.itnsource.com, accessed January 2006. Thanks to Larry McKinna, ITN's resident British Pathé expert, for clarifying this issue. It would appear that where films were classified well after the event without corroborating evidence, a nominal dating of 1 Jan was given. This film is dated between 1914 and 1918, as many were tiny fragments from uncategorized cans.
28. A. Melling, ' "Ray of the Rovers": The Working Class Heroine in Popular Football Fiction 1915–25', *International Journal of the History of Sport,* 16, no. 1 (April 1998); A. Melling, 'Cultural Differentiation, Shared Aspiration: The Entente Cordiale of International Ladies' Football 1920–45', *European Sports History Review,* 1 (1998); A. Melling, *Ladies Football: Gender and Socialisation of Women Football Players in Lancashire 1926–1960,* unpublished PhD dissertation, University of Central Lancashire, November 1999.
29. See for example the Imperial War Museum, Women's Work Collection, (IWM,WWC) MUN 24/6; MUN 24/15; 24/17.
30. Matt Taylor, *The Leaguers: The Making of Professional Football in England 1900–1939* (Liverpool: Liverpool University Press, 2005) for a discussion of this wider issue.
31. A. Gibson and W. Pickford (eds), *Association Football and the Men Who Made It,* 4 vols., London, 1906, especially W. McGregor, 'The Origin and Future of the Football League', in Gibson and Pickford (eds), *Association Football,* vol. 2.
32. See the Pathé newsreel collection at http://www.britishpathe.com/ to search the entire 3,500-hour British Pathé Film Archive which covers news, sport, social

history and entertainment from 1896 to 1970. See also the ITN collection for some of the same items but also additional footage at http://www.itnsource.com/, for example, REF: BP010119191045, 'Football Match between Handley Page Girls and Ladies Sterling Football Club', Ilford, Essex, 1 January 1919; REF:BGU407201275, 'Ladies at Darlington Quaker Girls v. Terry's Chocs' (*sic*), 6 May 1935; REF: BGY502140342, 'Britain Beat Germany 4–0 in European Championship in Berlin', 1 January 1957; REF: BGY503290098, 'The First International Show Girls Soccer Tournament Brazil', 10 August 1960; REF: 5160, 'The Grimethorpe Black Diamonds Ladies Soccer Club' (Yorkshire Television interview), 1 January 1968; REF: BGY509180617, 'Eire: Woman Footballer to Play in Belgium's Leading Ladies Team',14 January 1975.

33. See for example http://www.britishpathe.com, accessed January 2005.

34. W. Vamplew, in *Pay up and Play the Game: Professional Sport in Britain* (Cambridge: Cambridge University Press, 1988) p. 63. I am not of course suggesting that Dick, Kerr were professional players.

35. J. Hill, *Sport, Leisure and Culture in Twentieth-Century Britain* (Basingstoke: Palgrave, 2002), p. 3.

36. Ibid., pp. 59–74.

37. Reader-oriented criticism and reception theory came to prominence within Anglophone literary studies in the 1970s and have had a major influence on media, film and television studies. While the historian Jonathan Rose developed the idea of studying audiences as well as texts in 'Rereading the English Common Reader: A Preface to a History of Audiences', *Journal of the History of Ideas,* 53, no. 1 (March 1992): 47–70 and *The Intellectual Life of the British Working Classes* (New Haven, CT: Yale University Press, 2002), there is now a vast literature debating fundamental questions about the canon, stylistics, and reader/audience response including in cyberspace, for example, K. Hellekson and K. Busse, *Fan Fiction and Fan Communities in the Age of the Internet* (Jefferson, NC, and London: McFarland, 2006).

38. Barbara Jacobs, *Dick Kerr's Ladies* (London: Constable and Robinson, 2004).

39. See http://www.bbc.co.uk/radio4/womanshour, 2 September 2004, BBC, Woman's Hour interview with some of the post–World War Two Dick, Kerr players, accessed 12 January 2005.

40. *The Times,* 18 December 1917, Personal column.

41. For those interested in pursuing the various local teams there is a wealth of articles in regional newspapers; see for example 'Sportsman's Parade XLVIII: Mr Len Bridgett', *Stoke Evening Sentinel,* 22 January 1955: 'with the help of Mrs Bridgett and other members of the family, he formed the Stoke Ladies Football Club, which remained undefeated in its five years' existence, and won the English cup in 1922'; and 'Here and There: Team of the 1920s'; *Coventry Evening Telegraph,* 20 November 1989, covering the career of the Coventry City Ladies FC including player names, family relationships and contact details.

42. *The Times,* 3 January 1921, p. 7.
43. 'Ladies at Football England v France by a Special Correspondent', *The Times,* 7 May 1920, p. 6.
44. Gail Newsham, *In a League of Their Own!* (Chorley: Pride of Place, 1994), pp. 51–53.
45. 'Football by Night', *The Times,* 12 January 1924 (captioned photograph of the event).
46. Born Elinor Maud Dawe, Retford enjoyed a varied career that included singing at nearly every music hall of note in the United Kingdom, playing Prince Fortune in *Cinderella* at the London Opera House, being principal boy at La Scala and making a tour of South Africa in the 1930s; *The Times,* 30 June 1962, p. 10 (Obituaries).
47. *The Times,* 29 October 1975, p. 16 (Obituaries).
48. V. Toulmin, 'Traveling Shows and the First Static Cinemas', *Picture House,* no. 21 (Summer 1998): 5–12; see also J. Wilkinson, 'Early Experience with a Kinematograph Machine', *Kinematograph and Lantern Weekly,* 8 (March 1917): 16, as kinema operators and press photographers were at the matches.
49. John Adderley, 'Women's Football', *BBC Nation on Film,* London, 10 November 2006.
50. See Green, *A History of the Football Association,* pp. 289–292.
51. Ibid., p. 289.
52. 'Traffic Alteration at Croydon', *The Times,* 5 February 1926, p. 19. In this case the trams ran for women only after the Manchester City v. Huddersfield match.
53. Newsham, *In a League of Their Own!,* seems to do this in particular with her analysis of Alfred Frankland and Dick, Kerr in general.
54. Minutes of the FA Council Meeting, 2 July 1921, punctuation as the original.
55. Minutes of the FA Emergency Committee, 23 August 1921 to 3 October 1921, Item 36.
56. Football Association Consultative Committee Item 5; Women's Football Matches, 5 December 1921.
57. 'News in Brief', *The Times,* 6 April 1921, p. 7.
58. 'To Play, or Not to Play', *Athletic News and Cyclists Journal,* 12 December 1921.
59. Her Majesty's Stationary Office, *The Sex Discrimination Act* 1975: 1 The stated aim was to establish 'An Act to render unlawful certain kinds of sex discrimination and discrimination on the ground of marriage, and establish a Commission with the function of working towards the elimination of such discrimination and promoting equality of opportunity between men and women generally.'
60. Equal Opportunities Commission, *Football Association and Nottinghamshire FA v Theresa Bennett,* Newark, 1978: 2: Sir David Cairns in his ruling gave this insight: 'The expression "average woman" does not mean a woman of the age which is the mean of all the ages of all the women in the country, nor a

woman of the age which is the mean of all those who play football, nor an age which is a mean of all the ages of girls under 12. The words "average woman" do not envisage any arithmetical average at all, but means something like "the ordinary woman" and, in the context of sport, "the ordinary woman of the sort of age and sort of physical characteristic who would be likely to engage in that sport"'.

61. Harry Smith, Team Manager, Crosfields Under-Elevens 'A' Team, *Women's Football Fourth Report of Session 2005–06 Report, Together with Formal Minutes, Oral and Written Evidence* (House of Commons: Culture, Media and Sport Committee), 22 June 2006, p. 65.
62. John Whittingdale, Chairman, Culture, Media and Sport Select Committee, personal communication, 14 November 2006.
63. Green, *A History of the Football Association,* p. 534.
64. See Taylor, *The Leaguers: The Making of Professional Football in England 1900–1939,* for a discussion of this wider issue; for example, there were 997 registered players in 1911 and 2,123 in eighty-eight clubs by 1925.
65. Though Worcester City was alphabetically the last club listed, it didn't have quite the same ring to it; my apologies to the supporters.
66. 'Clubs and Charity', *Athletic News,* 17 January 1921.
67. Football Association Emergency Council minutes, 21 March to 22 April 1922, Item 143.
68. 'To Play, or Not to Play', *Athletic News and Cyclists Journal.*
69. See, for example, in the newspaper article included in the chapter on the United States in this book: 'Many of the girls discarded their caps at this stage and disclosed tresses bobbed in the prevailing fashion.': 'Women's Team Plays Coasts to 4 to 4 Tie', *Pawtucket Times,* 7 October 1922. In terms of uniform, Dick, Kerr wore an identifiable football strip from the first game, indicative of their attitude toward playing football and in contrast to some infantilized women's uniforms such as gymslips and adapted works costumes, as is discussed in *A Game for Rough Girls.*
70. REF:BP25052283412, 'Eve and the Noble Art', London: Pathé PLC, 25 May 1922, at http://www.itnsource.co.uk/.
71. 'FA Sharply Criticised', *Stalybridge Times,* 19 September 1947.
72. 'Sea and Spa. Holiday Attractions Everywhere', *The Times,* 28 June 1921, p. 8; 'Big Decorations in Little Streets', *The Times,* 3 June 1953, p. 8.
73. 'News in Brief', *The Times,* 14 March 1922, p. 9.
74. 'Royal Ceremony at Waterloo. The Mons Trial', *The Times,* 22 March 1922, p. 16.
75. 'Loss of the L 24', *The Times,* 12 January 1924, p. 12.
76. REF: BP01112665003, 'Miners' Wives Football for Charity', London, Pathé PLC, 1 November 1926, at www.itnsource.co.uk.

77. REF: BP09043176713, 'Aren't Girls Wonderful?' London, Pathé PLC, 9 April 1931, at www.itnsource.co.uk.

78. Council Minutes item 34: 'It has been brought to the notice of the Council that so-called football by women players is in contemplation in various parts of the country ... The Council therefore calls upon all county Associations to take such steps as may be necessary within the territory under their control to see that clubs and officals do not loan their grounds or provide facilities for irregular football by women participants' (16 December 1946).

79. *Corinthian Ladies versus Lancashire Ladies Programme* notes, Manchester Athletic Club Ground Fallowfield, 20 August 1952.

80. *FA News,* October 1961, p. 104.

81. REF: BP030266201103, 'Queens of Soccer', 3 February 1966, at http://www.itnsource.com.

82. Minutes of the FA Council, 1 December 1969, item 37, layout and punctuation as the original.

83. Minutes of the FA Executive Committee, 16 December 1970, Item 16, and 19 January 1971, Item 46.

84. P. Gregory to Dr H Käser, Secretary, FIFA, 20 July 1973, WFA Collection.

85. E.A. Croker, The Football Association Correspondence File, WFA collection 10, July 1984.

86. P. Gregory to Dr H Käser, Secretary, FIFA, 2 June 1974, WFA Collection.

87. H Käser, Secretary, FIFA, to Pat Gregory, 20 June 1974, FIFA Correspondence File to the Football Association.

88. P. Gregory to Dr H Käser, Secretary, FIFA, 6 July 1974, WFA Correspondence file.

89. The First International Show Girls Soccer Tournament, Brazil, 10 August 1960, at http://www.itnsource.co.uk/.

90. Minutes. Joint Consultative Committee for Women's Football. Lancaster Gate. 3 October 1974.

91. FA Minutes of Match Permit Subcommittee, 30 June 1973, Item 8, women's football, pp. 109–110.

92. FA Minutes of Match Permit Subcommittee, 25 February 1974, Item 6, women's football, pp. 64–65.

93. Minutes of the meeting of the 1981 FIFA Technical Committee, Item 1, Women's football and competitions. Discussed by Group A 17/18, Zurich: FIFA House, December 1981.

94. Ibid.

95. Select Committee on Culture, Media and Sport, Second Special Report, Appendix 2, Reply from the Football Association, 17 October 2006.

96. The paraphrase of this assertion came on Women's Hour with Jenny Murray, 16 June 2005, available online at www.BBC.Women's Hour.

97. Daniel J. Cohen and Roy Rosenzweig, *Digital History: A Guide to Gathering, Preserving, and Presenting the Past on the Web* (Philadelphia: University of Pennsylvannia Press, 2004), available online at http://chnm.gmu.edu/digitalhistory/exploring/1.php. It explores the Internet's global computer network to share information in commonly agreed-upon ways. Previously, in the 1980s and early 1990s, the most intense energy in digital history centred not on the possibilities of online networks but rather on fixed-media products like laserdiscs and CD-ROMs.
98. Google, at http://www.google.co.uk/search, accessed 28 November 2005.
99. The *Journal of Multimedia History* and the *Journal of the Association for History and Computing* have taken this e-route, as have more than 400 other history journals. History News Network (HNN) is a more popular publication that combines history and journalism, prompting conversation and debate on the Web.

# $-4-$

# Waltzing the Matildas
## Women's Football in Australia

We find in a continent containing only 5,000,000 souls four football games played during the winter, vis., Australian Football, Northern Union, Rugby Union and Soccer. My contention is that Australia will be playing nothing but soccer in ten years' time if things go along as present. If the FA decided to spend some of its funds upon a touring team or teams, the Association game would, I feel sure, be in full charge in this country five years afterwards. What we need is a really first class exposition of soccer in each of the States. The game here is improving rapidly but Billy Meredith and one or two others would be fleet enough to walk around us. It is some picturesque play that we sadly need.[1]

Give Girls a Fair Go. Is the average Australian aware that this country has a women's national soccer team? The answer is simple—no. The main reason is that since 1975 Australia's women's team has played only three matches in Australia. Besides the women's team lacking public identity with Australians, a further injustice exists for the girls who make up the national team. Each player is responsible for her own air fares and accommodation wherever the national team has to travel. Every player is responsible for her own gear expenditure. Each girl forfeits wages whilst travelling and, because of the nature of their code, cannot be compensated financially.[2]

In the year after the first excerpt appeared in *Athletic News* in England, Australia played what has been called their first national association football match against New Zealand in 1922 (the latter won 3–1).[3] More than fifty years later, the initial official women's international for The Matildas involved the same countries. To put this in context of the inception of Australian Rules football in 1858 and the Rugby Tests against England from 1888 is to see how the sport generally, and women's participation especially, appear to have lagged behind as great sporting traditions, and in particular rivalries, have been constructed. As the second extract implies, the women's soccer team were hampered by a lack of resources from 1969 to 1995 to the extent of playing several unofficial and the first eight authorized representative games against the New Zealand SWANZ (as the women's team are called). Fortunately, the ambitions of the women players have overcome the lack of means, and their enthusiasm had already developed beyond this traditional rivalry. Twenty-five years to the day after they had played the first A-international recognized by the Australian Football Association (AFA), in 1979, the team had played 169 games and travelled to five of the six FIFA regional confederations (the exception being Africa). However, if 2003 saw the reduced circumstances of the Women's World Cup on an international scale, on the domestic stage, upheaval of national and state governance structures in the sport meant a difficult time for association football as a code. The wider processes relating to the establishment of football, show transformations followed by periods of retrenchment and restructuring of which the women's game has been frequent, if an unintended, casualty.

It has already been seen that events such as the Women's World Invitational Tournament held in Taipei and subsequent editions of it were to pave the way for the more recent recognition of international women's soccer by FIFA. In spite of the financial and travel difficulties outlined earlier, Australian women's teams already took part in the wider networks of international competitive play, which preceded that official involvement. They had competed in the Asian Ladies Football Confederation (ALFC) 1978 tournament against teams from Austria, the US, Sweden, Denmark and Thailand. In 1980 Australia, along with Papua New Guinea and Fiji, founded the Oceania Women's Football Association, which effectively acted as the organizing body until the FIFA-affiliated confederation for Oceania (OFC) created a women's committee in 1991. By 1984 the quasi-allied status was more FIFA-focussed than ALFC-minded, as is indicated by Gagg's response to a letter proposing a Women's World Cup qualifier in the region;

> Point 1: In the new regulations for a Women's World Cup, which will be elaborated by FIFA, your proposal could possibly be taken into consideration.
> Point 2: You are right in assuming that the Asian Ladies' Football Confederation has not been authorized neither by FIFA nor the Asian Football Confederation. The step you took to become a member of the Oceania Football Confederation has been the only legal solution.
> Point 3: FIFA has already elaborated a project for a Women's World Cup, which has been sanctioned by both the FIFA Technical Committee and the Executive committee. In 1985, at the latest in 1986, the first Women's World Cup will be organized.[4]

Following the ALFC developments, in addition to the 1978 and 1981 Women's Invitational Tournaments in Taipei, the inaugural Oceania Cup in Noumea in 1984 involved New Zealand, Fiji and New Caledonia. It was described in enthusiastic terms by the correspondent who, unlike the players, appears to have been a guest courtesy of his sponsor:

> I had the pleasure of travelling with the team thanks to Mr Roger Wellings' Sportwell tours company. I only wish the average Australian could have been in Noumea to see a bunch of young attractive females, wearing green and gold and doing battle for Australia. They did a fine job, despite being beaten for the Cup in the Final against rivals New Zealand.

Australia is coached by Jimmy Selby ... a young clean-cut Australian professional, well-educated with very sound knowledge of soccer.[5]

The awareness of increasing levels of international and regional interest led Elaine Watson (adopting a presidential title seemingly popular in world football) to write to FIFA on behalf of the Australian Women's Soccer Association (AWSA) to illustrate the discrimination against women coaches the same year:

Many women who have wished to pursue a career in coaching soccer have found restrictions imposed on their full participation in all aspects of advanced coaching courses. In many cases, limitations have proved detrimental to their chances of passing such courses (or even taking part at all). Here in Australia, such physical sports as Rugby League and Australian rules Football have no such rulings on their coaching courses, with the result that between 1/4 and 1/3 of their accredited coaches are female, and as we would like to see women qualifying to coach soccer players (whether men, women or juniors) we believe that full participation in all courses is a must. In view of the fact we are talking about a teaching/learning situation and not a competitive one, what is the FIFA ruling in this particular area?[6]

By 1995 Australia had ousted New Zealand (which competed in the first World Cup in 1991) to represent the OFC in the second Women's World Cup in Sweden. It reported participation growth in women's soccer at 30 per cent each year and aimed for gold in the 2000 Olympics by undergoing intensive training at national camps.[7] The situation appeared to be generally promising; from the mid-1990s, Australian male players have made a significant contribution to the Premiership in England. Nevertheless, there is a relative lack of depth in women's participation compared with men's soccer. Currently, there are 449,000 registered male players in Australia, whereas female registrants total 58,000. Both the men's and the women's team finished penultimate in the Sydney competition, and the promise of a decade ago seems unfulfilled. In large part this has been affected by the difficult place of association football in Australian sports culture. The lack of Olympic status for women's soccer was also a factor in the women's team being overlooked for talent identification programmes until 1996. The most popular female participation sport in Australia is netball (more than 350,000 registered athletes and an estimate of 1.2 million players in total, with popularity in commonwealth countries dating back to the nineteenth century), and, though it received its Olympic recognition as late as 1995, the dominance of basketball in the games has brought some representation for the related discipline.

Unlike the Matildas, the male nickname, Socceroos, was expected by the Football Federation Australia Ltd (FFA) to fade away.[8] The national governing body that was to become a limited company in response to fiscal and procedural irregularity was refounded in 1961 and reaffiliated with FIFA in 1963 after paying fines for financial and technical indiscretion. However, since then, name changes around whether to call the game 'soccer' or 'football' reflect the problematic placing of the association game. Following the relaunch of 'football' in the title in early 2005, the hope was that the men's national team would simply be called Australia. This proved to be a brief experiment. As the writer in the *Athletic News* indicated in the twentieth century, it is not just upheaval within the sport or patriarchal governance structures with which those interested in the association code have to contend in the twenty-first. The challenges which mean that soccer has struggled against rugby-based games throughout its history in Australia have not especially helped female involvement in the sport. Against this longer history, establishment of a national infrastructure and changes to Australia's place in the international framework are relatively new; for instance, a national player registration scheme was launched in 2006. That year, Australia became a full member of the Asian Football Confederation (AFC), leaving the Oceania Football Confederation (OFC) and becoming part of the Vision Asia initiative. The executive body reached the conclusion that, given the enormous potential that the Asian market offered through an association with Australia (the AFC is the second largest behind UEFA with forty-six members), the case did not need to be discussed by the FIFA Congress.

In spite of the political controversies that have occurred within and around the rules and regulation of national and international associations, there is plenty of recent success in Australian women's soccer at various levels. At Women's World Cup China 2007, Matildas' team captain, Cheryl Salisbury, will be the first to play in all four finals tournaments that Australia has qualified for (Sweden in 1995, US in 1999 and 2003). Salisbury, along with fellow national team players Alagich, Golebiowski and Murray, played in the professional league Women's United Soccer Association (WUSA); Forman, Tann-Derby and Wheeler are all 1995 and 1999 WWC players. The three Australian match officials who participated in the FIFA U-19 Women's World Championship Thailand 2004 had their first top-level appointment; namely referee Jaqui Melksham and assistant Sarah Ho (both twenty-five and from Brisbane and Sydney, respectively) and Michelle Treloar (age thirty-three, of Canberra). All three had previously officiated at the four-nation Australia Cup and the U19 Oceania qualifiers in Papua New Guinea. The appearances continued the recognition of Australian female match officials at major international tournaments following appearances at the Olympics in 1996 and 2000 and at the Women's World Cup 2003. In 2006 Julie Murray continued an already impressive career to became one of fifteen FIFA Ambassadors of Women's Football. Begun as the Ansett Australia Summer Series, the Women's National Soccer League (WNSL) began in 1996 with six clubs and continued until 2004. In the final year it briefly expanded to seven teams with the addition of the Western Wave of Western Australia; the first growth since the 1996–1997 season. Coached by Alistair Edwards, a Socceroo, assisted by Scott Miller, a national team and Glory player, and the former Matildas goalkeeper Tracey Wheeler, the team's branding was said to be inspired by the healthy, outdoor, beach-oriented lifestyle of western Australia. Sponsorship, by Midland Brick, was the first for a women's national soccer league team. It was a short six-game development in spite of the hype. Credited as the top domestic women's league and offering the opportunity for many of Australia's world-class players to stay on home soil, the league was dominated by the Queensland Sting (the Queensland Institute of Sport) with four titles, though the NSW Sapphires (New South Wales Institute of Sport) and the Adelaide Sensation (as the SA Sports Institute Pirates) have also won. Its suspension has meant that top players must again travel abroad if they wish to play at the highest level, and a national league has yet to be reinstated. One of the aspects which makes Australia comparable with other large countries with harsh landscapes is that there are a comparatively few large conurbations in a small number of states. In this sense, Britain's moderately small size, many counties and combination of towns and cities should perhaps be expected to produce quite different forms of sports competition in general. This is certainly the case for women's football, where intervillage, intertown, intercity and intercounty competition in Britain are in contrast with the intracity organization of women's football in Australia to a much more marked degree. In the challenging circumstance of the distance to be covered and the overall lack of resources, including pitches, it is unsurprising that most teams in the WNSL were centred in or near various specialist institutes of sport.

As a nation, the general consensus has been that Australia has had an outstanding success rate in a wide range of international sports. The influences include demographic trends, natural and human geography, cultural attitudes, politics and economics. The male-dominated sports culture persists, especially in terms of participation, in spite of the temperate climate, open spaces and, in particular, seacoast, as Doug Booth's *Australian Beach Cultures* shows.[9] Vamplew and Adair have suggested that 'Australia was not a militaristic nation ands sport perhaps was the cement that bound the nation together.'[10] Perhaps the intensely aggressive approach toward victory is also a significant factor in this mix. The focus of political will with regard to sport in Australia could be summed up as 'playing is fun, winning even better'. The attitude may owe something to the nineteenth century, but the mixed national economy which supports the current infrastructure surrounding sport also has a long legacy. Following the recent Olympics, in spite of maintaining fourth overall, the cost of each gold medal was cited in the media in an overall move to par down elite funding in sports which gave a poor return in Athens in 2004 (with seventeen gold, sixteen silver and sixteen bronze against sixteen gold, twenty-five silver and seventeen bronze in Sydney). A survey of articles in *Sporting Traditions* serves to highlight the literature on women and sport and physical education as a late grower, particularly feminist analyses of sport.[11] An increasing range of texts since Sydney 2000 have asked whether all Australians have been allowed to participate in, and to shape, the nation's sporting past and present. Indigenous populations including Aborigines, women and ethnic populations have consistently been identified as excluded and marginalized in the cultural and social aspects of Australia's heritage.[12] The mechanisms by which some have been included and some excluded are particularly significant in this most sporting of nations.

However, some of those women who have worn the green and gold for Australia on the soccer pitch are now belatedly being recognized. For example, Sue Monteath and Jane Oakley were amongst eleven inductees to the 2004 Australian Soccer Association Hall of Fame (HOF), established in 1999. The Hall of Fame recognizes players and nonplayers for their contribution to the sport on a national basis with a system of three distinct but equivalent groups. Monteath held a national place for more than ten years and was inducted with a distinction. Oakley's coaching, administrative and development work were recognized by a Roll of Honour. Some benefits have been less forseen. The demise of Women's USA has been used by countries like Australia to boost their coaching portfolio; for example, Tom Sermanni, who had previously coached the New York Power, became the Matildas' coach for the second time after the 2004 Olympics. Robbie Hooker, his assistant coach in New York and an ex-international for Australia, became head coach of the ACT women's programme.

The major challenge to the sport is not one of infrastructure or a set of principles by which it should be administered and managed. Put simply, soccer has image issues that it would take a shrewdness of PR gurus (or whatever the collective noun rightly is) to reform, regenerate and legitimate. While not yet having read an academic version of Markovits and Hellerman, I find hints of 'Australian exceptionalism' here:

> Traditionally, it has not been 'aesthetic' sports but those sports hegemonically viewed as legitimate tests of manhood which have been the catalyst for idolisation, proving Connell's (1990) point about hegemonic masculinity, that 'to be culturally exalted, the pattern of masculinity must have exemplars who are celebrated as heroes' (p. 94). In Australia, such sports include rugby league, rugby union and Australian Rules football, while soccer players are generally regarded as soft.[13]

Whether this has helped or hindered female development is open to question. As several players introduced to soccer preschool or as extracurricular activity (mainly through the influence of fathers, brothers, boys and girls in the street) have noted, the early socialization of 'falling into' a sport is a very underresearched topic. Usually, where I met a player, I also encountered their families; yet entry into the informal football culture did not necessarily bear out this 'soft' focus. As in other case-study nations, football is one of many social activities and games and is not always a determining feature of interaction, which can be mixed or single-sex. This is unlike later, more formal single-sex clubs into which participation becomes siphoned as a degree of participation in sport is institutionalized. For example, players frequently mentioned netball as a point of comparison with their own experiences, especially with regard to stereotypes surrounding its female appropriateness.[14] As with other case-study nations and other codes, this physical challenge, the demanding nature of the skill base and the exertion are aspects of the appeal. Josie, age sixteen, also played basketball and netball:

> You can really get into soccer—more so than other sports, we want to show what we're made of. That we can take the contact and that we are up to the skill level. I prefer to play at adult level because its faster, you need to be fitter and your skills need to be there. If they try to give me a bit of a shock, you know, 'hard first challenge' and all that, I don't notice and use my speed.

There is something to the hegemonic exclusion of Association football in Australian sports culture, though. Grant Jarvie assesses the twin forces of globalization and internationalization and in particular questions the simplicity of framing contemporary sport purely in global or local terms: 'It has been suggested that nationalism is becoming obsolete as a result of globalization and that the role of sports in the making of nations is weakening. Global sport has presented fundamental challenges to local and national sport, but it has also created the opportunity for sport to be more international.'[15] If qualification at the 1974 World Cup Finals competition meant that soccer in Australia had arrived, Captain Johnny Warren's memoir, entitled *Sheilas, Wogs and Pooftas*, indicates the somewhat second-rate status of the sport among his contemporaries: moreover, the feat was not to be repeated until 2006.[16] The National Soccer League (NSL) was established in 1977 and was arguably the first truly national football competition in Australia. This league, and Soccer Australia, were disbanded in 2004 and replaced by the A-League and by the Football Federation Australia, respectively. The A-League is currently negotiating to maintain the inclusion of the ailing franchise New Zealand Knights, who wished to surrender their licence to field a team in the Hyundai A-League at the conclusion of the season. At the same time, the FFA has signed a major deal with Nike to support its national teams. The wider question of building a sporting nationalism based on soccer is too large to consider here, but this broader lack of support is punctuated by more localized enthusiasm and a degree of multinational participation.

What then of the history of association football and woman's participation which led to the formation of a National Squad in 1979? As the *Athletic News* article indicates, strong links among Great Britain, Australia and New Zealand help to explain the presence of football of various codes from the mid-1800s on. Ray Crawford suggests that the magazine of the Presbyterian Ladies College in 1876 had an appeal for football players.[17] In terms of school sport, there is some continuity with both the English and United States cases in that most state-provided education was coeducational with a single-sex provision for the privileged few during the first fifty years of the twentieth century. It seems that Boyd was overoptimistic in his appraisal of soccer; though it seems to have been popular in and around Sydney from the 1880s, most football was played to rugby or hybrid rules.[18] There had been recorded games of

Australian Rules football since 1858 and the establishment of the Victorian Football Association in 1877. Early soccer enthusiasts appeared keen to preserve its British character at this time with the establishment of the Anglo-Australian State Associations in 1884. By 1896 the British Ladies Football Club referred to in the chapter on England were being reported as a source of both social and sporting controversy in the *Melbourne Herald*. A cartoon in the *Melbourne Punch* in 1899 ridiculed the idea of women who appear to be playing either rugby or Australian Rules codes, and the popularity of these sports with women seems to have been more extensive than soccer. Just before World War One, working-class migrants from Great Britain and other European countries seem to have broadened the appeal as social distinctions became less clear. If both the Americans and the Australians were to have their own rules as a refusal to imitate their ex-colonizer, there were examples of some success for both rugby and association codes. Against this background of so-called indigenous and colonial codes, Marion Stell refers to women's football teams formed in Perth and in Melbourne, but it is unclear under what rules.[19]

Like munitionettes football in Britain, Peter Burke has identified Australian rules played by female employees of large companies in Perth, Western Australia, including the Foy and Gibson department store.[20] This competition appeared to build upon cricket matches for female retail employees which had begun some years before and were recorded in journals like *Draper of Australasia* in 1911, often being played for charitable causes. The impact of proprietors of large Perth retailers such as Boans, Bon Marche, Brennans and Charles Moore Economic stores arguably came to be more significant than that of industries which allowed women to enter in wartime. That is, participation in football fitted into ongoing occupational structures more than the changed nature of work in war. The same year the Australian Soccer Association was formed, *Table Talk*, a society journal taken over by the *Melbourne Herald*, felt sufficiently provoked to ask 'Should Women Play Football?' and showed teams of women, dressed not unlike their European counterparts, playing in front of mixed crowds in some finery, with the match in Melbourne preceeded by 'one recently played in Ballarat'.[21] The oval ball, however, suggests that this publicity was linked with rugby or Australian Rules, though the first women's interstate game took place in 1921 and another was played in 1925 between the Reds and the Blues at Brisbane. There are also references in personal collections to women's teams in Carlton, Sydney and Brisbane from 1925 to 1933.[22]

As with the growth of the game in the US, some commentators explain its popularity as a result of ethnic differentiation and hence minority interest. However, Majumdar has noted that the dissemination of football was not a one-way process. In the late 1920s, the Australian-born Anne Kelleve took the lead in promoting cricket and to a lesser extent soccer in the Anglo Indian schools in Kerala and beyond.[23] However, Rowe et al place the rise of participation in the sport until the early 1970s as 'a sport marked by its subjectivity: a composite migrant came to stand for it ... The supposed lack of exemplary nation-state sentiment in the game—its ethnicity—has been recuperated as actiology again and again by critics, commentators and administrators.'[24] The appeal in the *Athletic News* looked to have some success by the outbreak of World War Two, with some 1,200 clubs. At the close of hostilities, the Sydney Sports Ground women's game shown by Pathé newsreels in 1944 again demonstrate not only a degree of play, put predictably by the commentator as 'these girls get a kick out of soccer', but also a presentation to a live and wider audience.[25]

The large-scale postwar immigration of migrants affected eastern and southern Europeans 'who happened to be footballers by profession' in a wider context of the White Australia Policy.[26] The year 1972 saw what has been called the hyphenated Australians as the assimilationist policies began to give way to a more multicultural ethos, with identification of both birth-nation and chosen nationality. Above country-specific factors, the one-nation-one vote policy of FIFA also affected the domestic situation as the New South Wales Federation of Soccer clubs split in 1957 from the Australian Soccer Football Association and therefore was not recognized by the International Federation. The inclusion of Austrian, Dutch and Israeli professionals without transfer certificates led to FIFA's exclusion of the Australian FA at the 1960 Congress, as well as AFC's denial of membership in 1964 and of eventual entry to the men's World Cup in 1965. In terms of the national situation, Dyck for instance acknowledges that most clubs grew out of the social establishment of teams but cautions against 'the reduction of the game to merely an ethnic sport' as a one-dimensional aspect of Anglo-Australian dominance of sport.[27] The names of clubs like Aston Villa in Brisbane (around since at least 1964) and Ipswich United in Queensland balance with Brisbane Eastern Suburbs, Weston Creek, Mindil Aces to support this point. The New South Wales connection seems to be especially important for women's football. The year 1974 saw the formation of the Australian Women's Soccer Association referred to in the Introduction. Player-administrators such as Leonie Parker and Trixie Tagg indicate that there was considerable activity before the Association's eventual consolidation into the Australian Soccer Federation, and as a consequence both were awarded with life membership of the NSW Women's Federation in 1984. As a detailed example, in 1972 Leonie's daughter had wanted to play, and so Leonie formed a girls' team, Killarney Heights, in combination with her daughter and her friends in the Manly district. She also formed the Manly-Warringah Women's Soccer Association and became vice president of the New South Wales Women's Federation. The Ku -ring-gai district association on Sydney's north shore seems to have provided their main opposition. After a five-year playing career, the spirit of committed familial voluntarism continued with her husband, Fred, serving as a referees' examiner. Leonie was a referee and coach for more than a decade, and her son Geoff played for the Killarney Heights club. As one of the first qualified women referees, Leonie was also assistant coach for the State Under-15 side.

The formation of a women's association was well placed to take advantage of these existing networks to play internationals; for instance, in 1975 New Zealand and Australia were invited to participate in the Women's Asian Cup in Hong Kong, and the current phase of development has grown from there. Women who pioneered aspects of female play have lately been honoured as Hall of Fame inductees; for example, Theresa Dees (born Theresa Jones in 1963) is a model of continuing participation. She came through the junior ranks as a goalkeeper to represent Victoria for eighteen years and Australia for ten years, playing eighteen internationals. Theresa switched to administration after retirement to become a national team manager and Victoria director/development officer. She was awarded the 2000 Australian Sports Medal and was inducted into the Hall of Fame in 2003. At the same session, the distinguished contribution of Betty Hoar was recognized. She was one of the pioneers of women's soccer in Victoria and a long-time administrator with the national women's body. Since 1974, she has had an active role with every Victorian Women's management committee, was elected to the national association in 1979 as treasurer and has remained on the board in various posts. Over a ten-year period, she managed Australian teams to New Zealand, Hawaii, New Caledonia and Dallas. In 1984 Betty was awarded Life Membership of the Victorian Women's Association, the Australian Women's Association, the Victorian Soccer Federation and also awarded the 2000 Australian Sports Medal.

The periodization of the development in Australia is consequently more difficult to summarize than most. If I have been increasingly critical of suggestions of discontinuity between the origins up to the mid-1920s and the establishment phase in the early 1960s on in my own work, the model almost seems elongated in this case. That is, with World Cup representation in 1995 and a national league in 1996, it could be argued that Australian women soccer players have succeeded disproportionately well, given that the establishment phase is just over a decade old. However, this would overemphasize a top-down approach and ignore a major element of a more in-depth, country-specific study that is waiting to be done. Life history accounts of the Sues, Janes, Leonies, Trixies, Bettys and Theresas would help to understand the whys and hows of the networks in women's sport, youth leagues, recreational, rural and urban participation and so forth. This consequently goes beyond being a female sport issue to touch on aspects of volunteerism, formation of sporting communities and familial networks as aspects of leisure organization. There may well be more subtle forms of continuity than recognition by sporting bureaucracies that are all the more noteworthy for their quiet ubiquity. As Joanne 'Joey' Millan put it more eloquently in a 1986 interview about the opportunities to travel she had experienced since national squad selection in 1981:

> Playing soccer for Australia, Joanne has travelled to Hawaii, New Caledonia, China, Taiwan and New Zealand. 'It is easily the best way to see some of the world by playing Soccer for your country. The fun and the memories gathered whilst on tour are invaluable.'[28]

By the mid-1980s nationally, Saints United of Sydney were the team to beat, and 'Ladies soccer' was a more integral part of the operations of many associations.

This was part of the problem, as the overlapping and opposing levels of competition, combined with a lack of Olympic cachet, meant that women's football was very much reliant on a voluntaristic and regional format. Walter Gagg's response to Elaine Watson's complaint about women's exclusion from coaching courses is a gallant blend of disingenuous sincerity:

> FIFA is well aware of the problems, particularly concerning women's participation in coaching courses. Nevertheless, this matter is to be ruled between AWSA and the Australian Soccer Federation and FIFA cannot impose any guidelines in this field. The question is also whether women's football organisation in Australia is integrated within the Australian Soccer Federation. If this applies, there should be possibilities for women to participate in coaching courses by ASF, even on an advanced level, and thus to pursue a career in football coaching. Wishing you every success.[29]

Of the 1984 Women's National Soccer Team, for example, midfielder Sandy (Pee Wee) Brentnall came from Western Australia, while the 'golden girl' sisters Joanne and Kerry Millman hailed from Queensland, as did Susan Monteath, while Renaye Iserief of Central Coast, Julie Porter of the South Coast and Julie Dolan represented New South Wales. A 2006 squad featured players from the following clubs: Melissa Barbieri (Victoria), Emma Wirkus (South Australia), Rhian Davies (New South Wales), Kate McShea (Queensland), Karla Reuter (NSW), Cheryl Salisbury (NSW), Heather Garriock (NSW), Kim Carroll (Qld), Collette McCallum (Western Australia), Joanne Peters (NSW), Lauren Colthorpe (NSW), Amber Neilson (NSW), Joanne Burgess (NSW), Caitlin Munoz (Canberra), Sarah Walsh (NSW) and Sasha McDonnell (Qld). While existing networks may have helped participation, some of the debates in the press also have continuities. Irene E. Sneyd, JP, an Australia Women's Soccer Association life member, felt obliged to make a case for the association on behalf both of a nationally-affiliated female interest group and the women of the New South Wales Federation who wished to remain part of the larger network:

> Having spent the last 27 years on soccer administration, with the final 12 years in women's soccer, I suggest I qualify as to knowing something about which I speak. It grieves me to see that the best (journalist) friend that Women's Soccer has had, John Economos, has recently had to share the Women's Page with a writer who is damaging the code he is writing about ... I question the method of this person, on questioning the need for the AWSA (in your issue April 15) I suggest he is playing politics ... Statements like this can be very damaging to the code, when many people give hours of their time for the benefit of others.[30]

It seems a contentious point, the extent to which women's soccer at this point could be called a national sport with ten affiliated regional associations. So the Matildas were to participate in a Women's World Cup before a Women's National Soccer League (WNSL) formed in 1996 with Queensland Academy of Sport the inaugural champions. This is not so unusual for countries represented at the international level, and a considerable debate remains about how far the existing networks of women's football rely upon earlier forms. A quite separate deliberation about whether women's national teams have been selected via rigorous means is likely to continue. What is more significant perhaps for the sport as a whole is that while WWC '99 in Los Angeles may have seen the largest crowd for a women's international at 93,000 in the Rose Bowl, the largest crowd of 88,000 for a men's club match in Sydney was achieved the same year.

While the 2000 Sydney Olympic Games were the most prestigious presentation of an international women's (and men's) football tournament in Australia to date, they were not without considerable controversy. The Olympic tradition is one which has led Vamplew to write:

> Occasionally too Australia has challenged the world. Indeed Australians have participated in every summer Olympics—one of three nations to do so—since the establishment of the modern game in Athens in 1896 ... success on this particular world stage had been limited with the exception of the Melbourne Games in 1956, the first and only time so far the Olympics have been held in the southern hemisphere. Revelling in the support of the home crowd and with many events being held 'in season', Australian men and women won thirty-five medals, thirteen of them gold. Disappointing later results, particularly the failure to win any gold medals in at the Montreal Olympics in 1976, forced Australians to realize that talent alone was no longer sufficient and led to the formation of the Australian Institute of Sport with a charter to apply sports science to the coaching and training of top-ranking sports people.[31]

Talent identification programmes in sport have taken on increasing significance of late. In Australia, this has come about as a result of greater competition between sports for athletically gifted participants.[32] Structured talent identification programmes are not new to Australia, with pioneering research conducted with the sport of rowing in 1988 and a coordinated national programme in operation since 1994. Such initiatives have had their success, with an Olympic gold medalist identified from the 1988 rowing programme and multiple world junior championship medalists and representatives coming out of the national Talent Search initiative. However, an alternative view of the Olympic games and female contributions to it alleges:

> Between 1948 and 1996 women won 40% of Australia's Gold medals at the Olympic Games despite comprising just 24% of Australia's Athletes. Similarly, between 1911 and 1990 women won 35% of Australia's Gold Medals at the Commonwealth Games in a period when they were allowed to participate in only 31% of the sports available and constituted 27% of all Australian athletes. Yet despite this astonishing performance women's sport generally receives about 2% of Australian media coverage, and much of it stereotypical, trivializing and sexually objectifying.[33]

While the IOC reputedly spent $230 million US to use the event to 'Celebrate Humanity', Dennis Phillips has also argued that it was an occasion to celebrate 100 years of women at the games with seven Australian women Olympians involved in the relay and Cathy Freeman lighting the torch.[34] Helen Lenskyj questions Samaranch's declaration of the social impact of the games implied by 'The Best Ever' either as a means of overcoming postcolonial racial tension or in addressing green issues.[35] At the Sport and Human Rights Conference in Sydney that preceded the Games, delegates were encouraged to recognize the 'owners of the land' as a way of acknowledging the contradictions of control and exclusion as a means of protection. The project to transform sport and society beyond the social and economic issues was symbolically embraced even if more pragmatic struggles over diversity remained. The prominence of Cathy Freeman also raised issues of race and ethnicity, not least the immigration that had provided so much of Australia's population causing interpretive conflict over whether racial diversity or unity should be the focus. Whether Sydney was able to build upon the success of Women's World Cup 1999 in either national or international terms for women's soccer is a moot point. Australian networks did not buy any rights for the 1999 event, though some highlights appeared on sports programs and news. By the 2003 World Cup, the Australian television companies were no more persuaded of public interest; there was brief coverage on SBS-TV's nightly Toyota World Sports, the World Game program (Sundays on SBS) aired a live interview with coach Adrian Santrac and captain Cheryl Salisbury, but otherwise fans relied on overseas pay TV such as ESPN or Eurosport. The main problem to affect coverage in Sydney was to be the dominating role played by the US channel NBC, which had a disproportionate effect on media coverage as a result of sustaining a 20 per cent drop in audience figures compared with viewership for Atlanta '96.

What Sydney 2000 undoubtedly did manage was to attract more than 1 million spectators to the men's and women's Olympic football tournaments, staged in Sydney, Melbourne, Adelaide, Brisbane and Canberra. In the men's tournament, Cameroon beat Spain in the final at the Olympic Stadium after a penalty shootout in front of 104,000 fans with an average of more than three goals a game; a figure rarely reached in a prestigious tournament. In the women's tournament, the US unsurprisingly began as favourites and had beaten Norway two-nil in the group stages, but a goal by Dagny Mellgren in extra time set the score at 2–3 for the first Olympic gold medal for the Scandinavian women. The FIFA delegation judged that the crowd in Sydney particularly had been good promotion for women's football in Australia and that even though the Australian teams were knocked out relatively early in the competition, it had not negatively impacted on crowds, an opinion not borne out by the figures. Both finals were played in Sydney, and Australia women's group games against Sweden and Brazil, respectively, were also played in the city. Nevertheless, the staging of the two finals was quite different. In a solid performance by the home nation, the Matildas ranked seventh overall, between Sweden and Nigeria. Having ranked eleventh place in Women's World Cup '99 out of sixteen and last place (of twelve) in Sweden '95, their standing after Sydney represented some improvement, but the team would not have qualified for the Olympic competition other than as hosts. The preponderance of team members from the Canberra Eclipse, NSW Sapphires, NNSW Horizon, SASI Pirates and QAS Sting indicate the impact of the national league combined with the all-time programme launched in July 1998 to develop the team in conjunction with the Australian Institute of Sport. For the first time, Coach Chris Tanzey had both the time and financial aid to develop a squad of twenty players. The men's team, although ostensibly in a youth competition, also came last but one in the sixteen-team tournament, placed between the Czech Republic and Morocco. Concern had been expressed as to the quality of Olympic competition as a 'youth and women's' tournament which was felt not to present Association football in the best light to an Australian audience keen to see the best proponents of their sport. The introduction of three 'wildcard' players over the under-twenty-three age limit set in the men's competition, was thought to have been vital in presenting competitive spectacle, with Viduka, Skoko and Lazaridis returning to play from Europe in the games.

The FIFA president took the opportunity to review football's place in the Olympic movement:

> Football was instrumental in spreading the Olympic message since the tournaments were staged in various venues. He remarked that the FIFA Executive Committee had been invited to the Olympics so as to appraise football's importance in the context of the Games and be better equipped to judge whether FIFA should rethink its role in the Olympics. The President said that the Executive Committee members would confer on the issue at a later stage ... He furthermore pointed out that the IOC President was adamantly against football withdrawing from the Olympics. However, the Executive committee would define the modalities of the Olympic football tournaments.[36]

Whether this included bargaining over quotas for the size of teams in future Games or involved other moves of diplomacy, the figures for women's competitions have risen since, as has been indicated, to ten teams in 2004 and twelve in 2008. There has also been some administrative change to develop a women's FIFA committee that would be comprised mainly of female representatives in line with the incremental target-setting of women sports leaders initiated by the International Olympic Committee. This began in 1981, when two women were elected to the IOC; since then, a total of twenty-one women have served as IOC members. At present, there are fourteen women members who represent 14 per cent of the total of 113 IOC members. In order to increase the number of women occupying leadership and administrative positions within the wider Olympic Movement, the IOC set the following goals: by 31 December 2005, the National Olympic Committees (NOCs), International Sports Federations (ISFs), and sports bodies belonging to the Olympic Movement should establish as a goal that at least 20 per cent of the positions in all their decision-making structures (in particular the executive and legislative bodies) be held by women. An initial target of having at least 10 per cent of positions within decision-making bodies held by women was set for December 2000 but was not met by many of the bodies concerned. Since 2003 there has been one woman on the IOC executive (equating to 6.6 per cent or a ratio of 1:15) and 'more than 30% of the NOCs and 29% of the ISFs have already achieved the 2005 target'.[37] Given the limited success of this and the outcome of related research which seemed to focus more on the 'problem' of women than on the processes of exclusion, the legacy of Sydney may be rather more positive for football than for women sports leaders, but not by much.

The relative status of the women's final match had already been cemented by moving it so that it preceded the men's, reflected in the minutes in terms of a flourish followed by a business-like tone:

> Peter Hugg, Tournament Director, concluded by saying that the Olympics had given excellent exposure to football, which he was sure would leave a legacy for the game in Australia. He thanked the FIFA President and the Chairman for placing their trust in Australia and stressed that the Australians would be delighted to host another FIFA event ...
>
> The General Secretary stated that the FIFA President, the IOC President Juan Antonio Samaranch and other IOC and FIFA delegates would present the men's medals after the final at the Olympic stadium. The gold, silver and bronze medals for the women would be presented after the women's final.[38]

Though there were some records set for attendance at women's football in 2000, the overall attendances were considerably down, with a total of 326, 215 for all women's matches in Australia compared with 550,926 in 1996, and average match attendance fizzling in the second phase to 15,000 (whereas they had been 20,000 in the first) compared to a steady 35,000 throughout Atlanta. The difference in female grass-roots participation no doubt accounts for much of the situation. It was not helped, though, by placing the women's final at Sydney football ground (where the men's competition had averaged 36,000), rather than at the Sydney Olympic Stadium (for that record-breaking 104,000). Discussion around the timing and date of this match had been lengthy, and this policy of consistently demoting the women's final was also an issue for Athens, where two groups of five originally had a women's final to be played after the men's on Sunday, 29 August, before it was subsequently reorganized to two three-team and one four-side group, with the eventual final preceding the men's on the Thursday.[39]

Meanwhile, domestically, the Independent Soccer Review Committee published a report in 2003 on the governance of Association football in Australia, more commonly called the Crawford Report. This highlighted in unflattering terms the critical state of association football in Australia, including the failure of the Socceroos to qualify for the World Cup and Confederations Cup plus an investigation by the

Australian Broadcasting Corporation's Four Corners programme into conflicts of interest and mismanagement at the Board level at Soccer Australia. The constant in-fighting between political factions and the concentration of voting and legislative powers in the hands of a relative minority of people was not a new issue in governing the code; nevertheless, the overt resistance to accepting the government enquiry, and even an initial refusal to accept its recommendations despite the balance of government and public opinion, was inappropriate in the current context.

Those who appear to be latecomers in the international sporting arena often possess few advantages other than surprise. Though as a code football took place before there was a fully fledged commercial consumer culture in Australia, the passion and numbers of players and support do not match that of the other codes listed in the *Athletic News* or against friendly sporting rivals upon whom focus public attention, as in cricket. The naming of the Socceroos and the Matildas perhaps reflects this unease and attempts to blend aspects of the culture with home-grown identity and pride. On an international stage, when the public hear the word 'Test' they are more likely to think of those long-standing rivalries in cricket and rugby than the tradition going back to the 1925 tour by a British soccer side. If we talk about football heroes and their public we are more likely talking about Australian Rules players and rugby stars than Kewell, Viduka and others who play overseas. Rather than creating a breathing space, this uncertain situation impacts on women soccer players, as the harsher disparagement of the sport is supplemented by attitudes to women athletes generally. However, as the brief survey of women's involvement indicates, disbelief as to women's long-term involvement will, it is hoped, give way to a different kind of astonishment over the scope of their contribution. While still in an era of firsts, as indicated by the participation of the national women's futsal team under coach Gui Costa in the Cheetah Cup 2004, there is also much more sustained connection between women and association football in Australia still to uncover.

Consider this record for a sporting hero and the narratives that might be written about it: renowned as a commanding midfield player, with vision, touch and the ability to run off the ball; after her international debut at fifteen, one of the highest capped and the longest serving squad members; captain in the first World Cup finals tournament for which the team qualifies after which she is dropped from the national team before returning as striker two years later and with an audacious reputation as a scorer of crucial lone goals in major tournaments spanning almost two decades, Julie Murray should perhaps be one of the sporting icons celebrated as much as the international media personalities who carried the torch in Sydney 2000 and who provide spectacle beyond. There has yet to be an historic period about which to be nostalgic for Australian women in the game, though Sydney was certainly a significant event. However, Australian sport is hardly lacking in heroes, and the relative outsider status of soccer as a sport and the seeming newness of women's place in it internationally, mitigate against winning the public's admiration and celebration. In contrast to the women's football team, Australia confirmed their status as a great women's hockey side with a 3–1 win over Argentina, to win the Olympic gold medal in Sydney 2000, adding to their victories in Seoul in 1988 and Atlanta 1996. It remains, against the dominance of other football codes and the success of established women's sports, including team games, for the Australian public to give the Matildas a fair go.

# Notes

1. Alec Boyd, 'Australia Wants a Soccer Team', *The Athletic News and Cyclists Journal* (17 October 1921).
2. John Economos, 'Women in Soccer', *Australian Soccer Weekly,* 24 January 1984.
3. In the recently begun 'capping exercise', cap number one has been allocated by Football Federation Australia to Alex Gibb, 'who captained the Australian side in its historical first international match against New Zealand in 1922'; see http://www.footballaustralia.com.au, accessed 14 November 2006.
4. Walter Gagg, Head of Technical Department, *Letter to Elaine Watson Australian Women's Soccer Association (inc)*, 26 April 1984, FIFA Correspondence Files, Zurich.
5. Economos, 'Women in Soccer'.
6. Elaine Watson, *Australian Women's Soccer Association (inc) letter to Walter Gagg,* 8 June 1984, FIFA Correspondence Files, Zurich.
7. Sue Lopez, *Women on the Ball: A Guide to Women's Football* (London: Scarlet Press, 1997), p. 111; see also Marian Stell, *Half the Race: A History of Australian Women in Sport* (New South Wales: Angus and Robertson, 1991) for a more comprehensive history of women in sport from the colonial period to the present day.
8. Before 1 January 2005 it was known as the Australian Soccer Association (ASA), which succeeded Soccer Australia in 2003.
9. Douglas Booth, *Australian Beach Cultures: The History of Sun, Sand and Surf* (London: Frank Cass, 2001).
10. Daryl Adair and Wray Vamplew, *Sport in Australian History* (Melbourne: Oxford University Press, 1997).
11. See, for example, R. Cashman and A. Weaver, *Wicket Women: Cricket and Women in Australia* (Kensington: New South Wales University Press, 1991), which is revealing of attitudes toward women's sport in the media, for example, as well as the history of cricket.
12. Bernard Whimpress, 'Australian Rules Football', in Wray Vamplew and Brian Stoddart, *Sport in Australia: A Social History* (Cambridge: Cambridge University Press, 1994), pp. 19–40, which has rather more reference to women's involvement than Philip Mosely and Bill Murray, 'Soccer', in the same volume, pp. 213–231.

13. Ian Burgess, Allan Edwards and James Skinner, 'Football Culture in an Australian School Setting: The Construction of Masculine Identity', *Sport, Education and Society,* 8, no. 2 (2003): 202.

14. The Roy Morgan survey, which interviewed 100,000 people age fourteen and up over a four-year period, found that netball still exceeded football as a participation sport. It estimated that 1.2 million Australians in total played football, of which 348,000 were females. The increase in soccer participation over the years has been enjoyed across all states, in particular New South Wales (374,000 to 525,000), Victoria (184,000 to 271,000) and Queensland (142,000 to 223,000): 'Soccer Scores Goals as Number One Played Sport in the Country', Finding No. 3661, 11 August 2003. This implied steady growth increasing from 831,000 participants in March 2000 to more than 1.1 million in March 2004: 'Soccer Still the Nation's Most Popular Team Sport, Despite Overall Decline in Team Sports', Article No. 327, 26 June 2004. However, it should be noted that the study found a drop in female participation in team sports and in the under-fourteens especially.

15. Grant Jarvie, 'Internationalism and Sport in the Making of Nations', *Identities: Global Studies in Culture and Power*, 10, no. 4 (2003): 537–551.

16. See the Johnny Warren Football Foundation Vision, 'Achieving Johnny Warren's Dream of an Australian Team Winning the Football World Cup', at http://www.jwff.com.au, accessed November 2006.

17. R. Crawford, 'Sport for Young Ladies: The Victoria Independent Schools 1875–1925', *Sporting Traditions,* 1, no. 1 (1984).

18. Christiane Eisenberg, Pierre Lanfranchi, Tony Mason and Alfred Wahl, *100 Years of Football: The FIFA Centennial Book* (London: Weidenfeld and Nicholson, 2004), p. 43.

19. Stell, *Half the Race: A History of Australian Women in Sport*, p. 13, which Peter Burke, in 'Patriot Games: Women's Football during the First World War in Australia', *Football Studies,* 8, no. 2 (2005): 5, suggests may come from a West Australian newspaper report of 23 May 1895.

20. Burke, 'Patriot Games: Women's Football during the First World War in Australia'.

21. 'Should Women Play Football?' *Table Talk,* 28 July 1921. My thanks for this reference to Debbie Hindley.

22. Photographs of Myra Kawulak courtesy of Debbie Hindley, Murdoch University, Perth, WA.

23. Boria Majumdar and Kausik Bandyopadhyay, *A Social History of Indian Football: Striving to Score* (London: Routledge, 2005), p. 157; see also the role of Brajaranjan Ray and, for an overview, ch. 10, 'The Gendered Kick: Women's Soccer in Twentieth Century India', pp. 152–167.

24. David Rowe, Geoffrey Lawrence, Jim McKay and Toby Miller, *Globalization and Sport: Playing the World* (London: Sage, 2001), p. 118.

25. REF: BP140244136411, 'Feminine Football', at http://www.itnsource.com, accessed 14 February 1944.

26. Pierre Lanfranchi and Matthew Taylor, *Moving with the Ball: The Migration of Professional Footballers* (Oxford: Berg, 2001), p. 232, especially the factors defined as 'pushing' migrant workers to 'a future in the new land, Australia', as well as the 'pull' dynamic, including 'the sun, the beaches and the hospitality'.

27. Philip Moore, 'Soccer and the Politics of Culture in Western Australia', in Noel Dyck (ed), *Games, Sports and Cultures* (London: Berg, 2000), p. 118.

28. John Economos, 'Joey Is Jumping for Joy', *Australian Soccer Weekly*, 6 May 1986, p. 21.

29. Walter Gagg, Head of Technical Department, *Letter to Elaine Watson Australian Women's Soccer Association (inc)*, 22 June 1984, FIFA Correspondence Files, Zurich.

30. Irene Sneyd, 'Letter page', *Australian Soccer Weekly,* 6 May 1986, p. 21.

31. Wray Vamplew, 'Australians and Sport', in Wray Vamplew and Brian Stoddart, *Sport in Australia,* p. 5.

32. D. Colquhoun and K.E. Chad, 'Physiological Characteristics of Australian Female Soccer Players after a Competitive Season', *Australian Journal of Science and Medicine in Sport*, 18, no. 3 (1986): 9–12; J.A. Davis and J. Brewer, 'Physiological Characteristics of an International Female Soccer Squad', *Journal of Sports Science*, 10 (1992): 142–143; J.A. Davis and J. Brewer, 'Applied Physiology of Female Soccer Players', *Sports Medicine*, 16 (1993): 180–189; D. Hoare, 'The Australian National Talent Search Program', *Coaching Focus,* 31 (1992): 3–4; and D. Hoare, 'Talent Search: A Review and Update', *Sports Coach* (Spring 1998): 32–33, for the growth in sports science articles relating to women's participation.

33. David Rowe et al., *Globalization and Sport: Playing the World,* p. 2.

34. Dennis Phillips, *Australian Women at the Olympic Games*, 3rd ed. (Petersham, UNSW: Walla Walla Press & Centre for Olympic Studies).

35. Helen Lenskyj, *The Best Olympics Ever? Social Impacts of Sydney 2000* (New York: State University of New York Press, 2002).

36. FIFA, *Minutes Meeting Number 6 of the Organising Committee for the Olympic Football Tournaments,* 27 September 2000, Sydney, p. 2.

37. International Olympic Committee, *Women in the Olympic Movement—Women in Sport Leadership Evaluation of the 10%–20% Objectives,* Department of International Cooperation and Development, November 2006.

38. FIFA, Minutes, *Meeting Number 6 of the Organising Committee for the Olympic Football Tournaments*, p. 2.

39. FIFA, *Minutes Meeting Number 2 of the Organising Committee for the Olympic Football Tournaments,* 29 October 2002, Zurich, Attachments 4 and 15.

# Conclusion

## To Play or Not to Play

The much talked of football match between British Ladies has been played, and the world has not moved an inch out of its orbit ... There was an enormous gathering, the number in which has been estimated variously at from seven to twenty thousand. the true number probably approached ten thousand the procession along Park-Rood to Nightingale-lane was close to continuous ... As a display of football it was execrable ... as a public exhibition to which anyone is admitted on payment of a shilling nothing is more degrading. Ignorance as to the insults to which they would expose themselves may be a lame excuse for Saturday's proceedings, but it is difficult to believe that any one of those who took part in them would again submit herself to the coarse and ribald remarks about their figure and their costumes and their movements which must have reached their ears from the time they entered the field to the time they left it.[1]

Mariel Margaret Hamm boasts 242 international caps and 144 international goals. Nike are reported to pay her $1m a year, with the company selling four times as many No. 9 Hamm replica shirts as those of other players, male or female. Other endorsements are thought to double Hamm's income, but in many ways she eschews the spotlight. She recently made the cover of *Sports Illustrated* under the headline: The Reluctant Superstar. 'Everybody in our society wants the female sports figure to be glamorous, gorgeous and smiling every minute,' says Heinrichs. 'Let's value the qualities Mia has: she's intelligent, articulate and humble. She has become the complete player.'[2]

Writing ten years after the first excerpt, Gibson and Pickford in *Association Football and the Men Who Made It,* with all the benefit of a decade of hindsight, announced that 'Lady Footballers ... subsequently became as extinct as the dodo so far as the Metropolis was concerned.' Fortunately, with the assistance of a longer and less parochial view, these rumours have proven premature. Michael Oriard, in his study of American Football (or 'gridiron') has identified women playing this code as early as 1895.[3] As has been noted, there are brief references to Australian Rules the same year as the British Ladies Football Club played at Crouch End and still more to rugby. The PR China shows a much longer history of women participating in football of various kinds. Real Madrid sent its first 'socia' card to a woman in 1926, there were women's teams in Czechoslovakia since the 1930s, physical education teachers in the US, and a tradition of female works teams in association and other codes. 'Boy can they play!' ran the slogan of the inaugural FIFA Women's World U19 Championship, held in Canada in 2002, marking the moment of female youth players in officially sponsored international competition. At the same time, there remain national associations that do not recognize women's football.[4] A turning point came on 22 August 1998 when forty Iranian women took their place in a football training session at Tehran's Hejab Stadium, as, since the start of the Islamic revolution, women had been forbidden to play football.[5] In 2004 a national football association that had previously provided a woman General Secretary to the Confederation, faced a complaint of discrimination filed by the Human Rights Commission because of the decision of New Zealand Soccer not to enter the female Oceania qualifying tournaments for both the Olympic Games and the U19 World Championship.[6] Citing initiatives, the New Zealand Soccer board rejected the claims and offered to host the inaugural FIFA U-17 Women's World Cup in 2008. Also in 2004, the Nigerian team, which had won their fourth successive African Women's Championship, were presented with cash gifts of $7,000 US each by President Olusegun Obasanjo at a special reception. In order to receive the bonus money owed them by the Federation, the team had staged a very public four-day sit-in at their hotel in Johannesburg after the conclusion of the championship. Evidently, the marginalization of women at administrative level and the lack of widespread support for women players mean that fundamental issues of control are as contentious now as they have ever been.

In spite of numerous differences, the gender order of national football associations, confederations and FIFA exhibit structures similar to those of other conservative sports federations where, for example, women are underrepresented in executive and policymaking bodies and women's football is put in a separate committee or section. There are a very few exceptions; one is Norway, where a system has operated since 1985 which Kari Fasting has termed a 'mild quota' of having at least one woman on each of the central committees.[7] It is hardly surprising that it should be the first women to sit on the Norwegian Football Association (NFA) Committee, Ellen Wille, also the first female speaker at a FIFA event, who publicly prompted Havelange to host a world championship for women. There remains a bedrock of traditional sport ideology about roles and systems which the new developments, although encouraging, can sometimes obscure.

In the Introduction, the lack of respect given to WFA material was not seen to be malicious, but there is plenty in the case studies to indicate a degree of ruthlessness. In the spring of 2005 FA Learning published an interview with the head of national teams, Sammy Lee (a former professional player with Liverpool and Queens Park Rangers) in which he expanded on the virtues of coach education:

> Coaching awards are a fundamental part of the English game now with the introduction of mandatory qualifications at the top level and, in my view, this is crucial for the game and for all British Coaches. I am pleased that Coaching is becoming more professionalised, more standardised and therefore aligns us with the rest of Europe ... Hopefully

we will continue to see opportunities in our game for 'home grown' Coaches besides players.[8]

What a head of national teams earns is subject to conjecture. What the 1997 case of Vanessa Hardwck indicates is that the Football Association would rather pay an additional sum of £10,000 to the £16,000 compensation already awarded by an Employment Tribunal when it was shown that it had decided to fail her for the Advanced Licence (then the top coaching qualification) before the final assessment meeting, when eight men who had worse marks and five with the same mark were passed. Lee passed his A Licence on that course. The diversification of coaching courses and the lack of transparency in the procedures make Lee's comments seem overly optimistic in view of these spiteful occupational cliques. While I am a fan of the first woman to hold the Pro licence as a player, it does appear that Hope Powell, the England women's national coach, was approached rather than the job being offered in open interview to any of the seven women who already held the A Licence in 2000. In 2006 the Luton manager, Mike Newell, launched a scathing attack on women officials; he was furious that an assistant referee, Amy Rayner, failed to award his side a penalty in the 3–2 loss to QPR. As a self-appointed critic of those who would taint the sporting spirit of the game via 'bungs', he demonstrates an equally self-referential sexism that is obviously irrational. In discussing these issues, media commentators have made the accusation that to do so is to show more of an interest in politics than football. To protect some of the world's highest paid and most prestigious occupations for male-only leagues and teams without reference to the law in the twenty-first century and to make this exception universal because of the peculiar logic of sport requires an interest in both. Furthermore, having done the practical aspects as well as considering the theoretical questions, when facing the vulnerability of being that lone representative of one's sex in a coaching or playing scenario, a different view of what sporting spirit might mean in Newell's vocabulary. This is not just in coaching and adult professions related to playing. When English boys of five and six are being trained in academies related to professional clubs in an increasingly scientific and specialized manner, precisely what is being protected? Does this 'story that we tell ourselves about ourselves' reveal more to do with politics or football?

There is much evidence to support the view that national associations, confederations and FIFA increasingly began to intervene in women's football out of fear that unaffiliated profit-seeking organizations or private individuals would organize tournaments. The development of a Women's World Championship—titled the Women's World Cup from 1995—is a case in point. Whereas it could be said that the attitude of FIFA prior to the 1960s had been to prevent the integration of women's football, expecting it to wither due to neglect, the growth of the sport meant that it became an imperative to control it by incorporation. UEFA was the first confederation to set up a committee for women's football, in 1971, with the inaugural conference on women's football organized in Zurich on 22 March 1973. Among the findings at this conference were that eight nations already had national competitions with international friendly matches, women's football in Italy was operated by commercial organizations that (shockingly) paid considerable transfer fees for good players, and a vote of five for and thirteen against for a resolution to introduce an international women's competition. Having decided to do nothing, the committee did just that for several years. However, successive unofficial international tournaments and conferences organized by businesspeople from Hong Kong to Italy led, in 1980, to the second conference on women's football, also in Zurich. In some rather unsubtle scheduling, UEFA called their meeting the same day as the Italian conference convened in the Valley of Aosta, and the 'problem' of commercialization was discussed extensively. Equally significant, that year, the IOC entered into negotiation with international federations in order to reduce the number of teams in team sport events. FIFA maintained sixteen teams in the men's final competition, provided that women's football was not introduced as an Olympic sport.[9]

Consequently, as with developments in many countries, until adoption by FIFA, international organization of women's football was characterized by considerable influence exerted on behalf of autonomous clubs and women-only federations, given the limited degree of centralization. The absence of widely recognized directives gave a large amount of independence to a variety of actors. Thus the fears that women's football would be commercialized or that an international women's football association could be founded which would threaten the unity of the sport directly contributed to incorporation. By establishing a separate committee, rather than integrating women's concerns into each committee, the international federation seems to have acted on the overriding political impetus to avoid giving into the wishes and demands of the advocates of women's football in any wholesale way. To control competition and commercialization by compartmentalizing it. For its part, women's football had been striving for international recognition, and this move seemed to offer a degree of success and prestige. It would have been a longer road perhaps to establish women's football as an Olympic sport without backing from FIFA. A degree of what could be interpreted as cooperation or collusion was entirely understandable, if, for some women administrators, it was unforgivable.

Speculation aside, what was lacking was intensive backing, full incorporation into the bureaucratic and executive systems, and fundamental change to the gendered nature of the sport's organization. What is still an issue is primarily a question of democracy and transparency. Put simply, the number of women in decision-making positions does not reflect the number of female members represented by the national associations or the federation as a whole, let alone the players. The related point is the issue of resources and the pool of potential women leaders who may find alternative employment until such time as the systems become more democratic. Sports organizations often bemoan difficulties in recruitment and retention of leaders without reviewing their own discriminatory practices. The question of representation and attention also remains. To address oversight in each of the central and elected committees of the federation, the quotas need to be more than mild. Few men and women want to be elected on anything other than merit, but until such time as the system as whole is reviewed, this rather ungainly means of representing women's interests will at least begin to move towards the 20 per cent and beyond representation set by the IOC for 2005.

The question of integration and control now seems to have taken a new twist, perhaps as a result of the change in governing body attitudes towards the old amateur–professional divide. If women's football was integrated in the 1970s gradually as a result of a wish to defend the commercial exploitation of female players, it is now being asked by key personnel such as Mr Blatter and Mr Johansen to court a degree of media coverage and to attract sponsorship in its own right. The most marketable asset they seem to focus on is the attractiveness of the players, who are asked to find sponsors among traditional female producers such as cosmetics and fashion. If the authorities have been keen to trumpet participation figures, then perhaps these could be used to lobby for increased representation to reflect the participation of women.

This about-face from those who, in their romantic paternalism, have restricted the development of commercialization in the guise of preventing exploitation is actually very shrewd mercantile policy. The entrance of football into underexposed sponsorship and related markets via the female player mirrors a wish to exploit new demand in general. However financially forward-looking this policy may be, its basis is a conservative attitude which has persisted since women have tried to be involved in football, since at least 1895. Having insisted upon central control of the women's game, the old guard are again voicing concern that the expansion of women's football should not be at the cost of men's football. A point often made during this study, be it at club, region or national level, was that the men's first team was considered *the* team, and some of this attitude is reflected in the idea of football and women's football. It appears to matter little that the women's team can be more successful in terms of trophies and medals, accomplishments which have often been used to argue that ever-more funds should be diverted to their underachieving male counterparts. As if there were some mythical pie which could be divided in only so many ways, women are now being told to develop financing in their sport. It is almost impossible from the documentation to identify what the costs and profits of women's football are and more difficult still to be sure how much is spent on female participation, as it can be subsumed into youth budgets, special initiatives and so forth, administered overall by the host national association. As the case of Mia Hamm and Nike has shown, the assumption that women players would have to break new markets in sponsorship deals is a misguided one. This latest episode indicates that the partial integration looks set to be a continuing problem until such time as a more radical review of women's representation in decision-making positions is made and acted upon.

Issues surrounding sexuality and gender appear to remain a key issue for the English players, much as the idea of 'butch' or mannish behaviour is linked with possible lesbian identity, particularly in contact and team sports considered to be traditionally male. However, this was expressed more in terms of the response to the question 'What do you think is the general opinion of women who play football?' than a discussion of the players' own sexuality:

> Well, I was shocked when a man who I worked with, he had a senior management role and had hired me so I was, you know, respectful of him until then, said, 'No, you don't play football do you? They're either dykes or bikes! I was shocked of course and offended and he saw that but he walked off laughing.

> I want to be accepted as a player, an equal on the team whatever the team. Being gay or straight seems to be a much bigger issue for girls teams because boys teams seem to be more about the football and not so much about people's sexuality but there are plenty of homophobic insults in men's sport too.

> I think it's funny when people are like, 'they're trying to be men but they'll never play as well because they are women' because it's so ridiculous! First if I wanted to be a man, which I do not, I'd get an operation or something! Second, come and play against me within the rules of the game and I'll let my football speak for itself. Third, why is your own sexuality so fragile you want to boost it by questioning mine through playing a sport I happen to have loved since I was a kid?

> Our coach makes me laugh. She's straight but she knows most of us are gay and she kind of gets carried away with being supportive in the team talk on match days—saying stuff at half time like 'Forget who is out there telling you what to do whether it's your Dad or Mum or boyfriend or whatever play your own game.' And we'll go 'Boyfriend coach?' and she'll go 'You know what I mean' and blush.

So the supposition that a female player is exhibiting aspects of her sexuality by playing the game produces multiple, sometimes contradictory stereotypes, as each of the case studies indicate. Despite the increasing numbers of women players, the dominant perception, often a source of masculine humour, as with the examples just given, is that men are interested in football only because men play. The logic of the stereotype therefore indicates that women are either playing because women play or in order to attract men. Because of the public perception that football is a sport that has been professionally and competitively all-male for most of its history, masculinity has been an unremarkable category. This is not to say that kinds of masculinities have not been developed in the male professional and competitive game from the underachieving-but-gifted typology to the student of the game to the natural leader. The fact that disagreements remain about the respectability of women playing football in British society in the early twenty-first century demonstrates some rather disheartening aspects of the culture. Equally depressing is the public relations overload that pits Sport England's top priorities against one another for funding that is linked to increased participation, which means that female development is little about equitable principles and has much (too much) to do with revolting management-speak about 'growing the game' and its supposed progressivism. In the run-up to 2012 this has tended to take one of two unappealing bureaucratic forms. The first is the equivalent of watching an embarrassing older relative disco-dance in public. The second is to hear freshly appointed nonplaying development officers cheerily announce the latest initiative, full of pride at vicariously wearing the three lions while simultaneously lacking any sense of irony or history. Either way, the clumsy attempts to 'represent' are about as convincing as watching New Labour politicians try to mime and clap along to 'things can only get better'. The tensions among social inclusion, social conscience and the responsibility of these administrations is part of wider expansionist portfolios which sees Football Association paid officials, for example, accept awards for 'coordinating' volunteers whose benefit is less tangible than nomination for awards in the Honours list. Even the most ardent fan would find it hard to glory in the self-congratulation if England women were to win WWC in 2007.

In contrast, if we ask what kind of women play football, or soccer in the US, rather different cultural conditions prevail. There are links between the rise of women's sports and 'equity' not least because of Title IX, the proven market for large women-only tournaments in Women's World Cup 1999 and for the women's professional league WUSA. Aligned with the rhetoric of equality is a degree of commercialization that is in marked contrast to the European context, and specifically the English example. This holds for endorsement deals, clothing and equipment in the High Street, for television and live attendance. The cultural representations of the US national team are also very different from those in the English example. The wholesome image of the players as smart, grateful athletes concerned to give back to their communities (including players and fans) is strong enough to withstand public scrutiny of Brandi Chastain's sports bra, televised to several nations. This is not to say that the stereotype of the collaborative, ethical, intelligent, maternal US national team player is any less about reinforcing normative femininity and heterosexuality than the English example. Nor is it operating in a sporting culture in which homophobia plays little part, as the cases of Australia and the US indicate (perhaps to a lesser extent with the milder 'tomboy' references in the PR China example).

There is, of course, a large market to sell to. Nevertheless, the focus on 'difference' links with the case studies more broadly because the domestic US market is effectively the pinnacle to which a women football player may aspire, as was evidenced by the influx of personnel to WUSA and the difficulties following its closure. While increasingly their male counterparts can take jobs in lucrative foreign leagues, the influential women players have to be astute, collegial and also pretty pragmatic in the choices that they make if they wish to continue to earn some part of their income from the sport. The place of these players in the culture of sport and more widely is not, then, free of tensions. While some would argue that they appear to have dominated the sport as a national team, this view can be at best only partial. The economic, professional and organizational barriers that they face mean that this acceptance of authority has been used to disproportionally allocate resources and funding to the male national team and to individual male professionals. Ironically, the class, the social status, the maturity of the college background has to be negotiated by the Women's National Team players as useful for marketability but also is used as an underlying narrative to distance them from the world of male professional team sport. They may be moral guardians of the game for the wider community, but the financial potential and reward are part of the difference.

In Australia, the continuities of football in a male-dominated sports culture are evident. With the development of the Australian code, like the American code, it is a sport that embraces different types of masculinities and also different body shapes. Furthermore, the alliance of the physical body with specific elements which are perceived to be somehow linked with certain kinds of masculinity, for example, weight and strength, are often used as arguments for the disparity between male and female participation. Others cite risk-taking behaviour and calculated infringement of rules as evidence of masculine validation, implied in being able to 'handle yourself' on the field. Shawn Ladda's work *The History of Intercollegiate Women's Soccer in the United States* indicates that in the US the intercollegiate ban in all team sports affected women's soccer broadly from the 1920s to the 1970s. There is plenty of evidence that girls were playing prep school and college football from the early 1900s. While we know the Dick, Kerr tour involved women playing against men, there was sufficient press coverage to indicate that, as with other European sports, the game was exported as similar to hockey and relatively egalitarian in its team composition. The section on the US discusses this broader history to suggest that the highly organized domestic sports leagues in a variety of codes, combined with a degree of international organization for association football, have served to make the popular cultural formation of the sport, in which women have been seen to engage more recently. In this, the US case study has continuities with the other examples, and a future study could look at the role of educational establishments as the site of female play in Australia, PR China and beyond.

In view of the widespread support for the independence of sports organizations and their right to coordinate both their own infrastructure and their own competitive rules, there is a need to question how democratic and transparent the methods of operation are. In theoretical terms, I have suggested that homophobia in sport reflects not only a fear of women's sexuality but also fear of the loss of male control of that sexuality, thus endangering the balance of power in gender relationships. It seems that we are in a phase whereby this has been used as an organizing principle historically in the social relations of football, but that same idea has been reconstituted in the contemporary atmosphere for a different form of control. That is, the wholesale exclusion of women as a group is no longer viable—large enough numbers of women across the world are showing that they can play football, and the depth of U17, U20 and adult competition provides continuing evidence. Consequently, these women have been vital in forcing the change of policy by the sports governing bureaucracies. However, in order to maintain male control of the sport and the form of women's participation, the challenge is to try to set norms for female players that are feminine-appropriate. This is an area of considerable scope for feminist-informed study and refinements to the process characterized in the Introduction as one of 'negative integration' will, it is hoped, follow in moving both the theoretical and the empirical discussions on.

The valorization of male athletes as possessing superior strength and muscularity (whatever their physical stature) is evident in changing the argument from one that suggests the female body as too weak to perform the sport to one that provides a protected arena for women's play. What is actually being protected is that heterosexual, heteronormative discourse and its binary construction.[10] The marginalization and consequent trivialization try to naturalize gender difference in bodies as fundamental. It is not some external attitude towards women that dictates this, the 'rules' tell us now, but something that is internalized and that inherently requires different treatment. While it is most encouraging that increasing numbers of women play football, therefore, there seems to be little end to this particular phase without a more radical revision of the distribution of power in the bureaucracies themselves. Whether sufficient numbers of women would support this next step or whether it remains to be pioneered by one or more individuals, perhaps from the elite level, is a question currently without an answer. In pursuing qualitative accounts that allow sportswomen to articulate their experiences as individuals and groups, we must seek a discussion that is historically and culturally located but must also be alert to differences in age, class, religious, ethnic and sexual identity, in addition to incorporating a range of differently-abled participants. If we multiply this by the various ways in which we experience and do identity to ourselves and others, it's an ambitious project. Because of that, a researcher could be only somewhat content with the outcome at any one time of trying to write it up, and I have been conscious of holding up a mirror to an amorphous and changing entity. Readers will be thankful that some points of definition and clarity do suggest themselves, however satisfied they are by the quality of that reflection.

The historical, structural and cultural contexts (by which I also mean organizational cultures) across the case studies make some of the specific points more widely applicable. For example, the underrepresentation of black, Asian and minority ethnic women in football internationally is an example of discriminatory practices in accessing sport that some women continue to face. The underrepresentation of African countries in top-level international competition is affected by issues relating to women's access to sport, the way that national football associations view women's participation, and regional and international factors. So the individual experiences draw out difference and diversity but also highlight similarities across these differing circumstances. It also raises the wider question of sport, leisure and women's access to resources across cultures. Women's football in each of the case-study nations here deserves a more in-depth study, but the situations in South America and in Africa are no less important.

Against the fundamental issues of female poverty, lack of access to education and denial of human rights, a discussion of the terminology of 'women's football' and 'football' may appear to be one of those semantic points of academic interest at best, at worst essentially pointless. Yet very few have asked why the distinction as it exists in its current form is important. Analyzing the relationship between the two is fundamental to understanding the future directions open to women players as a group and as individuals. Academics, legal practitioners and sports administrators can give their view of where aspects of the sport currently stand, but, if one is to understand in what direction football is heading and women's place in it, some further analysis is required. The concept of women's football as a subject of academic study in its own right is in its infancy, the lack of theoretical investigation in turn inhibited by a lack of data. This is made difficult partly by the multilevel aspects of the game in which myriad subsystems and subcultures exist, within nations as well as on an international level. However, an attempt to draw international comparisons is not a premature exercise because, though not vast, sufficient empirical material exists. The issue is not one about which sporting associations and federations can afford to be neutral. It is also timely, as this is partly influenced by the world-wide profile of the sport and its related forms.

'Capital of the New Soccer Nation. The idiotic but time-honoured songs, the beer, the hooliganism, the Spice Girls. US Soccer fans never acted much like the rest of the world, but Los Angeles soccer culture is at the Center of the fastest-growing sport in the country.'[11] Even while placing football as an aspect of modernity, much sport relies on nostalgia to create a golden era which did not quite exist, as women's involvement indicates. The way in which various bodies deal with women's football in overt and less obvious ways tells us about the way in which they wish to be seen. It is not possible, given the historical construction of football as a man's game, for the developments to be apolitical. Looking at the macro elements of international competition and regulation or the micro aspects of individual nations only would be less rewarding. There have been key individuals and groups that have shaped female participation, and, though they have done so without the institutional resources available to wealthy sports bureaucracies, their stories are an important part of the social and cultural history of the game. They are also too myriad to be told here, but that makes my point about the need for better empirical and theoretical understanding all the more forcefully. As Nettie Honeyball reportedly forecast:

It is a recognised fact that nothing is more conducive to a good complexion than good health, and we girls are already quite satisfied that in football we have found an invigorating, harmless, strengthening, and healthy recreation, and we all agree after each practice that we feel greatly benefited and refreshed. There are some prudes, no doubt who will vote the game improper as there is always a prejudice against women encroaching on what men consider their preserves. The female politician, clerk, cyclist &co., have had their turn of attempted suppression, but have more than held their ground, and so I think will the Lady Footballers.[12]

## Notes

1. *Hornsey and Finsbury Park Journal,* 25 March 1895.
2. Michael Preston, 'Quality Hamm', *The Sunday Times,* 5 October 2003, Section 2, p. 11. April Heinrichs was the national team coach and had been an outstanding US national team player.
3. Michael Oriard, *Reading Football: How the Popular Press Created an American Spectacle* (Chapel Hill: University of North Carolina Press, 1993).
4. The six confederations are the Asian Football Confederation (AFC); Confédération Africaine de Football (CAF); Confederation of North, Central American and Caribbean Association Football (CONCACAF); Confederación Sudamericana de Fútbol (CONMEBOL); Oceania Football Confederation (OFC) and Union des Associations Européennes de Football (UEFA).
5. Siavosh Ghazi, 'Iranian Women Put on Their Running Shoes', *UNESCO Courier,* Paris: UNESCO, April 1999, p. 20. As the article points out, misogynistic attitudes are not just a part of football; women had been granted right to full membership of the Marylebone Cricket club that same year, and ten honorary members were 'allowed to rub shoulders with men in the club pavilion—but only as long as their shoulders are covered'.
6. For example see http://www.fifa.com/en/media/index: 'There are over 20 million women footballers, 80% of whom are juniors or still in their teens, which demonstrates that the growing popularity for women's football is not only the prerogative of North America.' *FIFA Survey the Big Count 2000,* released 2001, accessed 10 January 2005.
7. Kari Fasting, 'Small Country Big Results: Women's Football in Norway', in Hong and Mangan, *Soccer Women and Liberation: Kicking Off a New Era* (London: Frank Cass), 2004, p. 155.
8. Sammy Lee, 'Interview with Sammy Lee', *FA Learning Insight,* The Football Association (Spring/Summer 2005), p. 10.
9. Dr H Käser letter re: women's football/The Olympic Games to Pat Gregory, Women's Football Association, England, dated 17 June 1980, private collection.
10. Even with recent initiatives such as the English FA's *Football for All* scheme, which is almost a paragon of political correctness: 'Football for All is about fairness. It's about doing things properly. About making sure everyone has a chance to be involved in football, regardless of ability, race or religion. About encouraging and increasing the involvement of groups at all levels of football

by recognising that inequalities exist and taking steps to address them. It's about making opportunities available where currently there are none. About using the power of football to build a better future. In order to achieve these objectives, Football for All has become a part of everything we do at The FA.' It covers racial equality, disability football, social inclusion and homophobia but does not cover gender equity.

11. Mike Hodgkinson, 'Capital of the New Soccer Nation', *Los Angeles Citybeat,* 16–22 October 2003.

12. 'The Ladies' Football Club', *Daily Graphic,* 25 January 1895, spelling and punctuation as original.

# Bibliography

Abrams, N. (2005), 'Inhibited but Not "Crowded Out": The Strange Fate of Soccer in the United States', *International Journal of the History of Sport,* 12, no. 3 (December): 1–17.

Acosta, V., and Linda Jean Carpenter (2004), *Women in Intercollegiate Sport: A Longitudinal, National Study Twenty Seven Year Update 1977–2004,* available at www.womenssportfoundtion.org.

Adair, D., and Wray Vamplew (1997), *Sport in Australian History,* Melbourne: Oxford University Press.

Adderley, J. (2006), 'Women's Football', *BBC Nation on Film,* London, BBC 10, November.

Adidas promotional leaflet (1999), FIFA Women's World Cup 1999, Los Angeles, CA.

Aldis, C. (2001), *British University Sports Association* files.

Allatt, C. (1988), *Analysis of Questionnaire with Reference to the Interest Shown in Girls in Full Time Education in the Playing of Association Football,* 19 September.

Allen, R. (1972), *Skinhead Girls,* New English Library.

American Physical Education Association (1923), *Preliminary Program of the National Convention,* Springfield, MA, 11–14 April 1923', *Mind and Body,* 30, no. 317 (April): 37–39.

Anderson, B. (1991), *Imagined Communities,* rev. ed., New York: Verso.

Andrews, D. (2000), 'Contextualising Suburban Soccer: Consumer Culture, Lifestyle Differentiation and Suburban America', in G. Finn and R. Giulianotti (eds), *Football Culture: Local Contests Global Visions,* London: Routledge.

Andrews, D., R. Pitter, D. Zwick and D. Ambrose (1997), 'Soccer's Racial Frontier: Sport and the Suburbanisation of Contemporary America', in G. Armstrong and R. Giulianotti (eds), *Entering the Field: New Perspectives on World Football,* Oxford: Berg.

Anon. (1895), 'Ladies football', *Penny Illustrated,* 23 February.

Anon. (1895), 'Ladies' football', *The Times,* 25 March.

Anon. (1895), 'Ladies' football', *Hornsey and Finsbury Park Journal,* 25 March.

Anon. (1895), 'The Ladies' Football Club', *Daily Graphic,* 25 January.

Anon. (1917), 'Personal Column', *The Times,* 18 December.

Anon. (1918), 'Radcliffe Athletic Association', *The Radcliffe Magazine,* October.

Anon. (1920), 'Ladies at Football England v France by a Special Correspondent', *The Times,* 7 May.

Anon. (1921), 'Ladies' football', *The Times,* 3 January.

Anon. (1921), 'Clubs and Charity', *Athletic News,* 17 January.

Anon. (1921), 'News in Brief', *The Times,* 6 April.

Anon. (1921), 'Sea and Spa: Holiday Attractions Everywhere', *The Times,* 28 June.

Anon. (1921), 'Should Women Play Football?' *Table Talk,* 28 July.

Anon. (1921), 'English Girl Teams Play Football for Charity', *Pawtucket Times,* 9 September.

Anon. (1921), 'To Play, or Not to Play', *The Athletic News and Cyclists Journal,* 12 December.

Anon. (1922), 'News in Brief', *The Times,* 14 March.

Anon. (1922), 'Royal Ceremony at Waterloo. The Mons Trial', *The Times,* 22 March.

Anon. (1922), 'British Women's Eleven Plays Fine Soccer', *Pawtucket Times,* 25 September.

Anon. (1922), 'Record Crowd to See Women in Soccer Game', *Pawtucket Times,* 28 September.

Anon. (1922), 'Women's Team Plays Coasts to 4 to 4 Tie', *Pawtucket Times,* 7 October.

Anon. (1923), 'Bridgetts United Win Women's FA Cup', *Stoke Evening Sentinel,* 10 July.

Anon. (1924), 'Football by Night', *The Times,* 12 January.

Anon. (1926), 'Traffic Alteration at Croydon', *The Times,* 5 February.

Anon. (1947), 'FA Sharply Criticised', *Stalybridge Times,* 19 September.

Anon. (1953), 'Big Decorations in Little Streets', *The Times,* 3 June.

Anon. (1955), 'Dolly Led Stoke (Ladies) to Victory in Cup', *Stoke Evening Sentinel,* 21 January.

Anon. (1955), 'Sportsman's Parade XLVIII: Mr Len Bridgett', *Stoke Evening Sentinel,* 22 January.

Anon. (1968), '1922 Cup Victory for Stoke Ladies', *Stoke Evening Sentinel,* 10 February.

Anon. (1968), 'Sports in Brief', *The Times,* 18 May.

Anon. (1972), 'Woman's Place Not on the Football Field', *The Times,* 30 September.

Anon. (1975), 'Lambert's Celebrate 50th', *Pawtucket Times,* 18 November.

Anon. (1976), 'They Were the Champions', *Stoke Evening Sentinel,* 12 March.

Anon. (1981), 'FAM Say No to Women's Soccer Control', *The Star,* 20 September.

Anon. (1983) (possibly Qiu Zhenqi), 'Women's Football in Ancient China', *National Women's Soccer Invitational Brochure,* Beijing, China.

Anon. (1989), 'Team of the Twenties', *Coventry Evening Telegraph,* 20 November.

Anon. (1992), 'Survivor Recalls Famous Team', *Stoke Evening Sentinel,* 18 April.

Anthony, David (1970), 'When to Kick Is Unwomanly', *Times Educational Supplement,* 10 October.

Armstrong, G., and R. Guilianotti (1997), *Entering the Field: New Perspectives on World Football,* Oxford: Berg.

Bailey, John (2004), 'The Great Women's Match of 1895', *Soccer History* Issue 7 (Spring).

Bains, J. (1998), *Corner Flags and Corner Shops: The Asian Football Player's Experience,* London: Victor Gollancz.

Bale, J. (1979), *The Development of Soccer as a Participant and Spectator Sport: Geographical Aspects,* London: Sports Council/Social Science Research Council.

Bale, J. (1980), 'Women's Football in England and Wales: A Social-Geographic Perspective', *Physical Education Review,* 3, no. 2: 45–62.

Bale, J. (1982), *Sport and Place: A Geography of Sport in England, Scotland and Wales,* London: Hurst.

Bale, J. (1993), *Sport, Space and the City,* London: Routledge.

Bale, J., and O. Moen (1995), *The Stadium and the City,* Keele: Keele University Press.

Bale, J., and Joseph Maguire (eds) (1994), *The Global Sports Arena: Athletic Talent Migration in an Interdependent World,* London: Frank Cass.

Banet-Weiser, S. (1999), 'Hoop Dreams: Professional Basketball and the Politics of Race and Gender', *Journal of Sport and Social Issues* 23, no. 4: 403–420.

Batt, P. (1973), 'Dates Have the Order of the Boot', *The Sun,* 17 April.

Battersby, K. (1994), 'Mohr Earns Germany First Leg Advantage', *Daily Telegraph,* 2 December.

Begbie, S. (1996), 'The Story So Far: Recent Developments in Women's Football in Scotland', *Scottish Journal of Physical Education,* 24: 6–17.

Bethell, A. (c1983), *Gregory's Girl* (an adaption of Bill Forsyth's original film script by Andrew Bethell), Cambridge: Cambridge University Press.

Beveridge, S. (1975), 'Edna—The Sad Soccer Star', *Sunday People,* 31 January.

Bhattacharya, N. (1992), *Hem and Football,* London: Secker and Warburg.

Birley, D. (1995), *Playing the Game: Sport and British Society 1910–1945,* Manchester: Manchester University Press.

Birley, D. (1995), *Sport and the Making of Britain,* Manchester: Manchester University Press.

Birrell, Susan (1994), 'Achievement Related Motives and the Woman Athlete', in Susan Birrell and Cheryl Cole (eds), *Women Sport and Culture,* Champaign, IL, and Leeds: Human Kinetics.

Birrell, S., and N. Theberg (1994), 'Feminist Resistance and Transformation in Sport', in D. Margaret Costa and Sharon R. Guthrie (eds), *Women and Sport: Interdisciplinary Perspectives,* Champaign, IL, and Leeds: Human Kinetics.

Blaikie, W. (1879), 'The Risks of Athletic Work', *Harper's New Monthly Magazine,* 58, December 1870.

Blatter, J. (1984), *General Secretary FIFA Circular 338 to All Associations 22 June,* FIFA Correspondence File, Zurich.

Blatter, J. (1995), 'The Future Is Feminine', *FIFA News,* Zurich, July.

Blatter, J. (2006), 'Promising Preparations for WWC 2007', *FIFA News,* Zurich, 19 March.

Boaler, J. (1994), 'When Do Girls Prefer Football to Fashion?' *British Educational Research Journal,* 20, no. 5.

Booth, D. (2001), *Australian Beach Cultures: The History of Sun, Sand and Surf,* London: Frank Cass.

Booth, Douglas (2005), *The Field: Truth and Fiction in Sport History,* London: Routledge.

Booth, Douglas (2006), 'Sites of Truth or Metaphors of Power? Refiguring the Archive', *Sport in History,* 26, no. 1 (April): 91–109.

Bourdieu, P. (1986), *Distinction: A Social Critique of the Judgement of Taste,* London: Routledge.

Bourke, W. (2000) (daughter of Alice Mills Lambert), essays, newspaper cuttings and eulogy provided by personal communication, 23 June.

Boyd, A. (1921), 'Australia Wants a Soccer Team', *The Athletic News and Cyclists Journal,* 17 October.

Bray, Jenny (1992), 'Women's Soccer Association of New Zealand (Inc)', *Letter to JS Blatter,* 9 November, FIFA Correspondence File, Zurich.

British Ladies Football Club Programme (1895), London: Mizen Printers, 23 March.

Broadbent, M. (1934), LD 7096.6 RG 27, *Alumnae Biographical Files for the Broadbent Papers,* Mount Holyoke College Archives, 1 October.

Broadbent, M. (1934) LD 7096.6 RG 27, *Alumnae Biographical Files for the Broadbent Papers,* Mount Holyoke College Archives, 6 October.

Brownell, S. (1995), *Training the Body for China: Sport and the Moral Order of the People's Republic,* Chicago and London: University of Chicago Press.

Burgess, I., Allan Edwards and James Skinner (2003), 'Football Culture in an Australian School Setting: The Construction of Masculine Identity', *Sport, Education and Society,* 8, no. 2.

Burke, P. (2005), 'Patriot Games: Women's Football during the First World War in Australia', *Football Studies,* 8, no. 2.

Carroll, S. (1999), 'The Disempowerment of the Gender Gap: Soccer Moms and the 1996 Elections', *Political Science and Politics,* 32, no. 1 (March): 7–11.

Cashman, R., and A. Weaver (1991), *Wicket Women: Cricket and Women in Australia,* Kensington: New South Wales University Press.

Cavan, Harry H. (1984), *World Women's Invitational Football Tournament Chinese Taipei Football Association,* FIFA Correspondence File, Zurich, 11 September.

Caudwell, Jayne (1999), 'Women's Football in the United Kingdom: Theorising Gender and Unpacking the Butch Lesbian Image', *Journal of Sport and Social Issues,* 23, no. 4: 390–403.

Caudwell, J. (2002), 'Women's Experiences of Sexuality within Football Contexts: A Particular and Located Footballing Epistemology', *Football Studies,* 5: 24–45.

Chang, W. (1981), *President ROCFA 'Welcome Speech', World Women's Invitational Tournament 1981,* Taipei, 11 October.

Chastain, B. (2004), *It's Not about the Bra: Play Hard, Play Fair, and Put the Fun Back into Competitive Sports,* New York: Harper Collins.

China PR Football Association (1991), *Football in China: Present Problems and Future Prospects,* 16 November, CFA document, Peking, China.

China PR Team Statement (1991), *China '91: 1st FIFA World Championship for Women's Football for the M&M's Cup,* Zurich: FIFA Archive.

Cheetham, S. (1994), *Gladys Prothero ... Football Genius!* London: Juma.

Chye Hin, T. (1981), *Vice President ALFC 'Re: Women's Football in Asia' 28th October 1981,* FIFA Correspondence File, Zurich.

Close, P., David Askew and Xu Xin (2006), *The Beijing Olympiad: The Political Economy of a Sporting Mega-Event,* London and New York: Routledge.

Cohen, D., and R. Rosenzweig (2004), *Digital History: A Guide to Gathering, Preserving, and Presenting the Past on the Web,* Philadelphia: University of Pennsylvannia Press.

Collins, S. (2006), 'National Sports and Other Myths: The Failure of US Soccer', *Soccer and Society: Special Edition Making It Happen: Fringe Nations in World Soccer Celebrating World Cup 2006,* 7, no. 2–3 (April): 353–363.

Collins, T. (2005), 'History, Sociology and the "Civilising Process"', *Sport in History,* 25, no. 2 (August): 289–306.

Collins, T. (2006), *Searching for a New Webb Ellis? Some Thoughts on the Historiography of Football,* unpublished paper, British Society of Sports History Conference, Lancaster, September.

Colquhoun, D., and K.E. Chad (1986), 'Physiological Characteristics of Australian Female Soccer Players after a Competitive Season', *Australian Journal of Science and Medicine in Sport,* 18, no. 3: 9–12

*Corinthian versus Lancashire Ladies Programme* (1951), Festival of Britain, Craven Park, 21 July.

*Corinthian versus Bolton Programme* (1952), Manchester Athletic Ground, Fallowfield, 20 August.

Crawford, R. (1984), 'Sport for Young Ladies: The Victoria Independent Schools 1875–1925', *Sporting Traditions,* 1, no. 1.

Crosset, T. (1990), 'Masculinity, Sexuality and the Development of Early Modern Sport', in Michael Messner and Donald Sabo (eds), *Sport Men and the Gender Order,* Champaign, IL: Human Kinetics.

Cubberley, H. (1932), 'Soccer for Girls', *Spauldings Athletic Library-Soccer for Women,* New York: American Sports Publishing Company.

Curry, G., Eric Dunning and Kenneth Sheard (2006), 'Sociological versus Empiricist History: Some Comments on Tony Collins's "History, Sociology and the 'Civilising Process'"' *Sport in History,* 26, no. 1 (April): 110–123.

Curtis, M., and C. Grant (2000), *University of Iowa Project on Women's Intercollegiate Sport and Title IX,* Iowa: University of Iowa Press.

Davis, J., and J. Brewer (1992), 'Physiological Characteristics of an International Female Soccer Squad', *Journal of Sports Science,* 10: 142–143.

Davis, J., and J. Brewer (1993), 'Applied Physiology of Female Soccer Players', *Sports Medicine,* 16: 180–189.

Davies, P. (1996), *I Lost My Heart to the Belles,* London: Mandarin.

De Coubertin, P. (1913), *1913 Olympic Review,* September, Lausanne: IOC Museum.

Diagnostic Research Inc. (1988), *The Wilson Report: Moms, Dads, Daughters, and Sports,* Los Angeles, CA.

Duke, V., and Liz Crolley (1996), *Football, Nationality and the State,* London: Longman.

Duval, L. (2000), 'The Development of Women's Track and Field in England: The Role of the Athletic Club 1920s–1950s', *The Sports Historian,* 21, no. 1: 1–34.

Economos, J. (1984), 'Women in Soccer', *Australian Soccer Weekly,* 24 January.

Eisenberg, C., Pierre Lanfranchi, Tony Mason and Alfred Wahl (2004), *100 Years of Football: The FIFA Centennial Book,* London: Weidenfeld and Nicholson.

English Schools FA (1986), *Curriculum Time Football Questionnaire,* September.

English Schools FA (1988), *Goodger and Auden Letter to English Schools FA,* 17 March.

English Schools FA (1988), *Report: Girls' Football Survey,* 19 September.

Equal Opportunities Commission (1978), *The Football Association Limited and Nottinghamshire Football Association v Miss T Bennett,* transcript of judgement, 28 July.

Equal Opportunities Commission (1999), *Hardwick vs the FA,* Employment Appeal Tribunal transcript, 30 April.

Espelund, K. (1995), *Developing Women's Football,* UEFA Youth Conference Paper.

European Commission Communication (1996), *Incorporating Equal Opportunities for Women and Men into All Community Policies and Activities,* Section 67, Luxembourg: Office for Official Publications of the European Communities.

European Communities Commission (1998), *Incorporating Equal Opportunities for Women and Men into All Community Policies and Activities,* Luxembourg: Office for Official Publications of the European Communities.

European Communities Commission Directorate-General for Employment and Social Affairs (2001), *Towards a Community Strategy on Gender Equality (2001–2005),* Luxembourg: Office for Official Publications of the European Communities.

Fasting, K. (1997), 'Sports and Women's Culture,' *Women's Studies International Forum,* 10, no. 4.

Fasting, K. (2004), 'Small Country Big Results: Women's Football in Norway', in F. Hong and J.A. Mangan (eds), *Soccer Women and Liberation: Kicking Off a New Era,* London: Frank Cass.

FIFA (1973), *Minutes of the First UEFA Women's Football Conference*, 22 March, Zurich: FIFA Archive.

FIFA (1974), *Letter from Dr H Käser to Mr T Croker 17 January*, FIFA Correspondence File, UEFA and the Football Association, Zurich: FIFA Archive.

FIFA (1974), *Letter from H Käser Secretary to Pat Gregory 20 June*, Correspondence Files to the Football Association, Zurich: FIFA Archive.

FIFA (1980), *Minutes of the Second UEFA Women's Football Conference*, 19 February, Zurich: FIFA Archive.

FIFA (1981), *Minutes of the Meeting of the 1981 FIFA Technical Committee Item 1 Women's Football and Competitions. Discussed by Group A Zurich: FIFA House 17/18 December*, Zurich: FIFA Archive.

FIFA (1984), *Walter Gagg FIFA Proposition pour l'organisation d'un tournoi mondial de feminin pour equipes representatives*, FIFA Correspondence File, Zurich.

FIFA (1985), *Willy Simonsen Norges Fotballforbund* Item 4, Oslo, 30 December, FIFA Correspondence File, Zurich.

FIFA (1986), *Minutes of Meeting with Peter Verlappen, General Secretary AFC*, 17 April, FIFA Correspondence File, Zurich.

FIFA (1986), *Minutes of the 45th Ordinary Congress Mexico City*, 29 May, FIFA Correspondence File, Zurich.

FIFA (1988), *Minutes of the 46th Ordinary Congress*, 2 July, Zurich: FIFA Archive.

FIFA (1991), *China '91: 1st FIFA World Championship for Women's Football for the M&Ms Cup*, Zurich: FIFA Archive.

FIFA (1992), *1st FIFA/M&Ms Symposium on Women's Football*, November, Zurich: FIFA Archive.

FIFA (1997), *Survey of Women's Football*, January, unpublished paper, Zurich: FIFA Archive.

FIFA (1997), Committee for Women's Football, *Minutes of Meeting No. 10*, 18 February, Zurich: FIFA Archive.

FIFA (1998), *Evaluation of the Questionnaire on Women's Football as at 30.7.97*, 2 March, Zurich: FIFA Archive.

FIFA (1999), 2nd Symposium on Women's Football, 8 July, Los Angeles Hilton and Towers, Los Angeles, CA.

FIFA (2000), *Minutes Meeting Number 6 of the Organising Committee for the Olympic Football Tournaments*, 27 September, Sydney.

FIFA (2002), *Minutes Meeting Number 2 of the Organising Committee for the Olympic Football Tournaments*, 29 October, Zurich, Attachments 4 and 15.

Fishwick, N. (1989), *English Football and Society: 1910–1950*, Manchester: Manchester University Press.

Fletcher, S. (1984), *Women First: The Female Tradition in English Physical Education 1880–1980*, London: Athlone.

Football Association (1921), *Minutes of the FA Council Meeting*, 2 July.

Football Association (1921), *Minutes of the FA Emergency Committee 23 August 1921 to 3 October 1921,* Item 36.

Football Association (1921), *Consultative Committee Women's Football Matches 5 December,* Item 5.

Football Association (1922), *Emergency Council Minutes 21 March to 22 April 1922,* Item 143.

Football Association (1946), *Minutes of the FA Council,* Item 34, 16 December.

Football Association (1969), *Minutes of the FA Council,* Item 37, 1 December.

Football Association (1971), *Minutes of the FA Executive Committee 16 December 1970,* Item 16, *and 19 January 1971,* Item 46.

Football Association (1973), *Minutes of Match Permit Sub-Committee 30 June,* Item 8.

Football Association (1974), *Minutes of Match Permit Sub-Committee 25 February,* Item 6.

Football Association (1974), *Minutes Joint Consultative Committee for Women's Football Lancaster Gate,* 3 October.

Football Association (1997), *Women's Football Alliance Minutes,* 21 November, Appendix D.

Football Association (2001), 'Developing Asian Girls Football', *On the Ball,* May.

*FOOTBALL Today,* Cradely Heath, West Midlands, May 1985–June 1986.

Foulds, S., and P. Harris (1979), *America's Soccer Heritage,* Manhattan Beach, CA: Soccer for Americans.

Fowler, T. (1896), 'A Phase of Modern College Life', *Harper's New Monthly Magazine* 92 (December 1895–May).

Francis, R. (2005), Chair, ERA Task Force, National Council of Women's Organizations; see http://www.equalrightsamendment.org/era.htm.

Frey, J., and S. Eitzen (1991), 'Sport and Society', *Annual Review of Sociology* 17.

Frost, H., and H. Cubberley (1923), *Field Hockey and Soccer for Women,* New York: Charles Scribners and Sons.

*Garden Party and Pensioners' Picnic 1960,* North West Film Archive, Manchester: Metropolitan University, accession number 1228.

Gavora, J. (2002), *Tilting the Playing Field: Schools, Sport, Sex and Title IX,* San Francisco: Encounter Books.

Ghazi, S. (1999), 'Iranian Women Put on Their Running Shoes', *UNESCO Courier,* April, Paris: UNESCO.

Gibson, A., and W. Pickford (eds) (1906), *Association Football and the Men Who Made It,* 4 vols, London: Caxton.

Glanville, B. (1973), 'Goals and Gals Don't Really Mix', *The Sunday Times,* 24 June.

Goodger and Auden (1978), *Letter to English Schools FA English Schools FA,* English Schools FA files, 16 July 2001.

Green, G. (1953), *A History of the Football Association,* London: Naldrett.

Gregg, L. (1999), *The Champion Within: Training for Excellence,* Burlington: JTC Sports.

Griffin, P. (1998), *Strong Women, Deep Closets: Lesbians and Homophobia in Sport,* Champaign, IL, and Leeds: Human Kinetics.

Guttman, A. (1991), *Women's Sports: A History,* New York: Columbia University Press.

Guttman, A., Karen Christensen, and Getrude Pfister (2001), *International Encyclopedia of Women and Sports,* New York and London: Macmillan.

Haliday, J. (1992), 'The Boot's on the Other Foot', *Derby Evening Telegraph,* 4 May.

Hall, M.A. (1996), *Feminism and Sporting Bodies: Essays on Theory and Practice,* Champaign, IL: Human Kinetics.

Hall, M.A. (2003), 'The Game of Choice: Girls' and Women's Soccer in Canada', *Soccer and Society,* 4, no. 2–3: 30–46.

Hamm, M. (1999), *Go For the Goal: A Champion's Guide to Winning in Soccer and Life,* New York: Harper.

Hamm, M. (2004), with Carol Thompson, *Winners Never Quit!* New York: Byron Press Visual Publications.

Handlin, O. (1953), *The Uprooted: From the Old World to the New,* Boston: Watts.

Hardy, Stephen H. (1996), 'Entrepreneurs, Organizations and the Sports Marketplace', *The New American Sport History,* Urbana and Chicago: University of Illinois Press.

Hargreaves, J. (1986), *Sport, Power and Culture,* Cambridge: Polity Press.

Hargreaves, J. (1994), *Sporting Females: Critical Issues in the History and Sociology of Women's Sport,* London: Routledge.

Hargreaves, J. (2000), *Heroines of Sport: The Politics of Difference and Identity,* London: Routledge.

Harris, H. (1938), 'America's Best Union', *Current History* 48, no. 1 (January).

Harris, J. (2001), 'Playing the Man's Game: Sites of Resistance and Incorporation in Women's Football', *World Leisure,* 43: 22–29.

Harris, J. (2005), 'The Image Problem in Women's Football', *Journal of Sport and Social Issues,* 29, no. 2: 184–197.

Harvey, A. (2005), *Football: The First Hundred Years,* New York and Oxon: Routledge.

Harwarth, Irene, Mindy Maline and Elizabeth DeBra, *Women's Colleges in the United States: History, Issues, and Challenges,* at www.ed.gov/offices/OERI/PLLI, accessed January 2005.

*Haslingdon Carnival 9 September 1950,* North West Film Archive, Manchester: Metropolitan University, accession number 578.

Havelange, J. (1991), *China '91: 1st FIFA World Championship for Women's Football for the M&Ms Cup,* Zurich: FIFA Archive.

Havelange, João (1984), *World Women's Invitational Football Tournament Chinese Taipei Football Association,* FIFA Correspondence File, Zurich, 11 September.

Hellekson, H., and K. Busse (2006), *Fan Fiction and Fan Communities in the Age of the Internet,* Jefferson, NC, and London: McFarland.

Hennies, R. (1995), 'Firm Bases—Scope at the Summit?' *FIFA Magazine,* Zurich, May.

Henry, J., and Howard Comeaux (1999), 'Gender Egalitarianism in Coed Sport: A Case Study of American Soccer', *International Review for the Sociology of Sport,* 34, no. 3: 277–290.

Highfield Oral History Group and the Sir Norman Chester Centre for Football (1993), *Highfield Rangers: An Oral History,* Leicester: Leicester City Council Living History Unit.

Hill, J. (1974), 'Take a Tip Revie—It's Time to Follow the Girls!' *News of the World,* 12 November.

Hill, J. (2002), *Sport, Leisure and Culture in Twentieth-Century Britain,* Basingstoke: Palgrave.

Hill, J., and J. Williams (1996), *Sport and Identity in the North of England,* Keele: Keele University Press.

Hirshman, L., and Jane Larson (1998), *Hard Bargains: The Politics of Sex,* Oxford and New York: Oxford University Press.

HMSO (1975), *The Sex Discrimination Act,* 12 November.

Hoare, D. (1992), 'The Australian National Talent Search Program', *Coaching Focus,* 31: 3–4.

Hoare, D. (1998), 'Talent Search: A Review and Update', *Sports Coach* (Spring): 32–33.

Hobsbawm, E. (1990), *Nations and Nationalism since 1870: Programme, Myth, Reality,* Cambridge: Cambridge University Press.

Hodgkinson, M. (2003), 'Capital of the New Soccer Nation', *Los Angeles Citybeat,* 16–22 October.

Holt, R. (1989), *Sport and the British: A Modern History,* Oxford: Oxford University Press.

Holt, R. and T. Mason (2000), *Sport in Britain 1945–2000,* London: Blackwell.

Hong, F. (1997), *Footbinding, Feminism and Freedom: The Liberation of Women's Bodies in Modern China,* London: Frank Cass.

Hong, F. (2001), 'Two Roads to China: The Inadequate and the Adequate (Review Essay)', *International Journal of the History of Sport,* 18, no. 2 (June).

Hong, F., and Tan Hua (2002), 'Sport in China: Conflict between Tradition and Modernity, 1840s to 1930s', *International Journal of the History of Sport,* 19, no. 2–3: 189.

Hong, F., and J.A. Mangan (2004), 'Will the Iron Roses Bloom Forever? Women's Football in China: Changes and Challenges', in Fan Hong and J.A. Mangan (eds), *Soccer Women and Liberation: Kicking Off a New Era,* London: Frank Cass.

House of Common Select Committee (2006), *Second Special Report: Women's Football 25 July 2006.* House of Commons Commission Publications: Parliamentary Copyright 19 October 2006; also available at http://www.publications.parliament.uk/pa/cm200506; accessed 11 July 2007.

House of Common Select Committee (2006), *Fourth Report of Session 2005–06: Responses from the Department for Culture, Media and Sport, the Football Association and the Football Foundation,* 19 October.

Howard, M. (1955), 'History of Physical Education at Mount Holyoke College 1837–1955', Mount Holyoke College Archives.

Howkins, A., and Lowerson, J. (1979), *Trends in Leisure 1919–1939,* London: Sports Council; Social Science Research Council.

Hulton Getty Picture Collection (1933), *Marks and Spencer's versus Invicta's at Queens Mead in Bromley Kent 8 June.*

The Imperial War Museum, *Women's Work Collection* MUN 24/6; MUN 24/15; 24/17.

International Olympic Committee (2000), *2nd IOC World Conference on Women and Sport: New Perspectives for the XXI Century,* 6 March, Paris.

International Olympic Committee (2000), *The Promotion of Women in the Olympic Movement,* Department of International Cooperation, February.

International Olympic Committee (2005), *IOC Report Women's Participation at the Games of the XXVIIIe Olympiad Athens 2004,* Department of International Cooperation and Competition, February.

International Olympic Committee (2006), *Women in the Olympic Movement—Women in Sport: Leadership Evaluation of the 10%–20% Objectives,* Department of International Cooperation and Development, November.

ITN Source (1914) BP010114189045, 'Can Girls Play Soccer? Well–Ilford Representatives Give Good Display', London: Pathé, 1 January.

ITN Source (1919) BP010119191045, 'Football Match between Handley Page Girls and Ladies Sterling Football Club Ilford, Essex', Pathé, 1 January.

ITN Source (1922) BP25052283412, 'Eve and the Noble Art', Pathé, 25 May.

ITN Source (1926) BP01112665003, 'Miners' Wives Football for Charity', Pathé, 1 November.

ITN Source (1931) BP09043176713, 'Aren't Girls Wonderful? Quaker Girls 3 Darlington, Durham', Pathé, 9 April.

ITN Source (1930) BP13113092624, 'Eve's Doing', Pathé, 13 November.

ITN Source (1935) BGU407201275, 'Ladies at Darlington: Quaker Girls v. Terry's Chocs', Pathé, 6 May.

ITN Source (1944) BP140244136411, 'Feminine Football', Pathé, 14 February.

ITN Source (1957) BP010157149729, 'Women's Football in Stuttgart', Pathé, 1 January.

ITN Source (1957) BGY502140342 'Britain Beat Germany 4–0 in European Championship in Berlin', Pathé, 1 January.

ITN Source (1957) BP050857149724, 'Germany and United Kingdom Ends with Draw', Pathé, 1–15 August.

ITN Source (1958) BP010158154511, 'Millions Take a Breather', Pathé, 1 January.

ITN Source (1959) BP020759158729, 'Football's a Girl's Game', Italy: Pathé, 12 July.

ITN Source (1960) BGY503290098, 'The First International Show Girls Soccer Tournament Brazil', 10 August.

ITN Source (1964) BGY505160012, 'Kenya: Prime Minister Kenyatta Tells of Independence Ruse', 4 August.

ITN Source (1966) BP030266201103, 'Queens of Soccer', 3 February.

ITN Source (1968) 5160, 'The Grimethorpe Black Diamonds Ladies' Soccer Club', Yorkshire Television interview, 1 January.

ITN Source (1975) BGY509180617, 'Eire: Woman Footballer to Play in Belgium's Leading Ladies Team', 14 January.

Jacobs, B. (2004), *Dick, Kerr's Ladies,* London: Constable and Robinson.

Jardine, C. (1992), 'The Boot's on the Other Foot', *Telegraph Magazine,* 23 February.

Jarvie, G. (2003), 'Internationalism and Sport in the Making of Nations', *Identities: Global Studies in Culture and Power,* 10, no. 4: 537–551.

Jarvie, G. (2006), *Sport, Culture and Society: An Introduction,* London and New York: Routledge.

Jewell, R., and David J. Molina (2005), 'An Evaluation of the Relationship between Hispanics and Major League Soccer', *Journal of Sports Economics,* 6, no. 2: 160–177.

Jinxia, D. (2002), 'Ascending Then Descending? Women's Soccer in Modern China', *Soccer and Society,* 3, no. 2: 1–18.

Jinxia, D. (2003), *Women Sport and Society in Modern China: Holding up More Than Half the Sky,* London: Frank Cass.

Jones, D. (1999), 'The Beautiful, Deadly Game', *The Guardian,* 6 November.

Jose, C. (1998), *American Soccer League 1921–31: The Golden Years of American Soccer,* Lanham, MD: Scarecrow Press.

Käser, H. (1980), letter, *Re: Women's Football / The Olympic Games to Pat Gregory Women's Football Association England,* 17 June, private collection.

Keating, F. (1977), 'Bridge of Thighs', *Guardian,* 16 May.

*KICK IT OUT* (1999), promotional material distributed by the Football Supporters Association.

Knight Commission, *Final Report of the Knight Commission on Athletics 2001,* available at www.knightcommission.org, accessed January 2006.

Knighton, M. (1929), 'Development of Soccer for Girls', *American Physical Education Review* 34.

Koppelman, A. (1994), *Why Discrimination against Lesbians and Gay Men Is Sex Discrimination,* New York: New York University Press.

Korr, C. (1986), *West Ham United: The Making of a Football Club,* London: Duckworth.

Ladda, S. (1995), *The History of Intercollegiate Women's Soccer in the United States,* unpublished D.Ed. dissertation, Columbia University, New York.

Lanfranchi, P., and M. Taylor (2001), *Moving with the Ball: The Migration of Professional Footballers,* Oxford: Berg.

Lee, M. (1932), *A History of Physical Education and Sports in the USA,* New York: John Wiley.

Leenders, T. (1991), *China '91: 1st FIFA World Championship for Women's Football for the M&Ms Cup,* Zurich: FIFA Archive.

Leigh, M., and T. Bonin (1977), 'The Pioneering Role of Madame Alice Milliat and the FSFI in Establishing International Trade for Women', *Journal of Sport History,* 4, no. 1 (Spring): 72–83.

Lenskyj, H. (2002), *The Best Olympics Ever? Social Impacts of Sydney 2000,* New York: State University of New York Press.

Leslie, J., and P. Burgoyne (1998), *FC Football Graphics,* London: Thames and Hudson.

Libman, G. (1990), 'Kicking up a Storm', *Los Angeles Times,* November 8.

Lightbown, C. (1990), 'Invincible Belles', *The Sunday Times Sport,* 29 April.

Lomas, J. (1983), 'Skills and Skirts', *West Notts and Derbyshire Recorder,* 29 September.

Longman, J. (2001), *The Girls of Summer: The U.S. Women's Soccer Team and How It Changed the World,* New York: Harper Paperbacks.

Lopez, S. (1979), 'An Investigation of Reasons for Participation in Women's Football', *Bulletin of Physical Education* 15.

Lopez, S. (1997), *Women on the Ball,* London: Scarlet.

Lorber, J. (1994), *Paradoxes of Gender,* New Haven, CT, and London: Yale University Press.

Luschen, G. (1970), *Cross Cultural Analysis of Sport and Games,* Champaign, IL: Stipes.

Majumdar, B., and Kausik Bandyopadhyay (2005), *A Social History of Indian Football: Striving to Score,* London: Routledge.

Mangan, J.A., and R. Parks (1987), *From 'Fair Sex' to Feminism: Sport and the Socialization of Women in the Industrial and Post-Industrial Eras,* London: Frank Cass.

Markovits, A., and S. Hellerman (2001), *Offside: Soccer and American Exceptionalism,* Princeton, NJ: Princeton University Press.

Markovits, A., and S. Hellerman (2003), *Women's Soccer in the United States: Yet Another American Exceptionalism,* in F. Hong and J.A. Mangan (eds), *Soccer, Women and Sexual Liberation: Kicking Off a New Era,* London: Frank Cass, pp. 14–30.

Markovits, A. and S. Hellerman (2003), 'The "Olympianization" of Soccer in the United States: From Marginalization in America's "Sports Space" to Recognition as a Quadrennial Event in American Mainstream Culture', *American Behavioural Scientist,* 46, no. 11 (July): 1533–1549.

Marschik, M. (1998), 'Offside: The Development of Women's Football in Austria', *Football Studies,* 2, no. 1: 69–88.

Mason, T. (1980), *Association Football and English Society 1863–1915,* Brighton: Harvester.

Mason, T. (1988), *Sport in Britain,* London: Faber and Faber.

Mason, T. (1989), *Sport in Britain: A Social History,* Cambridge: Cambridge University Press.

McCrone, K. (1988), *Playing the Game: Sport and the Physical Emancipation of English Women 1870–1914,* Lexington: The University Press of Kentucky.

McElroy, K. (1998), 'Somewhere to Run', in Lissa Smith (ed), *Nike Is a Goddess: The History of Women in Sports,* New York: Atlantic Monthly Press.

Melling, A. (1998), 'Cultural Differentiation, Shared Aspiration: The Entente Cordiale of International Ladies' Football 1920–45', *The European Sports History Review,* 1.

Melling, A. (1999), *Ladies Football: Gender and Socialisation of Women Football Players in Lancashire 1926–1960,* unpublished PhD dissertation, University of Central Lancashire, November.

Melling, A. (2001), 'Charging Amazons and Fair Invaders: The Dick Kerr's Ladies Soccer Tour of North America of 1922—Sowing Seed', *European Sports History Review,* 3 (Spring).

Mennesson, C., and J. Clement (2003), 'Homosociability and Homosexuality: The Case of Soccer Played by Women', *International Review for the Sociology of Sport,* 38, no. 3: 311–330.

Messner, M., and D. Sabo (1990), *Sport Men and Then Gender Order: Critical Feminist Perspectives,* Champaign, IL: Human Kinetics.

Miller, D. (1987), *A Survey of English Women's Football Clubs,* unpublished MA thesis, State University of California.

Miller, E. (2002), *Making Her Mark: Firsts and Milestones in Women's Sports,* New York: Contemporary Books.

Miller Lite (1993), *Report on Sports and Fitness in the Lives of Working Women, in Cupertino with Women's Sports Foundation, East Meadow NJ and Working Woman Magazine,* New York.

*Miroir des Sports July 1920,* weekly editions until 1921.

Mitchell, M. (1993), *Encyclopedia Brunoniana 1764 until 1993,* Brown College Archives.

Moore, P. (2000), 'Soccer and the Politics of Culture in Western Australia', in Noel Dyck (ed), *Games, Sports and Cultures,* London: Berg.

Morgan, J. (1977), 'You Can Call Me a Ladies' Man', *Daily Express,* 16 November.

Morgan, R. (2004), 'Soccer Still the Nation's Most Popular Team Sport, Despite Overall Decline in Team Sports', *The Roy Morgan Survey Article No. 327,* June 26.

Myotin, E. (1999), *Sports Socialisation of 11–20 year old Brazilian girls in the 1990s: A Social Psychological Study,* unpublished PhD dissertation, University of Loughborough.

Nelson, M.B. (1996), *The Stronger Women Get, the More Men Love Football: Sexism and the Culture of Sport,* London: Women's Press.

Newsham, Gail (1994), *In a League of Their Own!* Chorley: Pride of Place.

Newsham, G. (1998), *In a League of Their Own,* London: Scarlet.

Office of National Statistics (2001), *Social Trends No. 31.*

O'Neill, J. (1999), 'Awards Night Indicates a Growing Respect', *The Times,* 3 December.

Oriard, M. (1993), *Reading Football: How the Popular Press Created an American Spectacle,* Chapel Hill: University of North Carolina Press.

Owen, J. (1932), 'Sport in Women's Colleges', *New York Herald Tribune.*

Pannick, D. (1981), 'How the FA Kicks Girl Footballers off the Park', *The Guardian,* 16 November.

Pannick, D. (1983), *Sex Discrimination in Sport,* London: Equal Opportunities.

Parillo, B. (1999), 'Women's World Cup 1999', *Providence Journal,* 10 May.

Pauw, V. (1999), 'From Wishful Thinking to Development Policy', 2nd FIFA Women's Symposium, Los Angeles, CA.

Penner, M. (1999), 'Bare Facts Make These Two Heroes', *Los Angeles Times,* 11 July.

Pereira, C. (1976), ALFC General Secretary, 'Women's Football in Asia', 10 February, FIFA Correspondence File, Zurich.

Perriman, A. (1982), "'Girl 'Not Entitled to Play in Boys' Football Team'", *The Times,* 12 July.

Pettus, E. (1998), 'From the Suburbs to the Sports Arenas', in Lissa Smith (ed), *Nike Is a Goddess: The History of Women in Sports,* New York: Atlantic Monthly Press.

Pfister, G., S. Scraton, K. Fasting and A. Bunuel (1998), 'Women and Football—A Contradiction? The Beginnings of Women's Football in Four European Countries', *The European Sports History Review,* 1.

Phillips, D., *Australian Women at the Olympic Games, 3rd ed.,* Petersham, UNSW: Walla Walla Press and Centre for Olympic Studies.

Pierce, F. (1904), 'The Beginning of a Football Game', *The Radcliffe Magazine,* November.

Polley, M. (1998), *Moving the Goal Posts: A History of Sport and Society since 1945,* London: Routledge.

Powell, J. (1996), 'Sorry Ladies, You Can't Win a Man's Game', *Daily Mail,* 30 January.

Preston, M. (2003), 'Quality Hamm', *The Sunday Times,* 5 October, Section 2.

Pronger, B. (1999), 'Outta My Endzone: Sport and the Territorial Anus', *Journal of Sport and Social Issues,* 3, Issue 4.

Prudhomme-Poncet, L. (2003), *Histoire du football feminine au XXème siècle: Espaces et temps du sport,* Paris: L'Harmattann.

Richards, J. (2001), 'Our Kelly', *Total Football Magazine,* July.

Rideing, W. (1881), 'The English at the Seaside', *Harper's New Monthly Magazine,* 63, June–November.

Rimati, M. (1999), in Roger Le Grove Rogers, ed, *Women's Soccer World,* 1728 Mulberry St. Montgomery, AL 36106, March/April.

Roberts, E. (1984), *A Woman's Place: An Oral History of Working Class Women 1890–1940,* Oxford: Blackwell.

Roberts, J. (2006), 'The Best Football Team, the Best Platoon': The Role of the Football in the Proletarianization of the British Expeditionary Force 1914–1918', *Sport in History,* 26, no. 1 (April): 26–46.

Rose, J. (1992), 'Rereading the English Common Reader: A Preface to a History of Audiences', *Journal of the History of Ideas,* 53, no. 1 (March).

Rose, J. (2002), *The Intellectual Life of the British Working Classes,* New Haven, CT: Yale University Press.

Rowe, D., Geoffrey Lawrence, Jim McKay and Toby Miller (2001), *Globalization and Sport: Playing the World,* London: Sage.

Rowe, N., and R. Champion (2000), *Young People and Sport National Survey 1999,* London: Sport England Research.

Rudd, A. (1998), *Astroturf Blonde (It's a Man's Game—Sometimes),* London: Headline.

Russell, D. (1997), *Football and the English: A Social History of Association Football in England, 1863–1995,* Carnegie: Preston.

Scraton, S. (1992), *Shaping up to Womanhood,* Bucks: Open University Press.

Scraton, S., J. Cauldwell and S. Holland (2005), '"Bend It Like Patel" Centring "Race", Ethnicity and Gender in Feminist Analysis of Women's Football in England', *International Review for the Sociology of Sport,* 40, no. 1: 71–88.

Segar, C. (1981), 'AFC Want Total Control over the Women', *The Star,* 31 August.

Shulman, J., and William G. Bowen (2001), *The Game of Life: College Sports and Educational Values,* Princeton, NJ: Princeton University Press.

Smith College (1979), *The Smith Soccer Record Book, 1924–1979,* Smith College Archives.

Soccer Line (1994), *National Soccer Survey,* Florida: Soccer Industry Council of America.

Sports Council (England) (1992), *Allied Dunbar National Fitness Survey. Summary of the Major Findings and Messages,* London: Sports Council and Health Education Authority.

Sugden, J. and A. Tomlinson (1998), *FIFA and the Contest for the World Football: Who Rules the People's Game?* Cambridge: Polity Press.

Solomon, B. (1989), *In the Company of Educated Women: A History of Women and Higher Education in America,* New Haven, CT: Yale University Press.

Stell, M. (1991), *Half the Race: A History of Australian Women in Sport,* New South Wales: Angus and Robertson.

Talbot, M. (2000), *Gendering the Sport Agenda in Sport Decision Making,* European Women and Sport Conference, Helsinki, 6–8 July 2000.

Taylor, M. (2005), *The Leaguers: The Making of Professional Football in England 1900–1939,* Liverpool: Liverpool University Press.

Taylor, M. (2006), 'Global Players? Football Migration and Globalization 1930–2000', *Historical Social Research*, 31, no. 1: 7–30.

Tischler, M. (1981), *Footballers and Businessmen: The Origins of Professional Football in England*, New York: Homes and Meyer.

Tomlinson, A., and J. Sugden (1994), *Hosts and Champions: Soccer Cultures, National Identities and the USA World Cup*, Aldershot: Arena.

Toulmin, V. (1998), 'Traveling Shows and the First Static Cinemas', *Picture House*, no. 21 (Summer).

Tunis, J. (1935), 'Changing Trends in Sport', *Harper's Monthly Magazine*, no. 170, December 1934–May.

US Soccer Foundation (2003), *Soccer in the USA 2002–2003*, Chicago: US Soccer Foundation.

US Soccer Foundation (2005), *Annual Report 2005*, Chicago: US Soccer Foundation.

Vamplew, W. (1988), *Pay up and Play the Game: Professional Sport in Britain*, Cambridge: Cambridge University Press.

Verlappan, P. (1981), *Women's Football in Asia: Letter to Datin Teoh Chye Hin*, 28 September, Zurich: FIFA Archive.

Vertinsky, P. (1990), *The Eternally Wounded Woman: Women, Exercise and Doctors in the Late Nineteenth Century*, Manchester: Manchester University Press.

Vienna Declaration of Action (1993), adopted by the World Conference on Human Rights, Vienna, 25 June.

Viner, K. (1997), 'Sidelined', *The Guardian*, 21 January.

Wagg, Stephen (1984), *The Football World: A Contemporary Social History*, Brighton: Harvester.

Walvin, J. (1978), *Leisure and Society 1830–1950*, London: Longman.

Walvin, J. (1986), *Football and the Decline of Britain*, Basingstoke: Macmillan.

Walvin, J. (1994), *The People's Game: The History of Football Revisited*, 2nd ed., Edinburgh and London: Mainstream.

Wensel, M. (1984), 'The Diary of Julia Colt Butler 1889–1890', *Journal of the Rutgers University Libraries*, 46.

WFA Newsletters (1972–1988).

WFA Correspondence Files (1973), *P. Gregory to Dr H Käser Secretary FIFA*, 20 July.

WFA Correspondence Files (1974), *P. Gregory to Dr H Käser Secretary FIFA*, 2 June.

WFA Correspondence Files (1974), *P. Gregory to Dr H Käser Secretary FIFA*, 6 July.

WFA Correspondence Files (1980), *Women's International Soccer*, 3 June.

WFA Correspondence Files (1980), *Letter from H. Käser Secretary FIFA to Pat Gregory*, 17 June.

WFA Correspondence Files (1984), *E.A. Croker The Football Association Correspondence File*, 10 July.

WFA Address List 1992 (448/450 Hanging Ditch The Corn Exchange Manchester M4 3ES).

WFA News (1991), Action Replay, Fusion Creative Products Ltd., c1992.

Whimpress, B. (1994), 'Australian Rules Football', in Wray Vamplew and Brian Stoddart (eds), *Sport in Australia: A Social History,* Cambridge: Cambridge University Press, pp. 19–40.

Wilkinson, J. (1917), 'Early Experience with a Kinematograph Machine', *Kinematograph and Lantern Weekly,* 8 March.

Williamson, D. (1991), *The Belles of the Ball,* Devon: R and D Associates.

Wilson, T. (1938), 'The Contribution of an Athletic Programme to High School Girls', *Teacher's College Journal,* September.

Women's Soccer World (1999), *Women's Soccer World,* 3, no. 3 (August), Editorial and letters page.

Women's Sports Foundation (1989), *Minorities in Sports: The Effect of Varsity Sports Participation on the Social Educational and Career Mobility of Minority Students,* 15 August, New York: WSF.

Women's World Cup Los Angeles (1999), Official Programme and promotional material.

Woodhouse, D. (2001), *The Post War Development of Football for Females: A Cross Cultural and Comparative Study of England, the USA and Norway,* unpublished PhD dissertation, University of Leicester.

Yang, Mayfair Mei-Hui (1999), *Spaces of Their Own. Women's Public Sphere in Transnational China,* Minneapolis: University of Minnesota Press.

Yong, N. (2006), 'Full Speed Ahead', FIFA News, 1 September, available at http://www.fifa.com/.

Zhenqi, Q. (1982), 'Women's Soccer Has a Bright Future', *National Women's Soccer Invitational Brochure,* Beijing: PR China Football Association; Zurich: FIFA Archive.

Zhongcheng, S. (1982), ' "Pigtails" Soccer in China', *National Women's Soccer Invitational Brochure,* Beijing, China: PR China Football Association; Zurich: FIFA Archive.

# Index